THE CINEMA OF THE LOW COUNTRIES

First published in Great Britain in 2004 by
Wallflower Press
4th Floor, 26 Shacklewell Lane, London, E8 2EZ
www.wallflowerpress.co.uk

A catalogue for this book is available from the British Library

ISBN 1-904764-00-2 (paperback)
ISBN 1-904764-01-0 (hardback)

Printed in Turin, Italy by Grafiche Dessi s.r.l.

THE CINEMA OF
THE LOW COUNTRIES

EDITED BY

ERNEST MATHIJS

 **WALLFLOWER PRESS** LONDON & NEW YORK

24 FRAMES is a major new series focusing on national and regional cinemas from around the world. Rather than offering a 'best of' selection, the feature films and documentaries selected in each volume serve to highlight the specific elements of that territory's cinema, elucidating the historical and industrial context of production, the key genres and modes of representation, and foregrounding the work of the most important directors and their exemplary films. In taking an explicitly text-centred approach, the titles in this list offer 24 diverse entry-points into each national and regional cinema, and thus contribute to the appreciation of the rich traditions of global cinema.

Series Editors: Yoram Allon & Ian Haydn Smith

OTHER TITLES IN THE **24 FRAMES** SERIES:

THE CINEMA OF LATIN AMERICA *edited by Alberto Elena and Marina Díaz López*

THE CINEMA OF JAPAN & KOREA *edited by Justin Bowyer*

THE CINEMA OF ITALY *edited by Giorgio Bertellini*

FORTHCOMING TITLES:

THE CINEMA OF CENTRAL EUROPE *edited by Peter Hames*

THE CINEMA OF SCANDINAVIA *edited by Tytti Soila*

THE CINEMA OF BRITAIN & IRELAND *edited by Brian McFarlane*

THE CINEMA OF SPAIN & PORTUGAL *edited by Alberto Mira*

THE CINEMA OF FRANCE *edited by Phil Powrie*

CONTENTS

NOTES ON CONTRIBUTORS

BAS AGTERBERG teaches in the Institute for Media and Re/Presentation at the University of Utrecht, where he coordinates the Theatre, Film and Television Studies curriculum. He is also active as a producer of recent films by Jos Stelling (*The Waiting Room*, *The Gas Station*, *No Trains No Planes*). He is currently preparing a new production, *Duska*, and developing a centre for Film and Visual Culture (the Louis Hartlooper Complex).

DANIEL BILTEREYST is Professor in Film, Television and Cultural Media Studies at the University of Ghent. He has published widely on film, television and international communication. He currently directs research funded by the *Fund for Scientific Research* on non-fiction films in Flanders, and is a board member of the Flemish Audiovisual Fund.

PETER BOSMA studied Dutch Language and Literature, and Theatre Studies at the University of Utrecht. He designed and edited an Introductory Film Studies Course at the Dutch Open University (published as *Filmkunde*). He currently works at the Film Department of Theatre Lantaren/Venster in Rotterdam as a freelance lecturer and writer.

LEEN ENGELEN studied at the Catholic University of Leuven and at the University of Ulster, and has taught at the Department of Media Studies of the Catholic University of Leuven. Currently she is researching a PhD on the representation of World War One in Belgian fiction films of the interbellum. She has published papers on Belgian film history, representational aspects of World War One, and German, Polish and Spanish cinema.

JAN-PIETER EVERAERTS holds degrees in communication studies from the Catholic University of Leuven, and film technology from NARAFI. He has directed/produced over forty television programmes, written extensively on media, and is the author of five books on Belgian documentary film (including *Film in België*). He currently teaches at the RITS department of the Erasmus Hogeschool Brussels, is coordinator of the Flemish Documentary Film Network, and editor of the media watch E-zine *DIOGENE(S)*.

CATHERINE FOWLER is Reader and Course Leader of the MA Film: Independent Film and Filmmaking at the Southampton Institute of Higher Education. She has published in *Screen* and *The Historical Journal of Film, Radio and Television*, and chapters on Chantal Akerman and Belgian cinema in various edited collections. She is the editor of *The European Cinema Reader* (Routledge, 2002) and is co-editing a collection on Representations of the Rural in cinema.

WOUTER HESSELS teaches film history at the RITS department of the Erasmus Hogeschool Brussels. He is co-founder of the cinéclub Film Forest Brussels, and is a regular writer on François Truffaut's influence on Belgian cinema. With Ernest Mathijs, he co-edited *Waarheid & Werkelijkheid* (VUB Press, 2000). He develops artistic music-poetry projects with musician Marc Peire (*Verticaal Ritme, Ander Alfabet/Autre Alphabet...*).

BERT HOGENKAMP is a media historian at the Netherlands Institute of Sound and Vision, and holds a part-time professorship at the University of Utrecht. He has published extensively on the history of the documentary film and on film and the labour movement. His books include *De Borinage: De mijnwerkersstaking van 1932 en de film van Joris Ivens en Henri Storck* (*The Borinage: the miners' strike of 1932 and the film of Joris Ivens and Henri Storck*) (Kritak, 1983) and *Film, Television and the Left in Britain, 1950–1970* (Lawrence and Wishart, 2000).

MIKEL J. KOVEN is lecturer in Film and Television Studies at the University of Wales, Aberystwyth. His main research areas are exploitation cinema, Italian horror films, folklore and film, Jewish representation in film, Holocaust cinema and Classical Hollywood. He is the author of *Blaxploitation Films* (Pocket Essentials, 2000) and is currently working on a book-length study of the *giallo* film.

FRANK LAFOND is a PhD candidate studying Aesthetics at Lille University. He has published essays on the horror genre and film noir, in both French and English, and has edited a book on modern American horror film, a dictionary dedicated to the work of Jacques Tourneur, as well as an annual journal entitled *Rendez-vous avec la peur* (Editions du CEFAL, 2004).

ERIK MARTENS is a freelance film critic. His articles appear in the Flemish newspaper *De Standaard* and the entertainment weekly *Focus Knack*. He regularly contributes to other magazines and to

Flemish public radio *Klara*. Currently he is Editor-in-chief of the Flemish Film History DVD-project (for the Royal Belgian Film Archive) releasing, amongst others, *Mira*, *Crazy Love*, *Seagulls Die in the Harbour* and *The Man Who Had His Hair Cut Short*.

ERNEST MATHIJS is lecturer in film studies at the University of Wales, Aberystwyth. He has written extensively on Belgian cinema (*Daughters of Darkness*, *Man Bites Dog* and *S.*). Forthcoming publications include *Big Brother International: Format, Critics and Publics* (co-editor Janet Jones) and *Alternative Europe: Eurotrash and Exploitation Cinema Since 1945* (co-editor Xavier Mendik), both to be published by Wallflower Press in 2004. With Steven Jay Schneider he directs a book series on *Contemporary Cinema* for Rodopi.

XAVIER MENDIK is Director of the Cult Film Archive at University College Northampton, and also works as a documentary producer for Lippy Films. He has published widely on European cult and exploitation cinema, and has recently co-edited *Unruly Pleasures: The Cult Film and Its Critics* (FAB Press, 2000), *Shocking Cinema of the Seventies* (FAB, 2002) and *Underground U.S.A.: Filmmaking Beyond the Hollywood Canon* (Wallflower Press, 2002). A collection of his writings is forthcoming as *Fear Theory* (Wallflower Press, 2005) and he is currently developing a 6-part television series on extreme 1970s cinema.

PHILIP MOSLEY is Professor of English, Communications and Comparative Literature at Pennsylvania State University. He is the author of *Ingmar Bergman: The Cinema as Mistress* (Marion Boyars, 1981) and *Split Screen: Belgian Cinema and Cultural Identity* (SUNY, 2001). Also a specialist in Belgian francophone literature, other books include *Georges Rodenbach: Critical Essays* (Fairleigh Dickinson University Press, 1996) and translations of novels by Rodenbach and Guy Vaes.

STEVEN JAY SCHNEIDER is a PhD candidate in Philosophy at Harvard University, and in Cinema Studies at New York University's Tisch School of the Arts. He is editor of *Horror Film and Psychoanalysis: Freud's Worst Nightmares* (Cambridge University Press, 2004) and *New Hollywood Violence* (Manchester University Press, 2004), and co-editor of *Horror International* (Wayne State University Press, 2004). *Underground U.S.A.: Filmmaking Beyond the Hollywood Canon* (co-edited with Xavier Mendik) was published by Wallflower Press in 2002.

LIEVE SPAAS is Research Professor of Arts and Culture in the Faculty of Arts and Social Sciences at the University of Kingston. She is currently working on 'Remembering the Congo'. She has written extensively on film and cultural identity. Her recent publications include *The Francophone Film: A Struggle for Identity* (Manchester University Press, 2000), and *Le Cinéma nous parle* (University of Debrecen/Grant & Cutler, 2000). She is series editor of *Polygons: Cultural Diversities and Intersections* (Berghahn).

JOHAN SWINNEN teaches History and Theory of Photography, Film, Video and Visual Culture at the Free University of Brussels, and is general director of the Higher Institute for Fine Arts in Antwerp and vice-president of the European Society for the History of Photography. He is author of various publications (encyclopaedias, books, catalogues) and radio programmes, and has contributed to exhibitions and film-events. He is currently preparing a short film on Hadriaan Beverland.

VIVIANE THILL works at the Centre National de l'Audiovisuel in Luxembourg. She regularly reviews films for *Le Jeudi*, *Forum* and the television channel *RTL Télé Luxembourg*. With Michel Cieutat she edited a book on Oliver Stone (Editions Rivages, 1996), and co-wrote *Germaine Damar: Ein Luxemburger Star im deutschen Film der 50er Jahre* (CNA, 1995). She is currently working on a screenplay called 'Perl oder Pica' adapted from a novel by Jhemp Hoscheit.

PETE TOMBS grew up in the east end of London, watching more films than was good for him. After a career in bookselling he began to write about film for a wide variety of publications (including *The Guardian*, *The Independent*, *Sight and Sound* and *The Dark Side*). He is co-author of *Immoral Tales* (with Cathal Tohill, St Martin's Press, 1995) and author of *Mondo Macabro* (St Martin's Press, 1998). He currently lives in London and runs the company Boum Productions.

JAN UDRIS teaches film at Middlesex University and at Birkbeck College, London. His research interests include the ideologies of comedy and gender representation. He is the co-author (with Nathan Abrams and Ian Bell) of the textbook *Studying Film* (Arnold, 2001). He has also presented papers at international conferences and written articles for various European journals.

SOFIE VAN BAUWEL is a teaching and research assistant at the Department of Communication Studies at Ghent University, and a member of the Working Group on Film and Television

Studies. Her main academic research focuses on gender representations and feminist media studies. She is currently preparing a PhD on multiple gender identities and popular culture.

ANSJE VAN BEUSEKOM studied artistry at the Free University of Amsterdam and teaches Film and Media studies at Utrecht University. In 2001 she published her dissertation *Kunst en Amusement: Reacties op film als een nieuw medium in Nederland, 1895–1940* (Arcadia, 2001). Her research addresses the cultural reception of cinema, relations between cinema and other arts, and the role of cinema in the international avant-garde in the 1920s and 1930s.

HANS VAN DRIEL is Associate Professor in Media and Culture at the Faculty of Literature at Tilburg University. He has published widely on semiotics and on cultural and communicative aspects of an era of new media and film. His most recent books are *Digitaal Communiceren* (Boom, 2001) and *Internet & Communicatie* (Media Business Press, 1999). He also hosts the *Dutch Literature and Film Website*.

PAUL VAN YPEREN is a film historian, writing regularly for *Skrien*. He also published in *De Filmkrant*, *Movie, XL* and *Ons Amsterdam*, and is a collaborator of the Dutch Filmmuseum, the University of Utrecht, and Vara Television. He is one of the authors of the Film History course of the Open University, and co-wrote (with Bastiaan Anink) *De kleurrijke filmaffiches van Frans Bosen* (Arcadia, 1999), a book on film posters. With Bastiaan Anink he is preparing a book on the film poster collection of the Dutch Filmmuseum, and working for Premsela, the Dutch national foundation for design.

THOMAS WAUGH has been teaching film studies at Concordia University, Montreal, since 1976. He is the author of *Joris Ivens and the Evolution of the Radical Documentary 1926–1946* (diss. Columbia University, 1981) and *Show Us Life: Towards a History and Aesthetics of the Committed Documentary* (Scarecrow Press, 1984), as well as many articles and reviews on documentary film. More recent publications have focused on sexual representation, queer cinema and the national cinemas of Canada and India.

ACKNOWLEDGEMENTS

This book would not have been possible without the substantial aid of many people. Every author contributing to this volume deserves special thanks for their work, and for their ability to produce under stress, answering to various editorial requests. I enjoyed working with all of them, and hope to do so again soon. I also thank Yoram Allon, Hannah Patterson and Ben Walker at Wallflower Press.

I would also like to thank the Department of Theatre, Film and Television Studies at the University of Wales, Aberystwyth for allowing me to take the necessary time for this project while adapting to a new living environment in Wales. Particular thanks go to the University Research Fund for supporting the final research stages of this book.

Very special thanks to Harry Kümel for support, feedback and the preface, Jean-Paul Dorchain at the Royal Film Archive in Brussels for general assistance, and for providing stills; to Peter Bosma for putting me in touch with other contributors, and to Karel Dibbets for the help with the bibliography.

All images are courtesy of the pictures collection of the Royal Film Archive Belgium, except *Zuiderzee* (private collection Thomas Waugh); *Borinage* (Fonds Henri Storck); *Turkish Delight, Soldiers of Orange* (Nederlandse Film Compagnie); *Mariken* (Jos Stelling Archive); *Jeanne Dielman* (Paradise Films); *Twice a Woman, The Vanishing* (MGS Film, George Sluizer, Jutka Rona); *A Question of Silence* (Sigma Pictures Productions); *A Wopbobaloobop a Lopbamboom* (Frankfurter Filmproduktion); *The Northerners, Character* (First Floor Features); *Left Luggage* (Mulholland Pictures, Ate De Jong); and *Rosetta* (Les films du fleuve). I thank them all kindly for their permissions. All stills in this book are reproduced in the spirit of promoting the films.

Ernest Mathijs
April 2004

Voor mijn ouders

PREFACE

Ernest Mathijs: *What do you think about writing a foreword for a book about the Cinema of the Low Countries?*

Harry Kümel: Frankly, I feel like a fish out of water among the academics, professors and pedagogues (or the odd film critic) who adorn the pages of your consummate compendium about our indigenous film industry. After all, I am merely a film director.

But you are also a teacher at film schools and occupy a chair at the Brussels Free University.

I am and I do – by default. Like most of my colleagues, it's impossible to earn a decent living by being just a filmmaker in these blessed, little, rich countries of ours. There remains, of course, the recourse to the wonderful world of commercials, but that remains a stop-gap too, albeit a gold-lined one. This makes the whole argument in your introduction, about the wish to judge our films on their own merits, rather dangerous. When we are truly active in our profession of choice – a rare occurrence, to put it mildly – we become, as it were, context ourselves, not the real thing … Coca-Cola-wise.

And what would that context be?

One: money. Two: language. Three: filmmaking in a small country.

And there are no drawbacks in similar or even more restricted production milieus like, say, Denmark or Sweden?

These are top-to-bottom subsidised industries, financed in part by a surreptitious pornographic production, whose recognition ebbs and flows with the activities of one internationally recognised director. Nowadays it is (for, to me, unfathomable reasons) Lars von Trier in Denmark. And look what has become of the reputation and quality of Swedish cinema since Ingmar Bergman is no longer active in filmmaking. Come to think of it, the same could be said of Italian cinema since the occultation of its Holy Trinity Visconti, Fellini and Antonioni (though, in the latter case, my personal film religion would have me rather say Mario Bava). And see what Almodóvar has done for Spanish cinema (although I would have liked to see Alex de la Iglesia included in this universal appreciation). But, of course, Spanish cinema is a special case, being the only instance in Europe of a film activity important enough to sustain itself – mainly thanks to its South American hinterland.

Maybe your 'context' is just the lack of one truly great filmmaker whose mere presence and endeavours could be sufficient to nurture the rest of the local industry.

Or maybe it is a European problem in general. But the emergence of one great director in the Low Countries would certainly do no harm. I mean, recognition, and the possibilities that come with it, can only be obtained through a 'star' to whom they can stick, like leeches, their political and bureaucratic fortunes. But even then I would have my doubts. In Holland they simply banish filmmakers who 'threaten' to grow above the mediocre pack, whether it be commercially or artistically, or both. Paul Verhoeven is a case in point. At the time, the then president of the Dutch production fund detested his success to such a degree that he had all of his projects systematically rejected, so that Paul could do nothing but emigrate to Hollywood.

In Flanders, on the other hand, they allow you to grow a little bit. But then you are expected to tow the political and bureaucratic line. And if you don't, beware! The example here being Stijn Coninx. After the success of *Daens* (1992), Stijn was slathered with all possible kudos and laurels Belgium could provide (and was nominated for an Academy Award), including being awarded a knighthood. This was, in a sense, normal, but not because of the film's craftsmanship. It was because of its theme, which reflected the official perception of the Flemish idealised 'reality' at the time; a mixture of Christianity and Socialism. So, Stijn was expected to continue along that line (he was even offered for a time to 'do' another Flemish priest – this time Father Damian). Unfortunately, he didn't. And retribution came fast: he was dropped like a hot potato and the Damian project was taken from him. So, you see, same result with different means in both countries, and with the same goal: never nurture a potential great artist, he could escape the clutches of your subsidy system. I don't how things stand with our Walloon brothers. I don't know a lot about that cinema *tout court*. Therefore, I'd rather not speak about it (allowing us to avoid a useless discussion concerning, for example, the socialising coquetries of the Dardenne Brothers).

In this respect I think Francophone and Flemish cinema are too far apart to compare them. Dutch and Flemish cinema are very different as well. Moreover, as a Fleming, you know the differences in mentality between Flemish cities like, say, Antwerp, Ghent and Ostend. Meaning, that you can't really discuss the cinema originating from these regions in one broad stroke either.

Well, just for argument's sake, let's keep them temporarily together. But let's move back to your initial points of contention: money, language and filmmaking in a small country.

OK. First, money. Producing films is getting more expensive by the day. It's obvious that a small region can no longer afford to produce them alone. Second, language narrows our international appeal to, at best, subsidised art houses. And, third, if those hindrances weren't enough, we simply don't have the artistic and production wherewithal to make internationally viable and authentic films on a continuous basis. Have you ever asked yourself why no films with a historical and/or political, and/or truly social relevant background, are ever produced here (while we have plenty of these to draw from)? Just try to find a native screenplay writer in the Low Countries, capable of accomplishing such a feat (that is, since the truly unique Hugo Claus gave up screenwriting). And if there are one or two of these rare birds still around, they have been taken up by the few producers we have to be hacks for the television channels. This offers them a living, but sends creativity down the drain. As for producers themselves, none are brave enough to tackle such 'delicate' subjects, except in a few timid cases that remain, at best, peripheral. We've got marvelous technicians, great actors, and two or three distinguished directors. But when it comes to screenplays and production, it's the land of the living dead combined with the Flemish fretsaw massacre.

Wouldn't co-productions provide a solution?

They would – and have – on a purely financial level. And they have been greatly encouraged by the European authorities. But since these co-productions are only viable in conjunction with a country with a larger production potential, the authenticity (the *eigenheid* to which you allude in your introduction) tends to get lost. Indeed it either ends by being swallowed up by the larger partner, or by the concoction of 'European subjects', which are even worse.

But you directed some quite successful co-productions, which were quite 'authentic'.

Maybe. But then, we ought to discuss what is 'authentic', and what makes a good film – what makes for a genuine cinematographic experience. And we can tackle this a bit later, when I have addressed the root of our problem. Here again, we must differentiate between Holland and Flanders, although, at heart, they deal with similar developments. Both industries were started on a false premise, or at least a premise that did not have the good of an indigenous cinema in mind. In Holland, the industry was given its first start in the 1930s, when the Dutch still thought they could get away with accomodating the Germans, as they had in the First World War. And that start was financed, for the greatest part, by UFA, who were trying to create some kind of minor branch of Dutch cinema. Thus, large studios and labs were built, together with the planting of the seeds of a financing (and film school) infrastructure – along the same lines as the Nazi cinema. This has continued until today, camouflaged as so many things emanating from that period, under a 'right-minded' veneer, but still working along the same 'foreign' lines. It is, for example, an open secret that today a great deal of Hollywood productions are financed with Dutch money. To compensate for this capital drain, a system was devised a few years ago in which Dutch capital was freed through tax shelters and transferred to local film production. This seemed to work for a time – until the Dutch authorities began to make noises about cutting this, because it cost too much.

Still, those financial means produced some good results. Take Alex Van Warmerdam, for example.

Sure, in art houses and the like. But name me one Dutch movie that has really 'made it' internationally, since the departure of Paul Verhoeven.

What about the Flemish scene?

Here we have to rewind our Time Machine to 1964, when the first (official) impulse was given to Flemish cinema through government incentives. Actually, that impulse was inspired by *De Witte* (*Whitey*, Jan Vanderheyden, 1934), and had been pursued in the 1940s and 1950s with a string of popular farces, and was aesthetically preluded by *Meeuwen sterven in de Haven* (*Seagulls Die in the Harbour*, Roland Verhavert and Ivo Michiels, 1955). But, for the sake of argument, as you say, let's keep that official 'impulse' at 1964. The then Flemish Minister of Culture, Renaat van Elslande, saw indigenous cinema as an instrument to initiate the federalisation of the country. This inconspicuous means (inconspicuous because of the cultural, financial and political unimportance of Flemish cinema at that time) was aimed to drive a wedge between our two cultures, and, with hindsight, succeeded in its purpose. So, just like in Holland, albeit on a different level and within a different timeframe, our cinemas were born under false premises if not auspices. And that worm has continued to gnaw at the fruit of a genuine cinema in both our countries to this day.

That is quite a bleak picture you paint. Moreover, I have some difficulty in believing the UFA connection you allude to.

And yet, it has been pervasive, albeit in a subterranean manner, on both sides of the Moerdijk (the river separating the Northern from the Southern part of Holland, and in fact the Calvinist from the Catholic tradition). Let me give you two examples. In fictional cinema, the Dutch Fons Rademakers and Flemish Roland Verhavert could be called 'fathers' of regional cinema. Both filmmakers came more or less of age just before and during World War Two. Both were 'fed' by the film and dramaturgical aesthetics of 1930s Germany. Verhavert's *Seagulls Die in the Harbour* was meant to oppose the 'vulgar' influence of the then popular Flemish film farces of Edith Kiel. Kiel had learned her trade in UFA in the 1930s, where she met Jan Vanderheyden, followed him back to Flanders in 1934, and assisted him to make *Whitey*, an almost perfect example of the UFA 'style' of the time. And, although *Seagulls Die in the Harbour* was supposed to counterbalance this heritage, Verhavert could not escape it. Its influence would continue to hold court over Verhavert's career and Flemish cinema in general. The same can be said of Rademakers, even though the influence in his case was of a different kind. Still, although officially inheriting Italian neorealism and, later, the cinema of Bergman, a fair part of Rademakers' style was derived from the same UFA lineage, and his work on stage during World War Two must have taken its artistic toll somewhere.

So, a parallel can be derived here. In both cases I am not speaking of direct content (which in art is secondary anyway), but always of aesthetics. Aesthetics which continue to plague us to this day, albeit in a different, yet unmistakable, guise and which reach further than the cinema of our little countries, permeating a great deal of contemporary European cinema.

What are these specific aesthetics, then?

To put it in a lapidary manner, and to limit it to fiction cinema, the style whereby a situation is staged and recorded in a more or less formal fashion. This approach stands in stark contrast to interpretative cinema, where technique and style and staging are elevated to metaphors of a content that reaches much deeper than the factual content. To put it roughly, the cinema of Murnau as opposed to that of Veit Harlan, or the montage of Eisenstein versus that of Leni Riefenstahl, or, closer to us, the cinema of David Lynch or Almodóvar against that of Ken Loach or Lars von Trier.

This has carried us far away from the cinema of the Low Countries.

Yes and no. In a sense, our little filmlands are metaphors for the bigger picture of Euroland. Simply put, and as I said already, the European cinema is for the major part a subsidised cinema. And when you say 'subsidy', you say 'bureaucracy'. In other words, instead of working for popes or princes as the Renaissance artists did, our filmmakers are working, whether they want it or not, for bureaucrats. And if one accepts the idea that totalitarian regimes are bureaucracies that have run amok, it is not surprising that the roots of our cinema plunge into quite a dark and fetid morass indeed.

But is that still valid today?

More than ever. Let me give you some examples – which again establish troubling parallels between the otherwise divergent Dutch and Flemish cultures. Take on the one hand either Rademakers' *De Aanslag* (*The Assault*, 1986) or, for that matter, Verhoeven's *Soldaat van oranje* (*Soldier of Orange*, 1977), and on the other hand Stijn Coninx's *Daens*. Both Dutch films support the fable that Holland was one big 'pièce de résistance' during World War Two. As for the Flemish film, for all its undeniable qualities and the filmmaker's honesty, it lives up to the official Flemish myth of Catholic and Socialist integration. In other words, these were perfect 'regime' films. That they also satisfied the audience's expectations is another story, although one could have one's doubts about these yearnings, given the fact that the press in our countries is subsidised too. And there are more recent examples. For instance, you have those turgid, often digitalised and proportionately expensive movies in Holland. And in Flanders, the recent local super-hit *Zaak Alzheimer* (*The Alzheimer Case*, Erik Van Looy, 2003). A rare example of a genre thriller, for all its attempts at trying to extirpate itself from the officially anointed groove, it remains bogged down in it. Indeed, if the plot irritates certain Belgian sore spots (child pornography, rivalry between police forces, endemic corruption) it debilitates its own intentions by reducing them to mere fairytales – again at the service of the authorities it is supposed to castigate. Is it surprising then, that all these films have, in a sense, the Germanic look and feel of old to which I alluded earlier? Naturally, this 'style' remains hidden behind 'modern' trickeries, like hip editing and digital effects, which handily pull the wool over one's eyes. But it is still there for anyone to see.

What, for you, are genuine films then? Films that are truly 'authentic', inasmuch that they are not 'at the service of the Prince' and that they connect at the same time with tradition, culture and modernity. In a word, art?

Let me answer that with far better advocates of art than myself. First, Ruskin in his biography of Turner, when he asks himself what makes a true artist. He defines it as one capable of expressing the soul of a nation; to have considered meaning and to use a language of signs that reaches beyond literal representations, while feeling that the human condition is tragic, since inexplicable forces control it. Proust (who greatly admired Ruskin) put it more succinctly. It is not the reflected thing that counts, but the reflection itself. And it is only with this approach that one can appreciate simultaneously, say, *Citizen Kane* (Orson Welles, 1941), or John Ford, and the films of Mario Bava. And perhaps, at the end of a very, very long day, some of the worthier exponents of one's own national cinema.

Still, I have great confidence in some young men and women of the upcoming generation, some of which I have the privilege to school in the arcane art of cinema. In contrast to previous generations, and thanks to the simplification of techniques (digital recording, reduced light and sound requirements, home editing), their foreknowledge of cinema has become extraordinarily extensive in the span of a few years. This might possibly free them from the shackles and obligations that some of us were subjected to, and this bodes well for the future.

Interview with Harry Kümel, March 2004

INTRODUCTION

Cinema in the Low Countries and the Question of Cultural Identity

The history of cinema in the Low Countries (The Netherlands, Belgium, Luxembourg) is over-loaded with self-doubt. Its discourse is governed by a culture of complaints: complaints of small budgets, the disinterest in/of audiences, insufficient expertise and incompetence, of lack of support (from private companies and the state), of political interventions, moral concerns, aesthetic failure, and of cultural irrelevance. Such remarks come not just from the industry itself (producers, directors, screenwriters, actors), but also from viewers, local boards and governments, and the press. Films from the Low Countries always seem to have to compete with, and address, a massive historical (and topical) burden of such anxiety.

It should be no surprise, then, that discussions of Low Countries films often seem to put a heavy emphasis on context as well. As work by Bart Hofstede and Chris Peeters *et al.* demonstrates, much effort has gone into moral manifestos, policy-guidance reports, audience-preference research and comments on business performances (Morlion 1932; Hofstede 2000; Peeters *et al.* 2000). It has become part of Low Countries film studies to stress contexts, but although contexts are of crucial importance in the study of cinema, such studies usually lack one important approach: they hardly care about the films themselves, often reduceing cinema to a sociological phenomenon (a curiosity), an economic enterprise (a commodity) or a source of concern (a threat). They hardly ever take film as film and frequently appear unable to move between discussions of contexts and the texts themselves. It almost seems as if film discourse in the Low Countries could do away with discussion of what actually happens on the screen.

This is not to say that studies of Low Countries cinema that do take the intrinsic relationship between text and context into account do not exist. They do, but they are few and far between. Most of them are confined to reviews, two-page critiques at the most, and to the occasional academic interest of mainly foreign critics and scholars like Peter Cowie, Frédéric Sojcher and Philip Mosley, whose approaches in most cases tend to be wide-sweeping, or Carol Jenks and Ivone Margulies, who ignore the origin of the films. Critical studies of particular Low Countries films, *as* Low Countries films, take up only a small proportion of that output. The main problem with this is that, while there is ample material available on Low Countries cinema, it all seems to work top-down, reducing films to unique or symptomatic examples of trends and debates (refusing them their own discourses and qualities). This, then, makes an approach on Low Countries cinema that wants not just to balance, but connect textual with contextual arguments, very difficult.

Perhaps the most obvious example of these difficulties lies in the selection of Low Countries films that is presented here, and how they have been discussed. Although hundreds of films from the Low Countries deserve specific attention, I have tried to account for as much diversity and coherence as possible. The selection will inevitably not please everyone, and, admittedly, there are some glaring omissions. A few of these are hard to overcome; there is for instance a real research gap in studying films of the 1940s, 1950s, and even 1960s. Others are the result of my own perception of Low Countries cinema discourse, in particular, the emphasis on the 1970s. Throughout, however, I have tried to present as balanced a selection as possible. In all honesty, I think the list of films discussed in this book is a solid mix of what cinema of the Low Countries represents.

Probably more important than *what* is being discussed here is *how*. As a central approach, this book aims to put its focus on the critical discussion of the film text in relation to its context. Acknowledging contextual surroundings in which films are created, the goal is to put the film text at the centre of every discussion. Hence, close analysis and, to a somewhat lesser degree, reception and ancillary discourse analyses are the main methodological tools employed in this book. In doing so, this collection first of all tries to advance textual arguments and discourses on individual Low Countries films, with the aim of offering possibilities to work upwards towards larger issues, combining text and context to produce insights into how these films work. This approach also limits the scope: working bottom-up, with a focus on individual texts, makes it virtually impossible to address a representative sample of Low Countries cinema within a single volume, and even more difficult to systematically connect Low Countries cinema with other cinematic trends and discourses in the rest of the world.

Like everything in the Low Countries, this volume is a compromise. In compiling it, a careful balance between nations, languages, periods, styles and influences had to be taken into account. The result is that this book presents twelve Dutch, eleven Belgian (three explicitly described as Flemish, two as Walloon – most referring to both language communities) and one Luxembourgish film; in six languages (Dutch/Flemish, French, English, Lëtzebuergesch, Yiddish and German); from 1914 to 1999 (encapsulating the twentieth century). With the exception of one, they are all feature films. Three of them are documentaries. Nine are debut films. I have decided to implicitly allow historical issues to enter by organising the essays chronologically. Not only does this provide the most logical order, it also allows the reader to see how Low Countries cinema has evolved, from the earliest beginnings to the most recent period, encompassing a century of filmmaking.

One crucial guide in putting together both selection and approach has been the question of cultural identity in relation to Low Countries cinema. Cultural identity is always a slippery concept. It is increasingly being used and referred to in the study of media (and film in particular) to discuss the relationship between on-screen characters, circumstances, and backgrounds and real-life contexts. Yet it is very hard to define. Zygmunt Bauman and Stuart Hall see cultural identity not as some fixed and abstract notion of what constitutes a certain group of people, but rather as a continuous re-mapping of values and habits, innovations and desires that govern a community in its trajectory through the modern world. At the same time they see the conscious quest for cultural identity as a utopian attempt to produce fixed meanings. Cultural identity is an issue central to contemporary film studies, and it has a particular significance for Low Countries cinema.

First of all, there is the issue of the region itself. As authors like Catherine Labio and J. C. H. Blom & Emiel Lamberts have pointed out, the very concept of 'the Low Countries' is problematic. It groups together three territories (The Netherlands, Belgium and Luxembourg, together the BeNeLux), bordered (some say boxed in) by three historically dominant cultures: the British to the west, the French to the south, and the German to the east. It is one of the most densely populated areas in the Western world. Linguistically, historically, politically and culturally many demarcations and unions influence the Low Countries. There are five officially recognised languages (with films produced in all of them): Dutch, Fries, German, French and Lëtzebuergesch. Variations within and among these languages, like Flemish, complicate the relationships between language groups, with important cultural consequences, in financing films for instance. Historically, all three territories have gone through significant changes, sometimes imposed upon them. All have, at one point in history, been more or less politically dominated, sometimes occupied, by the other. The current borders hold since 1839, but there are still many affinities and kinships across borders that precede that date. After World War Two, the Benelux-union between them was the direct predecessor for the European Union. It is this Benelux-heritage, together with references to when the entire region was politically unified (at various times throughout the seventeenth, eighteenth and nineteenth centuries) which momentarily holds the Low Countries together as a concept. Politically, the Low Countries are best known for their consensus politics (the Dutch Polder model being the most famous example), which guarantees proportionate political representation, making local politics a colourful mix of compromises, coalitions and debates, again with political affiliations sometimes crossing borders. Culturally, the connections between them are very strong, ranging from traditional inter-cultural exchanges (such as language unions), co-productions (theatre, film), overlapping cultural markets (literature, popular press) and cultural policy (mutual support as well as protectionism).

Given such complicated connections within the Low Countries, many debates inevitably revolve around the question of what it means to be part of the region, and how to define one's own cultural identity in relation to it; what does it mean today to be Dutch, Belgian or Luxembourgish? With what and who does one feel affiliated, and how is identity self-presented? As one among many other cultural artifacts, local cinema inevitably addresses issues of cultural identity. Even from the early stages of production, concepts of local cultural markets influence the shape and content of Low Countries cinema. Film culture(s) in the Low Countries, both practice and reception, have been affected by local political and cultural agendas (such as language, state-supported production and criticism, a relation to national public and private broadcasting, festivals, pressure groups and controversies, and so on). Most of these agendas explicitly use *and* refer to cultural identity. Yet there is a general failure to describe just *how* cultural identity informs Low Countries cinema. As a result, much of the film production in the Low Countries is said to fail to connect to its own tradition and culture, precisely because there does not seem to be any agreement on how cultural identity is portrayed. In other words, even if Low Countries cinema were to represent issues of cultural identity, no one would know it because no one has been taught to look for it. It is now high time we started, because the beauty of many Low Countries films lies in their depiction of local cultural issues.

Another reason for a focus on cultural identity is the above-mentioned complaint of a culture of self-doubt. Because of the questioning of a straightforward way of getting to know Low Countries culture, these films inevitably address questions rather than answers; they are about 'who am I?' instead of 'this is I'. They thus provide even more uncertainty, making their placement into ready-made categories or types almost impossible. This means that Low Countries cinema is never genre cinema, and is almost always self-reflective, tied to reality while failing to question it. If this sounds too negative, it is at the very least never propagandistic or colonising. Moreover, the resulting uncertainty about the cultural status of films made and watched in the Low Countries makes the business of looking for meaning in these films (and connecting that to contexts) one of cultural relevance: it may provide reasons why these films are to be complained about, why they are perceived as threats, why local audiences do not want to see them.

What, then, are the most recurrent themes and issues in Low Countries cinema? Judging from reviews and comments it seems that they are mostly concerned with ways of dealing with *eigenheid*, a concept that is difficult to translate, pointing simultaneously at characteristic properties, individualities and even oddities of who people are and how they belong in their respective environments. *Eigenheid* refers to the different ways in which people define their own being against or in relation to that of others. What is interesting in Low Countries cinema is that this not only shows itself in the interaction among characters but also between characters and landscapes, cities, ideologies and any other cultural discourse. The link to reality, to 'what is really out there', also seems to be the defining element here: as long as something is real it can be interacted with. So, generally, Low Countries films focus on representations of the real (or what is perceived as such) and tell the story of the dramatic interaction, often in terms of anxiety or memory, between a character and that (part of) reality (for more on this, see Mosley 2003).

Sounds vague or esoteric? It is, and critics often condemn Low Countries cinema for its lack of certainties. But why not see that as an advantage? The ambiguity and lack of clarity in Low Countries cinema actually allows for quite a few interesting demarcations and concepts, making up a small thematic history of Low Countries cinema.

Interaction with the real fittingly describes the tradition in which Low Countries cinema has perhaps made the most impact, internationally and historically: that of the documentary. The very first Academy Award for a Low Countries film was awarded in 1960 to Bert Haanstra's *Glas* (*Glass*, 1958), in the category of short documentary. Besides Haanstra, almost everyone is familiar with the names of Henri Storck and Joris Ivens, two 'revolutionary' filmmakers, not only capturing on camera social reality since the late 1920s, but also engaging with reality. There has been much talk about how documentary filmmakers intervene with the subject they are filming, and how their own preferences are present in their productions. Both Ivens and Storck have never concealed their left-wing sympathies, and they have become paradigms for any kind of filmmaking relating to social reality in the Low Countries. It was therefore unavoidable that in a book otherwise devoted to fiction feature films, at least a couple of documentary films would appear: *Misère au Borinage* (1934) and *Glass*, and the Ivens double-bill *Zuiderzee/Nieuwe Gronden* (*New Earth*) (1930/33) testify of the close connection between interaction with social reality, and attempts to change it; part of trying to come to grips with how groups of people define their (well-)being through their place in society.

Unsurprisingly, the documentary tradition has influenced many Low Countries film-makers, and the connection with reality permeates practically every other film discussed in this book. In some cases that connection is obvious. One of the most recent Low Countries films to receive major accolades, the Dardenne Brothers' *Rosetta* (1999), recalls much of the radicalism of Storck in its portrayal of 'urgent realism': life out there is a battle, and who we are is how we fight it. Similarly, the feminist films of Chantal Akerman and Marleen Gorris discussed in this volume point to how women have to fight a similar battle for recognition, resisting male-dominated practices, earning a right for their own representation. *Eigenheid* also becomes a formal battle here. Gorris' *De stilte rond Christine M.* (*A Question of Silence*, 1982) needs to revert to a narrative break – a dream sequence – to show the difference between the 'real world' and how life *can* be. Akerman's *Jeanne Dielman 23 Quai du Commerce 1080 Bruxelles* (*Jeanne Dielman*, 1975) needs to forcefully bend cinematic conventions of plot, narrative and tempo, almost destroying the story, to make the viewer see how 'real life' is. In every case, the connection with the documentary tradition remains essential. *Jeanne Dielman* tellingly features a cameo appearance of Storck, a way to pay tribute to a legacy, while also stressing how topical Storck's approach still is, and reminding the viewer, ever so subtly, that this documentary realism is a convention. This convention is not always broken in the most respectful of ways. *C'est arrivé pres de chez vous* (*Man Bites Dog*, Rémy Belvaux, André Bonzel and Benvoît Poelvoorde, 1992) goes to great lengths to disguise itself as a documentary, trying very hard to look real, even up to the point where one may mistake it for being unmediated and direct (a snuff movie, a home movie, found footage). It uses the formal devices of realism, in this case black-and-white photography, hand-held camera, direct camera address, real locations and amateur actors, to achieve a seemingly *cinéma vérité* look. Yet it tells a black-comedy horror story that is every bit as unreal as any other fiction film. A so-called 'mockumentary', *Man Bites Dog* thus questions our ready belief of documentary realism, urging viewers to reconsider their positions towards what they see as real.

Further away from the documentary legacy, but still very much in line with the interaction with reality is the historical realism, or authenticity, of many Low Countries films. Retelling, reshaping, or even occasionally anticipating historical events (of whatever magnitude) in Low Countries cinema always occurs through a fairly direct link with historical reality. Much effort is put into making films look historically real, and pundits are incredibly sharp in their comments on how real something should look. A case in point is *Maudite soit la guerre* (*War is Hell*, Alfred Machin, 1914), the oldest well-known feature film of the Low Countries, and a peculiar anticipation of World War One warfare. Released only weeks before the outbreak of the Great War, it has become a model for historical representation. Another, perhaps better-known example is Paul Verhoeven's *Soldaat van Oranje* (*Soldier of Orange*, 1977), for a long time considered to be one of the most authentic films dealing with World War Two. While being a commercial success and a unique blend between an entertaining story and a (minutely detailed) slice of history, it was still criticised for its apparent lack of realism by several critics, who thought Verhoeven was being too sensationalistic. Much of this over-emphasis on 'authenticity' (a word often used but hardly defined), that never seemed to have bothered Hollywood, is the result of critical anxiety. Given the importance of the interaction with reality for the quest for characters' identity and, hence, their own cultural identity, critics had to be able to trust that reality. And in order for it to be trusted, it needed to be authentic – it needed to be comparable with its real life counterpart, even if that 'real life' lies hundreds of years in the past, and could not possibly be known other than through such representations. In any case, the urge for authenticity is more the result of a dominant critical stance than of filmmakers' choices. So while Hugo Claus' screenplay for *Mira, of de Teleurgang van de Waterhoek* (*Mira*, Fons Rademakers, 1971) was seen as an example of authenticity in setting, it was criticised for its *oneigen* (unauthentic) use of language dialects. The bridge location in *Mira* has since become an official national landscape monument; the language use is still an issue (a recurrent problem, particularly in Flemish-language films – or should I say, with Flemish-language critics).

Authenticity in setting and language are also very much at the centre of minority identity films like, *A Wopbobaloobop a Lopbamboom* (Andy Bausch, 1989) and *Left Luggage* (Jeroen Krabbé, 1998). These films are included in this book because they tell the story of cultural encounters within smaller communities. They are not based on actual events, yet they are no less relevant than the bigger stories. Without actual history to hold on to, they rely more on stereotyping and metaphors, but they are nevertheless very straightforward in being representations about real life; *A Wopbobaloobop...* in describing Southern Luxembourgish culture and its contact with French and German influences, and *Left Luggage* in telling the tale of differences and difficulties in Yiddish cultural presence and identity in the Lowlands. It is symptomatic that in both cases real life comparisons are never far away: southern Luxembourg and Jewish culture fall well outside the main cultural scope of Low Countries cultures. Even within such a small and multi-faceted range, where everything seems to be an exception, they are the bigger exception. Equally significant, in both cases cultural identity and reality as a whole are seen as sites of contestation – something to be fought over, causing drama and distress – rather than something one feels comfortable with. Is it a coincidence that the main characters from both stories are, and remain, alone? Or could they be seen as examples of a nomadic cultural identity – never fixed, always dynamic, and impossible to represent?

Moving away from real life connotations, Low Countries cinema shows a remarkable relationship to other cultural representations, most notably painting, theatre and literature. In painting, the huge international reputations of Van Eyck, Bosch, Brueghel, Rubens, Rembrandt, Van Gogh, Mondriaan (or De Stijl in general) and Surrealism (and Paul Delvaux and René Magritte in particular) invite comparisons between pictorial styles. When films as diverse as *Mariken van Nieumeghen* (*Mariken*, Jos Stelling, 1974), the visually stunning *Les Lèvres Rouges* (*Daughters of Darkness*, Harry Kümel, 1971) and *Karakter* (*Character*, Mike Van Diem, 1997) can all be linked to local traditions in painting then this is an important source of inspiration for at least the visual look of Low Countries films. *Mariken*, Stelling's debut film, even bases its narrative structure on painting. Its depiction of peasant and pagan life in the late Middle Ages, and its miracle play source material, invite a Boschian and Brueghelian tableau style: rude and realistic. Yet *Mariken* is an isolated case (and not only for that reason – its finance structure makes it a most curious example of filmmaking). Generally, the inspiration from painting seems less structural than could be assumed. There is no denying the influence, as many essays in this book testify and as documentaries on painting demonstrate, but it remains unclear to what degree visual styles, or even narratives in Low Countries fiction cinema, can be structurally linked to painting traditions.

The same goes for theatrical influences. *De Noorderlingen* (*The Northerners*, 1992) by Alex Van Warmerdam is offered in this book as a film that draws its influences from both painting and theatre, and as a perfect example of Low Countries cinema at its most artful. It is also exceptional in that it drew far more attention (and viewers) than theatre-inspired films usually do. The Low Countries have a vivid theatre tradition, of international reputation, but apart from recurrent remarks about the 'theatricality' of acting performances, and not for lack of trying, this hardly leads to easy translations between stage and screen.

Far more important, in aesthetics as well as in policy, is the influence of literature. Ever since the advent of state-supported, community-regulated film financing, literature has played a pivotal role in Low Countries cinema. Part of that influence stems from a persistent rumour – as many times denied as confirmed – that the funding of productions depends on the *eigenheid* (in this case cultural origin) of the source material. Literature from indigenous origin supposedly always fares better with subsidy commissions. True or not, as Hans Van Driel has shown, it has led to a huge number of literary adaptations (see Van Driel 2003 for an overview of this issue). Given the quantity, it is not easy to categorise them, but a few distinctions stand out. As with painting, theatre and the documentary tradition, realism is an important aesthetic device in literary adaptations. Of all kinds of adaptations, it is probably the most attempted one, because it allows the marriage of two already established traditions: filmic realism and literary realism. Of all films attempting this marriage, this book focuses on Van Diem's *Character*, one of the most successful recent adaptations. It is based on a novel by Ferdinand Bordewijk, an author belonging to the New Realism school and, although framed in a highly stylised manner, the film adheres to a realistic depiction of events. The success of *Character*, which won an Academy Award in 1998?, is typical for the kind of appreciation high-profile literary adaptations from the Low Countries usually receive abroad (the majority of major prizes go to adaptations); a recognition of both fidelity (to the source) and classical auteurism. Much of this auteurism can be traced to writers rather than filmmakers. Within the Low Countries some writers, like Hugo Claus, or Harry Mulisch (from which Fons Rademakers adapted *De Aanslag* (*The Assault*), which won an Academy Award in 1987), are seen as safe investments: basing a film on their work is guaranteed to draw some state support and limited distribution, if only because of their reputation. This often leads to films in which the difference between novel and film becomes the major point of discussion, a source for aesthetic considerations of film language versus literary language, as the essay here on *Twee Vrouwen* (*Twice a Woman*, 1979), a Mulisch novel filmed by George Sluizer, demonstrates.

How all of this ties in with the issue of cultural identity is more complex. Much of Low Countries literature has been discussed in terms of representing or even shaping cultural identity: a result of the conscious attempts in the nineteenth century – both Catholic and Calvinist – to have literature play a culturally relevant role in 'educating' society. Needless to say, much of this education was part of an attempt to gain control over cultural representations and their possible meanings. With the coming of film, some of these attempts were renewed. The filming of *De Witte* (*Whitey*, Jan Vanderheyden, 1934), based on a realistic yet idyllic countryside novel (a so-called *heimat* novel) by Ernest Claes, is an example of such a struggle for control, which explains why much of the film's discussion in this book focuses on the context of its production and its public presence. Yet, as this and many other examples came to demonstrate, it proved a lot more difficult to force film (and filmmakers) to be seen along the same lines as nineteenth-century literature. Many writers and filmmakers consciously challenged traditional interpretations by introducing, especially since the mid-to-late 1960s, sexuality as a pivotal metaphor for the living of life. Probably the best-known example of this combination of resistance, flamboyance and sexual openness is Paul Verhoeven's international breakthrough film, *Turks Fruit* (*Turkish Delight*, 1973), which is discussed here in relation to its representation of sexuality. Recently heralded as the best Dutch film ever, it is an adaptation of a scandal-novel by Jan Wolkers. The film itself became a controversy too through its explicit on-screen depictions of sexual activity as well as for its openness in seeing sex as culturally important. With *Mira*, which also features graphic nudity, and the *Emmanuelle* films (starring Dutch actress Sylvia Kristel), *Turkish Delight* became an inspiration for many filmmakers, a number of whom cared more about the possibility of drawing audiences through sex and nudity, than about cultural identity. As a result, the cinema of the Low Countries has garnered a reputation for depicting more nudity (especially frontal nudity) than any other regional cinema tradition.

There is also the issue of filmic realism as a pure cinematic device. Whether Low Countries cinema proceeds from literature to make its own cultural claims, or just builds on what is already culturally present in the source material is still an ongoing argument. The one case on which most critics agree that film has made its own impact is with 'magic realism'; probably the closest Low Countries cinema comes to developing a style of its own. Originally derived from a Belgian literary tradition, magic realism became the centre of a filmic style that has also been described as 'filmic surrealism', '*mise-en-abyme*', 'fantasy realism' and even 'poetic realism'. Its main characteristic is the individualisation of cultural identity, narrowing it down to crises within one character. The film which put magic realism on the map is André Delvaux's *De Man die zijn haar kort liet knippen* (*The Man Who Had His Hair Cut Short*, 1965) – one of the films through which Low Countries cinema entered modernism, and an adaptation of Johan Daisne's novel. *The Man Who Had His Hair Cut Short* is a quest into identity crises – gradually revealing that we can no longer trust what we see or hear, reality becoming a dream. As discussed in the essay in this collection, magic realism focuses on the uncertainty of establishing a cultural identity, the surreal melancholy of everyday life. Minute details in language, visuals and behaviour cast doubts on the truthfulness of the very real settings in which characters live and travel, until we finally give up looking for truth and settle, with the characters, for quiet contemplation – death, lunacy or a surrender to strangeness.

Both *The Man Who Had His Hair Cut Short* and *Turkish Delight* are key films for Low Countries cinema, moving beyond established traditions and enabling the possibility of an *eigen* (own) cinema of cultural relevance. Few films have been able to follow this lead. Some of Harry Kümel's films succeeded. Two others, discussed in this book, are *Crazy Love* (Dominique

Deruddere, 1987) and *Toto le héros* (*Toto the Hero*, Jaco Van Dormael, 1991). Both films tell the story of a fractured protagonist whose quest for identity and self-knowledge leads to crime, despair, moral ambiguity and, eventually, death – or rather, self-destruction. The lives that *Crazy Love*'s Harry and the eponymous Toto lead – always longing to be someone else (dreamers believing their actual lives are somewhere else) – are templates for cultural self-doubt in the Low Countries. The way both stories are structured and broken down into fragments, and the ambiguous style which never reveals whether we are shown dream or reality, demonstrate how Low Countries cinema also formally addresses this cultural quest.

Does this mean all films from the Low Countries fit this reality/dream/identity framework? Well, yes and no. Of course there are exceptions. Many films consciously try to go against the framework. Apart from the fact that this, in a way, reinforces its importance, it also means that there are alternative models to be adhered to. A couple of important ones need some elaboration. Many filmmakers from the Low Countries have tried to create genre/Hollywood formula films – some believing it would lead to more success, others believing it was an aesthetic way out of the cultural constraints in which they felt trapped. Comedies of the 1930s and 1950s, exploitation films of the 1970s, and high-concept thrillers from the 1980s and 1990s all have their place within Low Countries cinema. Yet many of these films still show a curious preference for identity issues. Consider two films discussed in this book – Sluizer's complex, successful and highly influential thriller *Spoorloos* (*The Vanishing*, 1988), again an adaptation, in the end begs the question of the protagonist's identity and its main difference from the novel lies exactly in revealing the identity of the murderer/murdered in different ways. Similarly, Kümel may have intended *Daughters of Darkness* as a piece of commercial trash but the film meticulously dissects the relationship between four people, up to the point where the merging of identities becomes its central theme. The commercial success of both films should not distract from their significance as quests for identity.

Another important point is that of foreigners filming in the Low Countries. Douglas Sirk and Max Ophüls aside, few well-known foreign filmmakers have been active in the region. A notable recent exception may be Luxembourg which has attracted foreign interest as a location. Even then, identity quests seem to trickle through. In Ophüls' *Komedie om geld* (*The Trouble with Money*, 1936) the main character learns an important lesson about his own identity. The fact that he *does* seem to be able to come to terms with it even accounts for somewhat of a break from regular Low Countries cinema themes. In general, however, the quest for and inability to obtain a fixed cultural identity breathes through almost every Low Countries film.

Still, this does not mean that the international reach of Low Countries cinema is limited. As Bart Hofstede argues, this perceived limitation is a myth. Compared to other European countries, and put in perspective, Low Countries cinema culture appears to do fairly well on the international market, especially since the 1970s. There have been a string of international awards, noted festival appearances, commercial surprise successes (*Daughters of Darkness*, *The Vanishing*) and Hollywood star careers (Paul Verhoeven, Jan De Bont, Rutger Hauer, Jeroen Krabbé, Dominique Deruddere, Carel Struyken and the inimitable Jean-Claude Van Damme – 'the muscles from Brussels'). Sylvia Kristel, Monique Van de Ven, Willeke Van Ammelrooy and, recently, Famke Janssen, have been among the most gazed at female stars (especially among film students and scholars) and Chantal Akerman almost single-handedly put feminist cinema on an international platform. Ginette Vincendeau names her, with Marleen Gorris, as pivotal to the canon of European cinema. Artistic avant-gardes and fringe industries have also made international impact. The student and short film culture is active and receives international attention and acclaim on regular basis. The art films of Johan Van Der Keuken and Dutch video artists are world-renowned. The animation film industry in Belgium has been one of the most admired and successful worldwide, delivering animators for Disney, DreamWorks, Hanna-Barbera and others on an almost constant basis. Raoul Servais is one of the most celebrated animators alive. Generally, Low Countries cinema technicians are, as Philip Mosley rightly puts it, 'among the best trained' in Europe. International co-productions also witness the significant input of the Low Countries often without the recognition they deserve, as films like *The Passion of Darkly Noon* (Philp Ridley, 1995), *Une Liaison Pornographique* (*A Pornographic Affair*, Frédéric Fonteyne, 1999) and *Farinellli, il castrato* (Gérard Corbiau, 1994) demonstrate. And as a crossroads of cultural influences, Low Countries film events and institutions are of paramount importance for the distribution and preservation of worldwide film culture (as the reputation of the three national film archives – the Royal Film Archive in Brussels, the Dutch Filmmuseum in Amsterdam and the CNA in Luxembourg – have so often demonstrated). Low Countries festivals are also well-known and respected throughout the world, from Exprmntl in Knokke and the Documentary Film Festival in Amsterdam to the International Film Festival Rotterdam which showcases some of the finest talents in international cinema.

As this brief and incomplete summary shows, the borders between an identifiable Low Countries origin and sheer internationalism/globalisation are hard to define. How Belgian is, or has been, Van Damme? This puts the issue of cultural identity in yet another light, not diminishing the importance of the concept (for cultural identity in global perspective is of prime interest to everyone) but questioning the attainability of reaching even the most vague of answers to 'who am I?' Perhaps we will never know, but this has not stopped Low Countries filmmakers from asking.

There are many ways to see films: as entertainment, as a means of distinction, as a way of looking for belonging. In this introduction I have emphasised the importance of cultural identity as a way of making sense of Low Countries cinema. But let us not forget that, while addressing important distinctions and ambiguities between the *eigen* and the other, past and present, individual and collective, tradition and innovation, and dream and reality, Low Countries cinema also, and perhaps foremost, does what films all over the world do: it provides fun.

I hope this book transfers some of that fun to the reader.

Ernest Mathijs

MAUDITE SOIT LA GUERRE WAR IS HELL

ALFRED MACHIN, BELGIUM, 1914

Maudite soit la guerre (*War is Hell*, 1914, also known as *War Be Damned*) is considered a key film in Belgian film history because of its value as a film made on the cusp of modernity; a work that, like cinema itself at that time, was a broker between the old and the new. Its director, Alfred Machin, had tried his hand at several other occupations before turning to filmmaking. Although little is known about his childhood and youth, we do know that he was born in Blendecque, in the north of France near the Belgian border, in 1887, and that both his father and his mother died before his eighteenth birthday. After his military service, served in North Africa between 1897 and 1900, he worked as a photo *retoucheur*. Shortly thereafter, he worked as a photographic journalist for the Parisian magazine *L'Illustration.* In 1905 he started working as a cameraman for Ferdinand Zecca, who at the time was working with Pathé in Montreuil. He continued his Pathé career as a *chasseur d'images.* His adventurous spirit and an experienced guide, the German agronomist Adam David, eventually lead him to the heart of Africa. During two African expeditions (1908 and 1910), he became fascinated with the wildlife there, eventually bringing some animals home with him (six ostriches, three gazelles, two giraffes, two hyenas, a panther, snakes, a baby leopard, two lions, three apes, five wild cats and a crocodile), some of which would eventually appear or even star in his later fiction films. The anthropological reports, wildlife documentaries and hunt scenes that he brought from his expeditions were distributed by Pathé and became popular with audiences around the world. When he was not in Africa, he continued his work for the *Pathé Journal,* shooting newsreels in France and Holland.

In 1909, Machin completed his first fiction film. *Le moulin maudit* (*The Mill*) was shot in a small Belgian village near Ghent. Here Machin came to develop a style which became the trademark of many of his early fiction films made in the low countries (for example, *L'histoire de Minna Claessens* (*The Story of Minna Claessens*, 1912), *La Fille de Delft* (*A Tragedy in the Clouds*, 1914) and *War is Hell*: a dramatic linear love story combined with meticulous framing of typical landscapes and picturesque settings. There is evidence that in his youth he fostered a special affinity with Flemish culture and folklore, which he often used in his films.

In 1911, Machin returned from the French Riviera, where he was shooting a series of fiction films for Pathé, to take up the position of artistic director of *Hollandsche Film,* the Belgian-Dutch Pathé film production branch located in Amsterdam. This marked the beginning of his career as an independent director. In this position he directed no less than fifteen fiction films, mainly folkloristic rural dramas targeted at local markets. Machin was transferred to Brussels in 1912 to establish a Belgian film production branch: *Belge-cinéma Film.* The studio had its headquarters at a former recreational ground on the outskirts of Brussels, named Karreveld. *Belge-cinéma Film* was the first film production company in Belgium, and it would remain the only one until Hippolyte de Kempeneer founded his *Compagnie Belge des films cinématographiques* after World War One. Before Machin directed his first feature for *Belge-Cinéma Film* (*The Story of Minna Claessens*) only one fiction film had been made in Belgium: *La famille Van Petegem à la mer* (*The Van Petegem Family Goes to the Seaside,* Isidore Moray, 1912). As such, Machin became one of the pioneers standing at the cradle of Belgian fiction film production. As Catherine Fowler suggests in an essay on Machin, 'the dispatching by Pathé of Alfred Machin to Belgium might read initially as an act of colonisation of Belgium by Pathé', the major company thus gaining control over film exhibition, distribution and production in Belgium.

Although both Alfred Machin and *Belge-cinéma Film* were of French origin, his films can be seen as uniquely Belgian. Machin gave his films a local touch by using popular actors from Brussels theatres and traditional folkloristic settings and citing references to the great moments of Belgian history. He also anticipated the fascination for exoticism and frivolity peculiar to the cheerful and Burgundian Brussels mentality by producing amusing sketches starring his wild animals. In 1913, while working in Belgium, Machin directed his most accomplished film, *War is Hell*. Only a few months after its release, Machin was called up by the French army to join the war effort and was sent to Biarritz. In 1915 he became the Pathé-delegate for the *Societé Cinématographique de l'Armée,* with whom he would end up working until the end of the war. In 1917, he was given a special mission: he was to accompany D. W. Griffith to the battlefields of Verdun, where the famous American director wanted to shoot some scenes for his 1918 war film *Hearts of the World,* set in a French village during World War One.

The war years turned the tide for Pathé. In France the company was surpassed by competitor Gaumont and on the world market American companies quickly took over. In 1919, Machin was put to work in Nice. He eventually managed to purchase the Nice studio complex in the beginning of the 1920s, renovating the studio and renting the shooting facilities to such renowned directors as Leonce Perret, Germaine Dulac, Jacques Feyder and Jean Durand. In

1923, he had modest success with his comedy *Bêtes … comme les hommes* (*Animals as Stupid as Men*). The film, in which all parts were played by animals, was distributed by United Artists, and offered Machin some financial breathing space. The amelioration was only temporary. In the years between 1924 and 1927 his own film productions received a low profile. In 1929, the *Revue Belge du Cinéma* announced the death of Alfred Machin, stating that he was killed by one of his wild panthers. Other sources, however, claim he died of a heart attack.

War is Hell, the focus of this essay, holds a central position in Machin's oeuvre. The film marks his fifteenth feature and was produced by *Belge-cinéma Film*. Machin both wrote and directed the film. The cameramen were his usual collaborator Jacques Bizeuil and his young apprentice Paul Flon, who would later become one of the most important Belgian directors.

War is Hell tells the Griffithian story of two friends from unnamed neighbouring countries, who become separated by war and then, as rival airmen, mistakenly kill each other in ignorance. The Modzel family, Mr and Mrs Modzel and their grown-up children Lidia and Sigismond, receive a visitor from a neighbouring country. The young Adolphe Hardeff stays with them as he trains to become a pilot, together with his newfound friend Sigismond. Soon Adolphe falls in love with Lidia. The beautiful idyll is brutally disturbed by the outbreak of war. Sigismond goes into service and Adolphe returns to his country to join his army. When an enemy pilot destroys the aeroplanes and hot-air balloons of Sigismond's army base, Sigismond volunteers to pursue the attacker. Not knowing that it is his friend Adolphe who is flying the plane, he sets off in pursuit with great audacity. After a spectacular air duel and an emergency landing, Adolphe kills Sigismond with a shotgun and is killed himself when Sigismond's company set fire to the windmill in which he is hiding. Later on, one of Sigismond's fellow soldiers, Lt Maxim, visits the Modzel family ignoring the exact facts of the death of their son, to bring them his personal belongings. The soldier falls in love with Lidia. The young girl, whose hopes for a safe return of her fiancé Adolphe have already been shattered, agrees to marry him. When she finds out that her brother and Adolphe killed each other, she breaks the engagement and seeks solace in a convent. After one last inter-title *'chagrin d'amour dure toute la vie'* ('the sorrow of love lasts a lifetime'), the film ends with a close-up of the grieving woman.

Financial support for the film came from Pathé. However, according to some sources, the director also received important logistical aid from the Belgian Army who are said to have supplied him with one or two infantry companies, trucks, cars, cannons, zeppelins and aeroplanes. The Belgian Air Force was established in 1911 and even in 1913 the number of aeroplanes available for loan must have been limited. If this information is correct, the Army must have lent Machin almost all its planes and zeppelins. Although Machin was at the height of his career, this kind of support would have been unheard of. Motives for such a collaboration are unknown. We can only guess that the Army may have wanted to publicise the need to develop military aviation in case of a future war. The film was completed in September 1913 and should consequently have been released before the end of the year. This, however, was not the case. The first screening took place in May 1914 in Brussels, barely three months before the German Army invaded Belgium. The film ran for three weeks, indicating a reasonable success. Pathé-Frères took care of the international distribution, screening the film as far afield as New York, Paris, Marseille and Berlin.

Unintentionally prophetic, in the Belgian Pathé programme (14–20 May 1914) the film was announced with the eloquent message that war, although cursed, remains a necessary patriotic duty. Several elements in the film, for example the eternal grief and sadness of Lidia over the death of the two boys, offer the possibility for the film to be read as pacifist in intent. The director's fascination with modern technology and warfare, however, successfully complicates such an interpretation. Whether it was really the intention of Machin to make a plea for peace is still a source of contestation. The supposed pacifism might, however, have been the reason why Pathé initially postponed the première. In May 1914, an advertising campaign accompanied the French release. In these advertisements Pathé maintained a stony silence about the pacifist elements of the film, instead stressing the fact that with this film, they, before all their competitors, could inform the audience about the progressive technical devices a country has at its disposal to defend itself in a modern war. Preceding the release, advertisements in several cinema journals recommended the film for its spectacular scenes: a military airfield set on fire, an air duel, and the burning down of a windmill.

A few weeks after its release in Paris, the film was taken out of circulation and re-released under a new title – *Mourir pour la patrie* (*To Die For Your Country*). Most likely, it was then provided with new, more suitable inter-titles. The American critic W. Stephen Bush praised the film for its beautifully coloured, picturesque and spectacular depiction of war. From his review it is clear that in May 1914 America had yet to feel any immediate threat from the war that would soon set Europe on fire. As Bush commented, 'The film is full of the strange incidents of war and of episodes such as will be possible only in the war of the future. Of these latter the fight in the air and the destruction of a number of dirigible balloons is easily the most sensational.' War in the air was obviously still considered science fiction.

After a short rerun in 1918 the film was more or less forgotten until Francis Bolen and André Thirifays made reference to it in 1954. In a programme on Belgian national television Bolen showed a clip from both *War is Hell* and *A Tragedy in the Clouds*. In a subsequent newspaper commentary relating to the program, Thirifays compared Machin to D. W. Griffith. This marked the beginning of a slow re-appreciation of Machin, his oeuvre and his place in European film history. In the 1960s, it was Bolen who took great pains in restoring the two films. In 1968, Francis Lacassin was the first to write Machin's biography, and also managed to successfully catalogue most of his films. Although details about his life were scarce and most of his films seemed to be lost, this biography is still a standard work for research on Machin. Recently, Lacassin published an extended version of the biography, with new information and accompanied by many illustrations. Bolen, author of one of the earliest and most important film histories of Belgian cinema, devoted an entire chapter to the work of Machin in which he tried to reconstruct the director's conduct in Belgium on the basis of press articles and interviews. To a large extent, we owe it to Bolen's highlighting the achievements of Machin that he did not completely disappear from Belgian film history. In the 1990s, several European film archives joined together to rescue his films from obscurity. Consequently, numerous films were rediscovered and restored and Machin landed a place in film history. The picture remains incomplete but several new approaches to his work shed a different light on his rich legacy.

One aspect of *War is Hell* worth focusing on is the opposing ways in which the war is revealed and depicted. The representation of war oscillates between a depiction of traditional warfare and an anticipation of an unknown, modern world conflict. On the one hand, Machin shows the then familiar image of the war as comprising of huge cavalry and ground army charges. Because of the extensive use of long shots, real audience identification became impossible; the audience was too distanced from any personal involvement to fully realise the horror of what was happening on-screen. By not showing death and destruction, the conflict appeared devoid of any real consequences.

Before World War One, Belgium was politically and culturally mostly in the French sphere of influence. The two nations shared an official language, a geographical border and, to a certain extent, a set of cultural values. It appears that the ideas about warfare in pre-war Belgium were generated by images from the Franco-Prussian War in 1870, the last war that took place on French territory. After the Franco-Prussian War a series of radical changes took place so that by 1914 the European armed forces were using the very latest in artillery technology. The anachronistic officer corps failed to realise that the use of new weapons required the application of new strategies. The employment of traditional methods, whereby troops advanced towards each other across an open field, or where soldiers fought in close contact, were no longer the way to win a war. It was yet to be recognised that 'to see but not to be seen' would become the most important creed of soldiers fighting within a deadlock situation on the fields of World War One. Orthodox images of offensive warfare continued to be used in popular literature, painting, photography and cinematography until the advent of the war. From this background, the way in which Alfred Machin represented war was no great surprise.

Machin displayed a sensitivity towards the depiction of death and bloodshed. The same hesitation towards the use of violent war scenes is found in most of the photographs of the Franco-Prussian War and the Commune of Paris. Many photographers visited the battlefields, choosing to photograph desolated ruins instead of casualties. By the end of the nineteenth century, the horrors of the French-German conflict had faded into memory. In 1910, the French-Prussian War's fortieth anniversary was celebrated with commemoration and glorification ceremonies. The 1913 military painting exhibition in Paris exhibited a revival of paintings about the French defeat in 1870. The paintings did not focus on the original humiliation of the defeat, but reflected a strong disappointment that a chance for vengeance never occurred in the previous forty years. The exalted heroism in the immediate aftermath of the war had now disappeared, in favour of paintings with a true patriotic appeal. In the aftermath of the Morocco crisis of 1911, the whole of Europe experienced an awakening of patriotic feelings. The same sentiments are also reflected in *War is Hell* as Machin proved sensitive to a certain patriotic heroism. Bush's critique in the *Moving Picture World* stated: 'in this feature enough is shown of the horrors of strife and carnage to justify it's lurid title, but the glamour and glory of the tented field is by no means neglected'.

Similar sentiments were present in French films released at the beginning of the 1910s. France was still the world's leading film producer, exporting its films all over the world. References to the imminent war were implicit, but the use of allegories and patriotic iconography were enough to influence the audience. Showing manoeuvring armies was the dominant mode of representing military activity because it demonstrated strength and was seen to enhance the patriotic feelings of the audience. Film producers used images from newsreels, where wars had long been a rewarding subject. Because of technical limitations, many of the war scenes were re-enacted in a studio. The images that were shot at the front were mostly panoramic views of troops charging on the battlefield, filmed from a safe distance, as was seen in *War is Hell*.

A traditional image of warfare and a re-born patriotism can also be found in popular literature describing fictional imaginary wars. Between 1910 and 1914, in Europe and the United States, more than sixty stories about imaginary wars were published. They would take place in the near future and the adversaries would be existing countries. Most of the authors had political motives, attempting to alert the audience to the fact that their national army would not be prepared if war broke out. At the same time, they attempted to encourage the people and their leaders to do something about the situation. Although the wars were set in the future, the authors took it for granted that the next war would be fought more or less after the style of the last, and that war would continue in a relatively restrained and humane manner. This lack of imagination and foresight can be explained by a gap between the traditional knowledge about warfare and the fast developments in military technology.

In the air raid sequence, there is a completely different representation of the war. Prior to the outbreak of war, the air force base where the two main characters were being trained was represented as a playground where all the aeroplanes could be admired, touched and tested as if they were toys. The base was shot in a quasi-documentary style, with the camera slowly moving amongst the aeroplanes. When the war broke out, these toys changed into merciless, murderous machines, and one senses a strong fascination for these new technological possibilities within the film. Machin was a pioneer, already making his first aerial shots for Pathé in 1910. In the film, extensive use is made of hot-air balloons and aeroplanes, here also shot in a quasi-documentary style. Balloons had been used for military observation since the second half of the eighteenth century, yet the type of round balloon used in Machin's film fell out of use at the end of the nineteenth century in favour of the newer cigar-shaped balloons. A special balloon company was installed in the Belgian Army in 1910. Due to the large number of ground personnel needed, the army could employ a fleet of only four balloons, but in Machin's film there are a great number of inflated balloons at the army base. The enemy pilot doubtless understood the strategic importance of the balloons and as a result attempts to destroy them. Their destruction is filmed as an explosion of colour, through the use of tints.

Though the military use of hot air balloons was already cutomary in 1914, military aviation was barely beyond the earliest stages of development. The aviation branch of the Belgian Army dated from 1911. In 1914, the army had 24 aeroplanes and 37 pilots at its disposal. Over the course of World War One military aviation would develop at a high speed, though for the most part it was limited to observational assignments. Some experiments had been carried out with machine guns mounted on aeroplanes but there was little enthusiasm for their use on the field. In the film, an air attack is carried out by the pilot throwing grenades out of the plane. The first real air bombardments took place in the summer of 1914. The film was shot a year earlier; hence what is depicted in *War is Hell* is a surprisingly visionary anticipation of the unknown developments in aviation during World War One. Or, as Modris Eksteins puts it more generally: 'the First World War undermined the credibility of what was conceived previously as a determined civilisation. The war encouraged fragmentation and fantasy … it encouraged a culture of the event, which relied on technology and innovation.'

Although the air duel is shot from a long distance, it is easy to identify with what is happening. The audience would have familiarised themselves with the two main characters and their fate, more than the anonymous characters fighting on the battlefield. The connection between the bombing and the consequent destruction on the ground is more pronounced. On the other hand, no casualties were shown and there was such a beauty to the way the images were framed, audiences may still have been distracted from the harsh reality of the conflict. Whether this film bears witness to a certain idea of pacifism remains open to debate. It can be said, however, that whatever pacifistic tendencies the film may have, they are certainly countered by Machin's explicit fascination for war technology and his neglect to show its consequences.

In can also be noted that over the course of the film, a progressive individualisation of war takes place. The balloon scene stands midway between an impersonal representation of war, consisting of massive charges, and the air duel sequence in which the war became individualised by focusing only on two familiar characters as they fight to the death. And it is only by their death that the audience is confronted with the real consequences of war. However, Machin does not completely extricate himself from older notions of the glory of death in battle. When the parents are informed that their son died as a hero on the field of honour, the pacifist message of the film is lost amidst the championing of valour, bravery and patriotism for one's country.

In terms of pre-war Belgian cinema, *War is Hell* occupies a prominent place. The film reflects the atmosphere of the pre-World War One era during which society as a whole seemed to hesitate between tradition and modernity. In the representation of war, this duality is connected to Machin's moral ambivalence, in which he hovers between horror and fascination vis-à-vis warfare. Alfred Machin's contribution to film history can hardly be over-estimated. He explored the many possibilities cinema, as a new twentieth-century medium, offered for the expression of artistic and political ideas. He was both an individual artistic spirit and a commercial talent. Within the strict rules and regulations of a multinational company like Pathé, he managed to hold on to his artistic freedom and social commitment. Thanks to his originality, creativity and sense of adventure his rich legacy deserves an important place in Belgian and European film history; his efforts for *Belge-cinéma Film* gave the starting signal for the emergence of Belgian film production. For many years Alfred Machin has been neglected in European film history. Thankfully, his oeuvre now has a place it deserves.[*]

Leen Engelen

[*] For this analysis I used the version of the film as restored by the Nederlands Film Museum and released on VHS (45 mins.), and the copy of the Royal Belgian Film Archive (55 mins.). I would like to sincerely thank Mrs Gabrielle Claes of the Royal Belgian Film Archive for giving me access to the film. I would also like to thank Mrs Clementine De Blieck for her much appreciated assistance.

ZUIDERZEE and NIEUWE GRONDEN NEW EARTH

JORIS IVENS, THE NETHERLANDS, 1930–33 AND 1933

Two of the most significant films produced in the Netherlands in the 1930s were Joris Ivens' silent *Zuiderzee* (1930–33) and his radically transformed sound version of the same material made in 1933, *Nieuwe Gronden* (*New Earth*). These two great works may not have determined the future course of Dutch cinema, but they are undeniably the cornerstones in the career of one of the Netherlands' greatest filmmakers. At the same time, the films have deep roots in the Dutch political, social, cultural and cinematic scene between the wars. Therefore, my emphasis on the *textuality* of these two different film versions of the emblematically Dutch national epic, the mammoth Zuiderzee reclamation project, should not rule out reading the two films as traces of an artistic *process* – exemplary, dynamic and complex, encapsulated in the binary terms 'from epic to agitprop'.

By 1929, Ivens had already established a reputation as the most visible member of the Amsterdam avant-garde filmmaking community gathered around the association *Filmliga*. In that year, he agreed to make *Wij Bouwen* (*We Are Building*) for the *Nederlandsche Bouwvak Arbeiders Bond*, the Dutch construction-workers' union, on behalf of the film production unit within the Ivens family photography company CAPI. The film was to celebrate the union's twenty-fifth anniversary and to promote recruitment. Ivens was already the author of several internationally recognised short works, most notably *De Brug* (*The Bridge*, 1928) and *Regen* (*Rain*, 1929). But the union commission was the beginning of a completely new career phase, shifting from artisanal status to professional, and from a conception of film as personal artistic expression to that of film as a means of communication to specific publics, or, as he described it himself, 'the integration of an artist in society'. The next few years, the most prolific of his career, would see, in addition to the Zuiderzee films, the industrial commission *Philips Radio* (1931, his first sound film), the Soviet feature *Komsomol* (1932, his first major international project – an Ivensian hybrid of Socialist Realist narrative and sound modernism) and the Belgian *Misère au Borinage* (*Borinage*, 1933, the prototype of activist documentary, with co-director Henri Storck). Each of these was in its own way a breakthrough in documentary film practice, both artistically and politically, but Ivens would return regularly to Amsterdam to join his collaborators, to build on the project that would eventually become *We Are Building*.

The original conception of *We Are Building* was, as Ivens' first autobiography states, 'the pride and importance of a man who works with his hands, who builds factories, homes, schools, and dams ... the feeling of dignity, solidarity and force that comes through that pride ... and the fight through union for the rights of all labour'. Ivens tackled this apparently prosaic subject with an enthusiasm that must have baffled his friends in *Filmliga*. Eventually, the film would cover the construction of housing and offices in Amsterdam, factories and caissons in Rotterdam, chemical plants near Maastricht, dikes in the Zuiderzee, a new railway line in Kerkrade province, as well as documenting the sinking of piles in Amsterdam. There was also a survey of new architectural trends and glimpses of various union activities such as the 1929 Rotterdam congress. The Zuiderzee material, supported by the Dutch government to document the draining techniques in use, was the departure point for the feature-length *Zuiderzee*, completed several years later.

We Are Building's duration of over two hours displays an uneven style and is infused with Ivens' lyrical flair and analytic perceptiveness. The version deposited in New York's Museum of Modern Art archives by Ivens in the early 1940s is organised, like a series of notebook entries, around certain aspects of building (scaffolding, bricklaying, and so on) or union events. Despite the radical change in Ivens' subject matter, he was still developing his repertoire of three stylistic and syntactic modes accumulated during his avant-garde period: the modernist-inspired visual analysis that reflected such earlier influences as constructivism; the spontaneous lyricism that echoed the documentary improvisation practiced by contemporaries as divergent as Vertov and Flaherty and anticipated the post-war emergence of direct cinema; and the semi-documentary *mise-en-scène* that reflected mainstream aspirations and anticipated such later currents as Italian Neorealism. A fundamentally narrative syntax binds these elements together, ranging from shot/counter-shot tropes to an overall chronological exposition that led from initial preparations to the finished job. Narrative has implications for the project goals: every worker contributes to the totality and the narrative montage constantly keeps the importance of this contribution in view.

A commissioned film thus provided the terrain for Ivens' first concentrated exploration of labour, perhaps the most important single subject of his oeuvre, and for the first tentative staking out of an ideological engagement with labour. *We Are Building* articulates an attitude to the human endeavour to shape the world by physical effort, a tribute to its rationality, order and design, in short to its heroism. Patently romantic shots habitually depict a group of workers silhouetted against the sky, and the director's close attention to the work of a single bricklayer or metalworker implies an unstinting solidarity. In such passages, by avoiding the mannerisms of the cinema of personal expression, the artist subordinates his own subjectivity to the worker's. The worker expresses himself by his labour and the artist provides him or her with the technology for showing that labour to others, an important step towards a radicalisation of the relationship between artist and subject.

Ivens' left-wing political affiliations were clear already in 1929 and by the time of his first trip to the Soviet Union in early 1930 his connections with the Communist Party of Holland were taken for granted. Ivens later remembered that one of the original ideas for *We Are Building* had been to contrast the entrepreneur capitalist who smokes cigars in armchairs, 'building' for a profit, with the worker who pays with his sweat for the building of homes and cities. The union rejected this idea as being too combative, but a few hints of the initial conception remain. Meanwhile, parallel activist film activities were escalating, from involvement with the International Labour Defense, an international workers' aid organisation funded by the Communist International, to cinematography for an explicitly CPH-sympathetic denunciation of poverty in rural Holland (*Arm Drenthe*, Leo van Lakerveld, 1929), to the workers newsreel activism for the left-wing *Vereeniging Voor Volks Cultuur* (VVVC, the Association for Popular Culture).

We Are Building was an important landmark in Ivens' career, not only because it was the film in which he first expressed his political sensibility, but also because it was the film in which he first encountered the aesthetic and ideological contradictions surrounding committed filmmaking in capitalist society. The enthusiastic response that greeted the early instalments of *We Are Building* from diverse audiences – from *Filmliga* intelligentsia who championed a new indigenous talent, to workers' audiences in both the Netherlands and the Soviet Union who saw a new proletarian artist – may have been what inspired the filmmakers to continue this project over the next few years.

The final closing of the dike network on 24 May 1932 sparked the filmmakers' decision to assemble all of their material on the epic project into a final version, which became *Zuiderzee*. Shorter preliminary versions had been in existence since 1930, the year the Soviets had ordered 200 prints. Ivens' first autobiography dates *Zuiderzee* as 1931–33 while more recent filmographies by Dutch researchers Kees Bakker, André Stufkens and Hans Schoots give 1930. The discrepancies simply confirm that the project was ongoing over those years, with several provisional versions whose exact dates remain vague (the undated Dutch Filmmuseum version of the film entitled *Zuiderzeewerken* (52 minutes) shows the closing of a preliminary dike in July 1929, and the next stage the following year, and concludes with the sowing of the newly drained land; the Museum of Modern Art version does not include the draining and cultivation material, nor any expository intertitles with dates, and is thus not surprisingly seven minutes shorter). Ivens' collaborator Helen van Dongen (who gradually assumed responsibilities as his editor as the 1930s progressed) prepared two 'record' films of the dike construction and the reclamation for the government, and did so again in 1933, for the first cultivation in the newly-reclaimed sectors.

More than any other Ivens film, *Zuiderzee* has always been treated as an 'epic', as film theorist Bela Balasz famously called it. The 'epic' label is apt because of the universal accessibility of this strong narrative of conquest over the sea – in contrast to the more localised yet meandering focus of *We Are Building*. Generations of audiences have been caught up in this theme of human struggle against nature, articulated with most impact in the increasingly intense montage as the gap in the dike climactically narrows and then closes. Such aspects of the film may be one reason why the film is often said to have 'lasted' exceptionally well, but this universality may also have been a reason why an increasingly politicised Ivens would soon step beyond it towards a new specificity, directness and immediacy. Still the notion of 'epic' might be usefully recharged through its application to Ivens' Marxist vision of the human project of social construction, its collective heroics and monumental scale, and its profoundly materialist articulation in the idiom of documentary cinema.

The Marxist inflection of the epic mode is profoundly embodied in *Zuiderzee*'s collective iconography rather than the individualist terms of the traditional epic. Ivens' heroics of the worker, discovered tentatively in *We Are Building*, are consolidated here in the romantic affirmation of the proletariat as the dramatic subject of history and film, and of the working class's labour as prime impetus of both. This affirmation determines the logic of causality and sequence in the narrative structure of the film. Each phase of the gigantic project is clearly connected to the next, never viewed in isolation: the willow matrices are towed out into place in the water *so that* a ballast of rock can be dropped into them forcing them to sink *so that* they can serve as foundations for the earth and clay that is to be moved… The animated diagram-map and the colossal bird's-eye perspectives of the entire construction site monitor the gradual metamorphosis of the Zuiderzee into the tamed inland Yselmeer, the historical transformation articulated by the filmic narrative.

Ivens' heroics are also rooted in specific cinematic approaches to the proletarian subject. The camera's attitude is most typically a respectful medium or medium-long low-angle perspective of one or several workers, based in the cinematographer's intimate involvement in the local situation, always connecting a sense of the individual with the sense of the group. Choreographic configurations are exploited to the fullest in symbolic as well as rhythmic and visual terms. One famous sequence shows two perfectly synchronised columns of men, arms interlocked, carrying a huge concrete conduit pipe – the sequence lyricises collective labour and radiates Marxist idealism. In another *tour de force* sequence, Ivens analyses at close range a single worker's straining neck and bulging arms as he grapples with a huge boulder with which he must pave a dike embankment, his feet firmly braced in their clogs, as well as the surface of the boulder as he chips it and eases it into place. At the end of this sequence both worker and audience admiringly survey the completed embankment. A Soviet spectator was so struck by the authenticity of this sequence that he was convinced that the bourgeois Ivens was a proletarian in disguise.

Although *Zuiderzee* was filmed concurrently with Ivens' discovery of extended dramatic personalisation within Soviet Socialist Realism, the individual workers that do emerge in *Zuiderzee* are often 'composite' workers, ideal subjects constructed in the montage rather than the dramatised rounded characters that he was beginning to envision elsewhere. At the same time, the collective subject of *Zuiderzee* is not an anonymous synthetic mass but a collective of specific individuals frequently glimpsed with great expressiveness. One has only to think of the portly worker who emerges though a trapdoor onto the deck of a barge and strolls about surveying the work site with self-satisfaction, all the while balancing his huge soup bowl and spooning it down with gusto.

So much for the human element, but how does technology fit into this profoundly materialist epic by the artist who turned a bridge into a constructivist sculpture in *The Bridge*? Technology is no longer cast through the abstractionist aesthetics of the 1920s avant-garde. While *Zuiderzee* continues many of the conventions of the machine films of earlier years – there are balletic forests of swinging cranes and a continuous celebration of the graphic and kinetic force of dredgers and pumps – the technology is subordinated to the human project and rhapsodised only in its use-value. Every lyrical juxtaposition of crane movements immediately turns to the deposit of a load, the taking up of another, and then to a summation of the central situation of the dike in relation to the sea, all connected editorially to the worker in control. The ultimate term of reference is always the societal subject. The opening sequence of workers sitting on their lunch break as their children play declares the ultimate principle of history, the fundamental Marxist axiom that humankind reproduces itself through labour.

As an epic narrative, *Zuiderzee* must ultimately be situated as Ivens' most mature expression of 'indirect' documentary discourse. In *Ideology and the Image*, Bill Nichols identifies two basic modes of documentary address, indirect and direct, 'depending on whether the viewer is explicitly acknowledged as the subject to whom the film is addressed'. *Zuiderzee* marked the apogee of Ivens' development of the indirect mode, expressed in his silent narrative style. The direct mode, suddenly ushered into place by the new sound technology and almost immediately consolidated in the commercial newsreels, explicitly and directly acknowledges the viewer, and would be used almost exclusively by the expository sound documentary throughout its heyday (1930–60). The dominant diegesis of the classical sound documentary was almost always situated on the voice-over soundtrack, and could be pure narrative, pure exposition or, most often, a combination of both. By the time Ivens had completed the final version of *Zuiderzee*, his silent indirect narrative style had already been displaced by his abrupt disjuncture in filmic practice in *Komsomol* and was about to be permanently reshaped in *Borinage*. But it was to be the sound version of *Zuiderzee, Nieuwe Gronden* (*New Earth*), that marked his most radical shifts; in particular, his shift to the direct mode both in the image-sound realignment of the new format of voice-over narration and in the image-image realignment of the emerging compilation mode (the archival montage mode of which *New Earth* is a prototype). At the same time, imbricated in these formal realignments was Ivens' shift in the socio-political dimensions of filmic practice.

Zuiderzee was the last of Ivens' films to abstain from the socio-political intervention that would henceforth be his trademark. Still it cannot be denied that it is the last great silent documentary on the world stage and one of Ivens' finest films. Unfortunately it is doubtful whether *Zuiderzee* was widely distributed in its 1933 version. Not only was the silent documentary an increasingly obsolete format, but the work had already been widely exposed in its earlier versions and the activity – and harmony – of Ivens' avant-garde constituency was winding down. In any case, Ivens himself contributed to the immediate obsolescence of *Zuiderzee* by making his own shortened sound version, *New Earth*.

Ivens could no longer affirm an epic universe devoid of class conflict in which the rational effort of workers was rewarded with the harvests of victory. He could no longer affirm the strength and dignity of working people while repressing the societal context which frustrated and exploited that strength. The epic combat is reformulated: the struggle against nature in *Zuiderzee* becomes the class struggle of *New Earth*. Films using an indirect, narrative form to recount for passive audiences the victories of humankind would have to be replaced by films which provoked, challenged or 'agitated' these audiences, which addressed them directly in class terms, exploding the myths of worker-society unity with the clash of images with images and with words. The epic became agitprop. (I am using the term 'agitprop' neutrally outside of its more recent, pejorative, Cold War-inflected applications, to refer to a distinctive cultural and political tradition of documentary oriented towards social activism and grounded in the utopian or denunciatory rhetoric of emotion or persuasion, a tradition that has evolved continuously since the silent period.)

New Earth incorporated and consolidated three of the major formal and rhetorical innovations that *Borinage* was pioneering at the same time. Firstly, *Borinage*'s skilful use of its intertitles as a kind of interpretative and expository direct address becomes adapted as *New Earth*'s spoken and musical commentary. Next, the dialectical montage of *Borinage* is expanded into the masterful coda that transformed *Zuiderzee* into a milestone in yet another documentary genre, compilation: years earlier Ivens and his leftist friends of the VVVC had conducted clandestine experiments with the re-editing of commercial newsreels, of which *New Earth* was the artistic culmination. Thirdly, the mood of defiance in the soundtrack of *New Earth*'s coda and the denunciatory views of hunger and unemployment on the image track of this final movement endow the entire film with the affirmation of resistance and inevitable victory – in other words the 'prop' component of agitprop, 'propaganda' or the orchestration of collective feelings of refusal, solidarity and revolutionary fervour.

It was not aesthetic goals alone that dictated the reworking of *Zuiderzee*, but also the rapidly changing political and economic situation. Ivens' new formal discoveries were hastened and confirmed by the pragmatic requirements of the immediate conjuncture of the world crisis. The last images of *Zuiderzee* (Dutch Filmmuseum version) had been the sowing of the newly created fields. However, the actual sequel to the closing of the dike had confounded expectations. The 10,000 workers who had worked for ten years on the project had been forced into unemployment after the completion of the drainage. The forecasts for the new harvests had been fulfilled but as just one more unsalable surplus glutting the paralysed world markets. The children that Ivens had depicted would not have access to the fruits of their parents' labour after all. The new version of *Zuiderzee* would have to express the unexpectedly tragic ending of a national epic.

The first task undertaken by Ivens and Van Dongen was to reduce the running time of *Zuiderzee* by approximately two-thirds. This meant that the deliberate pace and step-by-step exposition of the original film had to be sacrificed. The more impressive sequences of *Zuiderzee* such as the conduit and boulder sequences were retained and situated prominently, but as symbols of the various stages of the project rather than precise information. When it came to the climactic closing sequence of which the filmmakers had been so proud, the triple dynamic of land, water and human perspectives was retained but Van Dongen was to remember some of the collaborators being sorry to see their masterpiece shortened. The revised coda covered first of all the settlement and cultivation of the newly-drained land, highlighted by long graceful aerial sweeps over the new fields and canals, epic vistas of horizons transformed.

It is when the camera turns to the harvesting, tracking through the ripened crops on a mechanical harvester, that Ivens springs the famous about-face on the public. As the grain pours across the screen, the sounds of a stockmarket floor are gradually superimposed, ushering in the montage coda aurally first of all. Ivens detailed this structural transformation in his first autobiography: 'the continuity of the *New Earth* follows that used in telling a joke. Three quarters of the story is told in an elaborate build-up to what seems to be a foregone conclusion and then in the last quarter you pull a switch not hinted at in the build-up. We show a tremendous engineering work that conquered the sea, that is going to bring happiness and prosperity to everyone concerned and then we say, "But…"'. The discourse of rationality and coherence symbolised by the plentiful harvest is punctured, replaced by denunciation, irony and declamation. This 'switch' can be seen symbolically as the actual point where the indirect narrative mode is replaced by direct address and a challenge to the system underlying the nation-building epic discourse.

The intensifying stockmarket noise introduced during the harvest visuals ushers in a collage of expository newspaper headlines detailing hunger marches and the international wheat crisis. There then follows a return to the idyllic view of a field of waving grain now transformed by the intervening collage into an image of devastating irony. The voice-over (performed by Ivens himself) has a discreet role until this point when the narrator fires off statistics of the rich harvest with mounting excitement, setting up the bubble that is about to be burst. Then come silhouetted files of unemployed workers, intercut with flashbacks to similar images from happier days when files carried coils for the dike construction. The next movement of the coda includes newsreel footage of hunger marchers in New York, demonstrators in London, and strikers again in the United States. The harvest motif then returns, intercut with close-ups of hungry children from *Borinage* and once-busy cranes now idle. The newsreel images continue of crops being dumped and burned, with the images of the children repeated. (Much of the 'newsreel' footage of the dumping of surplus food was re-enacted by Ivens and his collaborators on location in the Paris region and in the Joinville studios, a minor element of dramatisation in the film and a standard documentary device of the period.) The montage becomes more and more chaotic as continuing repetition of the children and harvest motifs are alternated with newsreel images of the Ku Klux Klan and the American Farm Board President's then notorious pig eating surplus wheat, jobless crowds, and clouds of smoke. The final images are low-angle close-ups of workers carrying off sacks of grain to be dumped into the sea, accompanied by the film's famous song:

> I would like to be in a country where
> The wind from the sea ripples over the wheat.
> In this land of fertile promise they ask for
> Workmen to throw the wheat into the sea.
> There is too much grain in the fields
> Bread seems to be a gift of the devil.
> One bagful brings too small a price.
> Throw half the harvest into the water,
> Throw it in my boy,
> What a winter it will be.

This ballad – Brechtian both in the bitterness of its declamatory style and in its distancing structural role in the film – provides a stunning climax to the film, matching as it does the alternation of idyllic images and ironic reversals. Under this song, the final images of the grain and the sea give an overall visual coherence to the film, underlining the final irony that the sea, the adversary of the workers during the first two reels of the film, should eventually claim the produce of the lands wrested from it – whose prophetic ecological thrust would become sharper over the decades.

The score also reflects this experimental potential of the new audio-visual medium. Hanns Eisler, Brecht's former collaborator who had composed the music for *Komsomol*, reworked many of the motifs from his famous score for *Kuhle Wampe* (1932), in many cases synchronising them precisely to the continuity of the new film and in some cases influencing the picture editing. The goal of using music in the same dynamic, 'direct', way as the sound effects and voice-over, asynchronously and structurally, was clearly an important one for the partnership. Ivens had explained to a *Cinema Quarterly* interviewer in 1933 that the score would 'constitute a dynamic factor in the completed film in contrast to *Regen* where the music [post-synchronised in 1932] was solely an accompaniment and where the score formed a self-contained composition'. As Eisler would describe it, he and Ivens were both proud of their accomplishment in providing an almost independent dramatic and ideological function to the music, at times atonal and urgent, at times plaintive and melodious.

The premiere of *New Earth* took place in Amsterdam in December 1933 and in Paris in early 1934. Ivens' by now habitual battles with censors all over Europe inevitably ensued with the result in France at least that the film was distributed without the montage coda (not without Ivens being enormously flattered after being told by a 'sweet little old lady' censor that his film showed 'trop de réalité').

The reaction to the film was generally warm wherever it was shown, including the Netherlands, though predictable ideological demurrers, like Paul Rotha's, dismissed the film as a 'naively propagandistic picture' with 'singularly disappointing ending'. Surprisingly, despite the stereotyping of American society in the montage sequence, Ku Klux Klan and all, the American reaction to the film was the most enthusiastic, primarily among the politically sympathetic film communities on the East and West Coasts. Otis Ferguson gave a glowing review, calling it 'more exciting than rapid fiction and twice as beautiful' (though with uncharacteristic obtuseness, Ferguson dismissed the coda as 'incidental'). The film was voted the second best foreign film seen in New York in 1936 by the National Board of Review.

It may have been the montage coda of the film, with its emphasis on the world context, that provided more of a hook to international audiences than the strictly Dutch setting of the earlier version. In any case the generosity of the American response encouraged Ivens' and Van Dongen's foothold in the American film community in 1936 and their decision after two years of unproductive work in the USSR to settle there for almost a decade. Disembarking in New York in February 1936, Ivens began more than half a century of almost continuous exile, maintaining the dialectical relationship of epic and agitprop that he had first hammered out in his homeland.

Thomas Waugh

MISÈRE AU BORINAGE BORINAGE

HENRI STORCK & JORIS IVENS, BELGIUM, 1934

Misère au Borinage (Henri Storck & Joris Ivens, 1934) – or just *Borinage*, as one of its makers, Joris Ivens, preferred it to be called – is regarded as a classic example of left-wing cinema. The film shows the aftermath of a lost strike in the Belgian Borinage coalfield. It was first released in 1934 as a silent film with Flemish and French intertitles. In 1935 Ivens made a sound version in Moscow, embedding it in a Soviet frame story. Finally Storck removed the intertitles and added a spoken soundtrack in the early 1960s. Although it is often unclear which version the authors have seen, *Borinage* is mentioned in virtually every handbook on the documentary film. Ivens regarded it as the film that changed his career by 180 degrees. A career – like Storck's – that spanned most of the twentieth century.

The publication in July 1933 of the pamphlet *Comment on crève de faim au Levant de Mons* ('How one dies from hunger at the Levant de Mons'), prompted a handful of members of the Brussels film society Club de l'Ecran to ask Henri Storck to make a film in the Borinage. In the pamphlet Dr Paul Hennebert, an active member of the Workers' International Relief (also known as the 'Red Cross of the workers'), clinically analysed how the abject poverty that had hit the miners and their families after the 1932 strike affected their health. The pamphlet would act as a guidebook for the filmmakers. Storck had made a couple of avant-garde shorts in his native Ostend and worked in Paris as an assistant to Jean Vigo on *Zéro de Conduite* (*Zero for Conduct*, 1933). He was not sure that he could master such a subject. He therefore asked his friend Ivens, who happened to be in Paris editing his most recent film *Nieuwe Gronden* (*New Earth*, 1933), to join him. Ivens did not hesitate. Like Storck, he had started making avant-garde films, but had recently spent many months in the Soviet Union working on a film about the building of blast furnaces in Magnitogorsk (*Komsomol*, 1932). Experienced cinematographer François Rents and photographers Willy Kessels and Sacha Stone completed the crew. The lawyer Jean Fonteyne acted as driver and general factotum. He was a leading member of the International Labour Defence, who knew the coalfield extremely well as he had been a counsel for the defence of countless miners charged with striking and other offences. Occasionally Fonteyne used his personal 16mm camera to record Ivens and Storck at work or cameraman Rents being asked for his identity papers by a police officer. Along with footage of a visit in 1935 by French writer André Gide and shots of the 1936 strike in the coalfield this material would be incorporated in the silent film *Autour du Borinage* (*Around the Borinage*, 1933–36).

There was no time or money for Ivens and Storck to write a script on the basis of in-depth research. Instead the filmmakers resorted to a method that Ivens has called creative research: 'It concerns the question how one can observe reality intently and with an open mind; how one can get down to the root of the matter and how one can record it instantly on celluloid in a film language that is as simple as possible.' Thus they discovered the splendid façade of the Provincial Institute for Hygiene in Mons and contrasted it with the hovels that lacked electricity or running water, in which the miners had to live. The oil lamps that the film crew had brought along for lighting purposes had a useful side effect: to the surprise and joy of the inhabitants the heat they generated detered cockroaches and other vermin which normally infested their dwellings. Given their background it was not surprising that the filmmakers saw some 'beauty' in this poverty and in this lay the danger of aestheticising their subject. As Ivens stated: 'We often encountered this danger of aesthetic pleasure, lights and shadows, symmetry or balanced composition that would undermine our purpose for a moment.' Instead the filmmakers wanted the images to be an indictment of their working and living conditions.

From the 1870s onwards, the Borinage region had attracted numerous artists, particularly from the Netherlands. Among them were the painters Vincent van Gogh, who lived in the region as a lay preacher for almost two years, Isaac Israëls, Hendrik Luyten, father Jan Toorop and his daughter Charley, and Harmen Meurs. Confronted with the problem of representing the dangerous but productive labour carried out underground (where it was too dark for painters to work and where suspicious companies who owned the collieries refused them access), they opted for symbolic representations: the landscape with its pit workings and slagheaps, miners on their way to or from the pit, men and women looking for pieces of coal high upon the slagheaps, women waiting at the pithead for news after a disaster, and agitation during a strike. Ivens and Storck were aware of these representations and made use of them for their film. They filmed, for example, the young miner Delplanck while he was returning from a day's work underground in order to make a statement about the kind of labour he was performing and the wages that he earned. They also spent a day on one of the slagheaps to film the men and women who were looking for tiny pieces of coal. The images of these men and women descending from the slagheap carrying heavy sacks of coal refer directly to those made by Van Gogh and other painters. But where these artists met the limitations of their art, cinematography by means of editing could reveal the absurdity behind these representations. For, as the film shows, thousands of tons of coal that the miners have extracted lie behind barbed wire going to waste, while these men and women have to risk their health on the slagheaps.

During their discussions with the miners and their families Ivens and Storck heard of incidents that were so significant and symbolic that they wished that they had been present with a film camera when these took place. They decided to adopt the highly controversial method of reconstruction: asking those who had been part of an incident to play it out once more in front of the camera. At that time there were two schools in documentary filmmaking. One was associated with Robert Flaherty, director of such well-known films as *Nanook of the North* (1922) and *Moana* (1926), that allowed for interference in reality – and hence reconstruction – in order to reveal its essence. While Russian filmmaker Dziga Vertov, famous for his *Man with the Movie Camera* (1929), was the representative of a school that refused any form of interference, trusting in the camera's ability to record life and in montage as a means of exposing the hidden relationships. Ivens had been at the centre of the controversy. He had resorted to reconstruction in his film *Komsomol* and had been attacked for this by Vertov and his associates. In the end the film, including the disputed sequence, was approved by the authorities. It can therefore safely be assumed that it was the Dutchman who suggested the use of reconstruction for the Borinage film.

In his pamphlet Dr Hennebert had written about an incident in the garden city of Monobloc, owned by the Levant de Mons colliery: 'At other times the inhabitants literally take by storm the houses which are under threat of being cleared; they sit down on the furniture, on the tables, and prevent radically and effectively all the measures that might lead to the execution of the injunction to clear the premises.' The filmmakers decided to re-enact this incident in front of the camera. But it was obviously not possible to ask the bailiff and the policemen concerned to join this reconstruction. Therefore a couple of police uniforms were ordered from a hire firm for theatre costumes in Brussels and smuggled into Monobloc. Two young workers could be persuaded to change into these costumes, but only after considerable discussion, as playing the role of a policeman was not considered an honour. Ivens and Storck used the symbol of headgear to their advantage. The bailiff manages to get inside a worker's house by donning a cap and so giving the impression that he is a worker. As soon as he is inside, he changes the cap for his hat. Still, the reconstruction lacked authenticity because of the presence of the fake bailiff and policemen.

Another incident of which Ivens and Storck had been informed concerned the demonstration in Wasmes in commemoration of the fiftieth anniversary of Karl Marx's death. In March 1933 workers from the Borinage had marched through the streets of this mining village, carrying a portrait of the writer of *Das Capital*, until the police dispersed the demonstration. When the filmmakers saw the portrait, a remarkable oil painting, depicting the philosopher with the eyes of a coal miner, they were so enthusiastic that they decided to reconstruct the demonstration, half a year after it had taken place. They placed the demonstrators in groups of three, with a distance of a few yards between each group, so that they could easily run away through the small side-alleys of Wasmes if the police arrived. Remarkably, the onlookers thought they were watching a real demonstration. At one point, they all clenched their fists and made the Red Front salute. As Ivens would later point out in his autobiography, it was as if the reconstruction had been absorbed by reality. In a similar way the re-enactment of a visit by Dr Hennebert to the poverty-stricken Mouffe family yielded shots that went beyond reconstruction. Knowing the dire state the family was in, the film crew had taken a sack of potatoes along. The way these were eaten in front of the camera (without taking time for the potatoes to cool off) not only formed a reference to Van Gogh's famous painting of the 'potato eaters', but it was also indisputable proof that the members of the Mouffe family were genuinely suffering from hunger.

The film crew was accompanied by two highly regarded photographers: Willy Kessels and Sacha Stone. Although Kessels, a Belgian architect, had only taken up photography as a profession in 1930, he had quickly made a name for himself. His stills were published as illustrations in books, as series in the illustrated press and were used in advertising. He contributed to the International Exhibitions of photography and cinematography in Brussels in 1932 and 1933. Stone had made a career in Germany in the 1920s. A representative of 'modern' photography, his work was included in anthologies such as *Foto-Auge* (*Foto-Eye*, 1929). In 1932 he left Berlin for Brussels. The stills they shot (Stone only a couple, Kessels around fifty) were used for publicity purposes. But, as Ivens explained in an interview with the Dutch communist daily *De Tribune*, they also had a political significance: 'at the same time while we were shooting the film we made in many cases stills too, for example of workers looking for coal on the slagheaps. These stills were ready in two days and our comrades used them in their political agitation. Thus the film contributed, even before it was finished, in organising the workers for the struggle.'

By the end of November 1933 Ivens and Storck came to the conclusion that they had to do something with the footage they had shot so far. The small amount of money put up by individual backers had run out. They had a diverse amount of material at their disposal: reportage-like footage, a number of reconstructions and newsreel stock shots from the 1932 strike. It was now a case of assembling this material into a whole, to edit a convincing argument. The plan for German writer in exile Berthold Brecht to write a prologue, commentary and concluding sequence, and for his colleague Hanns Eisler (who had also escaped the Nazis) to write the musical score, had to be cancelled due to a lack of funds. Both Ivens and Storck had considerable experience in what has been termed 'idea editing'. Each had, for example, re-edited existing newsreels, placing the shots in a different order to give them a new meaning. Ivens had done this in 1930–31 for a special newsreel of the Dutch workers' film society *Vereeniging voor Volks Cultuur* (VVVC) and more recently for the new version of his film on the reclamation of the Zuiderzee, *New Earth*. Storck had used newsreel footage from 1928 only for his surrealist shorts *Histoire du Soldat Inconnu* (1932) and *Sur les Bords de la Caméra* (1932).

Ivens and Storck remained fixed to the idea of a prologue and a concluding sequence. In the prologue they showed that the Borinage strike had to be seen within a larger context: the crisis of world capitalism. They made use of newsreel footage, including a remarkable sequence shot by an RKO-Pathé cameraman in Ambridge, Pennsylvania, showing how the police and their deputies sought the confrontation with and gunned at striking steel workers, armed only with sticks. In its argument, the prologue closely resembled the last part of *New Earth*, the film that Ivens had just completed editing. The Borinage film stressed that the 1932 strike was a legitimate act, given the increasing number of accidents and the recurring pay-cuts. It illustrated the wages question by means of the sequence on the young miner Delplanck, more than 25 per cent of whose pitiful earnings were shown to flow back immediately to the colliery. The film further consisted of a careful alteration between 'purely' documentary footage and reconstructed sequences. The latter enabled the viewer, if only briefly, to identify with certain characters. For example with the unemployed miner Augustin Cage who, along with his pregnant wife and children, was evicted for failure to pay the rent and had to cycle for miles to collect a loaf of bread from his in-laws, passing the shop windows of bakery after bakery on the way. Thesis and antithesis are stressed in sequences like the construction of a church, costing millions of francs, juxtaposed with the hut that has been cleared to keep dry the stones needed for the new 'house of God'. Towards the end of the film a change of emphasis becomes noticeable. The filmmakers wanted to make clear that although the 1932 strike had been lost, the daily struggle for a better future was continuing. A campaign for the distribution of free coal by a committee of unemployed men is given as an example. The film ends with a concluding sequence in which a number of key shots are repeated and it is proclaimed that only a socialist society can make an end to the exploitation of one man [sic] by another.

On 6 March 1934 *Borinage*, preceded by Walter Ruttmann's experiment in sound *Melodie der Welt* (*Melody of the World*, 1930), was premiered by the Club de l'Ecran in Brussels. Three days later it was screened for invitees only in the Amsterdam art house cinema 'De Uitkijk'. The film attracted criticism from the Belgian and Dutch press. Social-democrat newspapers condemned the film for its partial (read communist) point of view. René Jauniaux, critic for the Brussels newspaper *Le Peuple*, accused the filmmakers even of 'betrayal of what once – in days long gone by! – was called the sincerity of the artist'. The communist press on the other hand hailed it as 'a slap in the face of the reformism', as the Dutch communist daily *De Tribune* put it bluntly. Some liberal newspapers lamented the fact that aesthetically speaking the filmmakers had made a step backwards. According to the critic of the *Nieuwe Rotterdamsche Courant*, the film had shifted 'the centre of what is happening before the lens, while the most important conclusion that film aesthetics had reached so far was the understanding that film art only starts behind the lens'. Lastly the Catholic press showed a great interest in the person of Joris Ivens. He was presented as a model for Catholic filmmakers. Of course his politics were condemned, but at the same time it was pointed out that a great deal could be learned from his films. The highly influential Dominican Felix Morlion even approached Henri Storck in secret, offering him the chance to shoot a film for Catholic Action. He told the filmmaker that he would be amply rewarded. But there was one condition: Storck's conversion to Catholicism had to be made public. Although he needed the money, Storck refused.

The largely negative response to the film at its Brussels premiere led to a serious crisis behind the scenes. Officially, the film was owned by a company established by lawyer Jean Fonteyne, Education Par l'Image (EPI – 'Education by Means of the Image'). The idea was that EPI would make deals with distribution companies at home and abroad, which would then take care of the theatrical and/or non-theatrical release of the film. One deal had already been concluded: IFO, a Dutch distribution company with a library of Soviet films and closely linked to the Communist Party, had taken out an option on the film. However Pierre Vermeylen, one of the financial backers, suggested drastic changes in the film. As a former communist (he had stood as a candidate in the Borinage for the 1929 Parliamentary elections) and a chairman of the International Labour Defence, his views had to be reckoned with. Without changes, Vermeylen felt that the film's chances of making an impact were virtually non-existent for the simple reason that no one would show it. Ivens was prepared to make one concession: to omit a series of no less than ten intertitles quoting the interventions in Parliament during the 1932 strike by the sole communist MP Joseph Jacquemotte. But otherwise he was adamant that the film stayed the way it was, including the portrait of Lenin cut out of a newspaper, hanging on the wall of the room where the committee of unemployed miners was having its meeting, as well as the demonstration in Wasmes with the portrait of Karl Marx. Despite serious doubts, Storck decided to concur with his co-director. But Ivens found himself in a quandary. His communist supporters criticised him for failing to point out in the film that there was an alternative: socialism as it was being constructed in the Soviet Union. The IFO decided therefore to add the words, 'after *Borinage* the last reel of *Komsomol* as a contrast between the Borinage, and the Soviet Union', for a couple of screenings that the distribution company had organised for members of the Friends of the Soviet Union. However, that was only a temporary solution.

Vermeylen's prediction had been correct. In Belgium the film was booked only by a few film societies and political groups. Inevitably its length (approximately half an hour) and the fact that it had no soundtrack did not particularly increase its chances for theatrical exhibition. There is a persistent myth that it was not seen because it had been banned by the censor. This was false, as there was no single body in Belgium that had the authority to ban the film. In the Netherlands, where a national censorship committee existed with the powers to ban any film that formed a danger to the public order or ran contrary to good morals, IFO did not even submit the film. It is unclear whether the distributor feared that it would be banned anyway, so that it might as well spare itself the bother (and the costs), or whether it had come to the conclusion on the basis of the handful of private screenings which it had held, that there simply was no market for the film. In reality, the IFO chose to give up the option that it had taken out on the film. Only the Swiss distributor of the film would generate some income for EPI during the coming years.

Within a month of the premiere of *Borinage* Joris Ivens left for the Soviet Union to pursue his career with the Mezhrabpom Studios. Various reasons for his move have been given. Ivens himself has always maintained that the negative reactions after *New Earth* and *Borinage* made it impossible for him to pursue his career as a documentary filmmaker in his native country. However, in his biography of Ivens, Hans Schoots has pointed out that the filmmaker still commanded a great deal of support, both from the Dutch press and his friends from the film society movement. Schoots argues that Ivens may have sought a definite rift with his father and the business career that the latter had planned for his son (as opposed to the artistic career that Ivens himself had in mind). In the Soviet Union he was given the opportunity to re-edit the

Borinage film in the Autumn of 1934, in the sense that had already been suggested by Ivens' communist supporters. Together with Alfred Kurella, one of the many Germans in exile who had found a job at Mezhrabpom, Ivens wrote a script using the arrival of a Belgian workers' delegation at a construction site of the Moscow underground as a frame story. The Belgians are invited for tea at the flat of their Soviet colleagues. Prompted by a question about the situation at home, one of the Belgians began telling the story of the 1932 strike. Generally speaking the new version follows the story line of the original film. It ends with a sequence showing how, thanks to the revolution, the Soviet miners live in a 'Garden of Eden'. Jean Fonteyne, who secretly acted as a go-between for the Comintern and therefore had excellent contacts in Moscow, made all the footage, including the outtakes Ivens and Storck had shot in the Borinage, available to the Dutchman. Thus Ivens included shots of leading Belgian communists like Henri De Boeck and Joseph Jacquemotte, which had not been used in the original version and further enhanced the partisan character of the film. Hans Hauska, another German in exile, wrote a musical score in the same vein as his master, Hanns Eisler. Ivens shortened the title to *Borinage*, dropping the word *Misère* that he felt gave a wrong impression of the film. All the time co-director Henri Storck was left completely unaware of what was happening to the film.

It was this sound version that most audiences outside of Belgium saw between the mid-1930s and the early 1960s. When Ivens went to the United States in 1936 at the invitation of the New Film Alliance, he took this version with him. The New York State censorship board was only prepared to give a visa to the film if a shot showing Dr Hennebert examining the genitals of one of the Mouffe children and the commentary accompanying the sequence of the demonstration with the Karl Marx portrait were removed.

A cutting copy of the film, dating from the late 1930s, that emerged from the vaults of the Cinémathèque Française in the early 1990s is proof that there may have been other plans for the film, of which, as far as we can know, neither Ivens nor Storck were aware. It starts with an entirely different prologue, obviously compiled from French footage, showing World War One, the economic boom of the 1920s, followed by overproduction and crisis. It then follows a radically re-edited version of *Borinage*, using material from the Russian version only. It is highly likely that Jean Fonteyne acted as the source for the cutter(s) who worked on this version, but the rest is shrouded in mystery.

In the early 1960s Henri Storck discovered that there was demand for a number of his silent films, provided some kind of sound versions were available as audiences felt uncomfortable when they had to watch in complete silence. In the case of *Histoire du Soldat Inconnu* and

Sur les Bords de la Caméra the solution was straightforward: the gramophone music that Storck had selected at the time was put on the soundtrack. For *Borinage* he decided to drop the intertitles, which was simple because for laboratory technical reasons they had never been included in the original negative, and have the texts of the captions spoken as a commentary by film critic André Thirifays. A symbolic choice, for it had been Thirifays who had first approached Storck with the idea of making a film on the Borinage. Apart from the commentary (spoken in French only, while original captions had been bilingual: French and Flemish) the sound version was faithful to the original 1934 version. There is no doubt that it sparked off a 'revival' of the film. It was distributed widely, both in Belgium and abroad, and seen in classrooms, by film societies and at political meetings. It matched the spirit of the time perfectly. For many of the May 1968 generation the film became a symbol of what left-wing or radical cinema (*cinéma militant*) could achieve. The various books on Joris Ivens, in particular his autobiography *The Camera and I*, that first became available in English in 1969 and was subsequently translated in Dutch, German and other languages, only helped to reinforce this image.

After the death of Willy Kessels in 1974 Storck came into possession of the negatives of the stills that the photographer had made during the shooting of the film. Their often stunning pictorial quality helped to enhance the film's reputation even more and situate it firmly in a modernist context. The stills were an important feature of a book on the history of *Borinage*, published in 1983 by the present author and Henri Storck. Based on research of virtually all the primary and secondary sources available at the time, the book not only examined the history of the film itself and its versions but situated it in the broader context of the history of the Borinage region and that of the documentary film genre. More than ten years later, Willy Kessels would be at the centre of a controversy because of his collaboration with the Germans during World War Two, leading to a debate about the relationship between modernism and political movements that inevitably affected the Borinage film too.

While films such as *A chacun son Borinage* (*To Everyone His Own Borinage*, Wieslaw Hudon 1979) and *Borinage, das verratene Land* (*Borinage, The Betrayed Region*, Helmut Bürgel 1988) examined the relationship between *Borinage*, its makers and the Borinage region itself, it was left to two Belgian films to provide a real link between the film made by Ivens and Storck and the present day. In 1960, Paul Meyer made a feature film that was envisaging a future without mining for the Borinage. *Déjà s'envole la fleur maigre* (*The Lank Flower Has Already Flown*) starts with the arrival of an Italian family at a local railway station in the Borinage. Mother and children have come from their home country to join the breadwinner. But the economic prospects are none too bright, as a growing number of mines in the region are being closed. Interestingly, director Paul Meyer uses the film to reverse familiar images. The slag-heaps, for example, are no longer the metaphorical fields where the gleaners of the industrial age are gathering tiny pieces of coal. Instead they have become playgrounds for children, using baking tins for daring races downhill. In an interior monologue Domenico, an elderly Italian worker who is about to leave the region, gives meaning to the landscape: '*Borinage, paysage, charbonnage, chomage*' ('Borinage, landscape, coal mine, unemployment'). Almost forty years later Patrick Jean referred directly to the 1934 film in his *Les Enfants du Borinage: Lettre à Henri Storck* (*Kids from the Coal Land: A Letter to Henri Storck*, 1999). He discovers remarkable parallels in the same Borinage, despite the demise of the coal industry and the coming of the welfare state: families living in poverty and slum housing, being unable – usually just like their parents or even grandparents – to get out of the trap. In his compassionate film Jean gives a voice to these contemporary equivalents of the families Cage and Mouffe. Proof that the film made by Joris Ivens and Henri Storck almost seventy years ago, remains just as topical today.

Bert Hogenkamp

DE WITTE WHITEY

JAN VANDERHEYDEN, BELGIUM, 1934

De Witte (*Whitey*, Jan Vanderheyden, 1934) is a perfect case of emerging regional cinema, popular culture and nationalism in 1930s Belgium. Throughout the interwar period Belgium was celebrated by the big international production centres as one of the most liberal film markets in Europe. Besides the huge import rate and the strong position of the distribution arms of American and German corporations, Belgium has often been seen as a 'natural' extension of the French film market. The gravitational force from the French film industry was powerful in many directions. French film corporations such as Aubert, Gaumont or Pathé were present on both the distribution and the exhibition scene, while they also lured away Belgian creative personnel (for instance Jacques Feyder, Charles Spaak, Fernand Gravey). The openness of the small Belgian film market was increased by the lack of any serious state intervention plan to stimulating local production or diminishing the inflow from abroad. As a result, Belgium may have been quite unique in that it showed a fine cross-section of the international film output, probably more than elsewhere in Europe. However, it also included a weak local production, especially in the northern, Dutch-language part of the country where local film production had great difficulties in developing due to the small local market, the lack of sufficient financial means, technical equipment and know how, as well as due to the attraction of the French-language film scene.

Similar to what happened in other regions and countries, the introduction of sound prompted a growing demand for non-exportable material in the local language. Probably the most successful Belgian filmmaker and producer in playing upon the attraction of hearing one's own language has been Jan Vanderheyden (1890–1961), who produced in 1934 the first Flemish fully-fledged talking picture. Based on a popular novel by Ernest Claes, *Whitey* is commonly seen as a classical film and a milestone in Belgian film history.

Whitey is also an interesting case of an emerging regional cinema in Europe after the introduction of sound cinema. Though technically quite weak, the film attracted a wide audience and proved that popular cinema in a local language could be commercially viable. In the aftermath of *Whitey*, Vanderheyden produced nine films in the following five years, and in the French-speaking part of Belgium film production continued to flourish. Often artistically poor and relatively unambitious, these films tried to reach a local audience through the use of popular genres (mainly comedies and vaudevilles) or the exploitation of well-known literary works, often combined with casting local actors. Given the public reception of the film, and inspired by a materialist approach in relation to historical reception analysis, it is necessary to understand the social meaning(s) of *Whitey*. The production was a well-publicised public event and the film quickly became the target of external pressures with commercial, religious and ideological motives. Above all, however, *Whitey* needs to be located as a crucial stage in the growth of a Flemish film culture with clear links to folk art, popular culture and literature, as well as to the ideological struggle around them, more so since it uses a consensual strategy in drawing a conservative, even nostalgic picture of Flemish local communities threatened by modernist society.

This becomes apparent when we look at *Whitey* as a cult event, taking into account its production, influences, distribution and reception. When Jan Vanderheyden began conceiving his first feature film, he already had some experience. Since 1916 he had been involved in international film distribution, first in London and then Paris as an export manager for the 'Transatlantic Cy.', a firm that distributed Universal's films to the Western European market. In 1922, he went back to Belgium, where he became the manager of 'Soleil Levant Films', a national distributor specialising in American and French pictures. Four years later he became more involved in the distribution of German films, changing the name of the distribution firm into 'International Film Distributors' (IFD). With the arrival of sound, Vanderheyden and IFD specialised in dubbing German films (often from the Aafa – Althoff-Ambos-Film-AG – studio) into French, bringing him closer to the sphere of film production. During one of his visits to Berlin, he also got involved with a German woman, Edith Kiel, who worked as a dialogue supervisor for the UFA studios. Soon Kiel left Berlin, following Vanderheyden to Antwerp, becoming his life-long creative companion in writing and directing most of his popular films.

In most accounts of *Whitey*, the film is presented as quite amateurish, given the absence of technical experience or decent equipment in Flanders at that time. This might have been true, but it cannot obscure the commercial flair with which Vanderheyden launched his first movie; as an experienced and respected distributor, he succeeded in turning it into a cultural and media event of major significance. The announcement of the project, the choice of the main actors, as well as the shooting of the film itself were hugely publicised in the press. The search of the main protagonists for instance was staged as a huge public event, closely followed and covered by the media. The final election itself (11 April 1934) was organised as a public contest attended by leading literary and cultural figures.

The choice of adapting the eponymous novel *De Witte* by Ernest Claes (1885–1968) proved to be commercially interesting too, as this was one of the most popular and best-selling Dutch-language books, translated and successfully sold in various other languages. In the 1930s, Claes was a writer with a solid record in terms of book sales, public appearances and lectures, mainly within Catholic and Flemish-nationalist circles. With *De Witte*, his first novel published in 1920, he immediately became a widely acclaimed author. In it he used a loose narrative structure, as well as an unaffected style and a highly recognisable 'folk' language to tell the story and the boyish adventures of a youngster (Whitey) in a small peasant community in the Flemish countryside. Claes, who had close links with German cultural life, was clearly influenced by *Heimatkunst*. Acting against modernist literary and art movements, this German literary movement cultivated a nostalgic view of a well-ordered, traditional society. This included a tendency towards an idealised view of nature, glorifying the past and an unspoiled rural life. Acting against an urban development, it cultivated a specific pastoral life, using folk language, the stories of simple peasants, and humour. Many of these characteristics appear in *De Witte*. Controversial when it was published in 1920, it attracted criticism from extremist Catholic circles, and in the Netherlands, Claes had been attacked for the 'pagan' elements embedded in the character of the charismatic and playful Whitey.

Vanderheyden's choice to adapt the book was widely acclaimed in the press, where it was stated that Claes himself would be involved in the project. However, it soon became clear that Kiel did not see the filmic narrative potential of this anecdotal pastoral novel and she soon convinced Vanderheyden to use a stronger storyline. Inspired by her experience in German commercial cinema, she reworked Claes' novel into a love story around the protagonist's brother and the local innkeeper's daughter. Claes and more traditional Catholic critics were critical of this script's deviations from the novel, denouncing it as a concession to international commercialism and its promotion of cheap 'sex appeal'.

Kiel's involvement in reworking the original story showed how this first Flemish sound picture had a clear commercial imperative from the start. The adaptation of the novel also indicates how this form of regional cinema did not escape from basic conventions in international commercial cinema, in terms of story line, themes and protagonists. Also, in technical and cinematographic terms, *Whitey* would become highly influenced by contemporary German film standards. Vanderheyden's and Kiel's contacts with the Berlin studios lured German craftsmen to Belgium. These included camerawork (Ewald Daub), editing (Walter Von Bonhorst), sound recording and handling (Fritz Seeger and Hans Rutten, using the Tobis-Klang system). The interior sequences were shot in one of the best-equipped German studios, the Johannestal studio of the Aafa in Berlin (July 1934). In an interview in *Wereldrevue* three months earlier, Vanderheyden tried to justify these choices, claiming that 'lacking well-trained Flemish or Dutch personnel, we are obliged to appeal to the ultimate masters of the European film art: German technicians'.

In many interviews Vanderheyden tried to induce this German quality reference to his film project, thereby underlining the historical importance of *Whitey* for the future of Flemish cinema and Belgian film production. In retrospect it seems that the ultimate proof of Vanderheyden's sharp business acumen was that he was able not only to create high expectations about *Whitey* as a movie or to make it into a cult event, but that he succeeded in creating a collective feeling of living through a historical momentum for Flemish (film) culture.

However, this also inflated expectations and put additional pressure on the project, certainly in this period of harsh and wide political, economic and social crises. For Vanderheyden and IFD there were clear economic imperatives and commercial risks, given the high production costs of the film and the general recession in local distribution and exploitation. But what makes *Whitey* such an outstanding case is that the film project became, more than ever and before its actual production stage, the plaything of ideological and religious pressures. Especially Catholic circles looked at it suspiciously and tried to influence the adaptation of Claes' popular novel. In fact, if we look at the articles published within Catholic newspapers and magazines, the *Whitey* project was considered to be extremely important. In various articles, leaders of the powerful Catholic Film Action (Katholieke Film Actie, KFA) took to the defence of the project, and insinuated their influence on it. In the leading Catholic newspaper *De Standaard*, one of the leaders of the KFA, Felix Morlion, wrote in several articles how he received the script of the future film: 'from the beginning we received the script. Without being masterly, we think that the adaptation of Claes' novel is reliable, simple and healthy. ... It is remarkable how the producer himself has seen the necessity to retain the popular atmosphere, while avoiding everything that could affect the respect for the priest, or what could affect dignity and chastity.' If we want to understand this, we have to go back to the importance of the KFA with Morlion as one of its most influential leaders. Since the 1920s Catholic leaders had been active in film distribution and exploitation (the latter known as the Catholic Film Central). At the start of the 1930s, the Catholics extended their range of action by trying to influence the press in their film coverage as well as to put more pressure on commercial cinemas programming 'unhealthy' films. Therefore the KFA, which was supported by local bishops, installed a Catholic Film Classification/Censorship Board (1932). By 1933 the KFA claimed that they played a major role in film criticism in Catholic newspapers, which were extremely dominant in Flanders.

Within this offensive atmosphere and inspired by the successes of their American counterparts, the Legion of Decency, the KFA dreamt of building a mass organisation as well as of influencing what was considered the heart of all evil: film production. In many writings leaders of the KFA wrote about the necessity to enlarge the range of action from distribution and exploitation to production. As Morlion's book *Filmleiding* shows, these hard claims on influencing local production can be situated between 1932 and 1934.

When the *Whitey* project was announced, the Belgian KFA was in an extremely offensive state of extending its range of action, not least through recruiting local legions (called Catholic Film Legion, Katholieke Film Liga, KFL). Even from an international perspective, the Belgian Catholic film initiatives have been evaluated as quite exceptional. Especially in the Dutch-speaking part of Belgium, the KFA proved to be quite influential through its growing number of legions, small local cinemas affiliated to the Catholic Film Central, as well as through its influence on Catholic newspapers. Within this context it is clear that any local Flemish producer who tried to launch a film project with lucrative aspirations had to take the KFA into account.

Even before the actual shooting, leaders of the KFA published several articles in which they openly defended the project. In several articles photographs show how Morlion and other members of the KFA were present during the shooting itself, while in socialist newspapers film critics denounced the KFA's attempts to influence *Whitey*. In August 1934, one month before the premiere, Morlion wrote how:

> *Whitey* will be a healthy film. Simple rural life will be at the background of this movie but it will be essentially Catholic. Even the most puritan observer will not be able to criticise the love affair. … *Whitey* shows a direction, which we as Catholics can follow. … We live in a small country … but in terms of ideas we can play an important role. There is a sound Catholic soil on which we can build. There is a tradition of artistic creation, which can be transported into modern art forms.

When *Whitey* was premiered, on 13 September 1934, Vanderheyden's commercial flair again succeeded in gaining full public attention, supporting press coverage with additional advertising in newspapers and trade journals. The premiere was attended by many leading figures including politicians, writers, artists, as well as representatives from the KFA. The abundant press coverage was extremely mild, supporting this firstborn Flemish talkie. Some newspapers talked about an unexpected artistic triumph in all respects, whereby the main actor playing Whitey (Jef Bruyninckx) was seen as a revelation and a Belgian Jackie Cooper. Other newspapers, however, included more critical remarks in terms of technical or cinematographic insufficiencies, as well as in relation to believability. Trying to compare the harshness of real peasants' life with the one in the movie, some journalists denounced the romantic side in the movie. Within more Catholic newspapers some criticism was formulated about Kiel's intervention into Claes' novel, mainly with the intrusion of the love affair. However, *Whitey* proved to be an enduring success with audiences: the film first toured in most major Flemish towns, followed by a successful run in the Netherlands and Brussels; thereafter, it was projected in almost every cinema in Flanders. Even after World War Two and up to the 1960s, this mythical movie was programmed over and over again, mostly with a renewed success.

In the meantime Vanderheyden and IFD built on the film's astonishing success. In 1935 two new comedies were produced (*Alleen voor U/Only For You*, 1935; and *Uilenspiegel leeft nog/Uilenspiegel Still Lives*, 1935), with more projects to follow. For most of these films, Vanderheyden used Dutch studios, but in 1939 he launched his own production base in Antwerp. By that time he was considered the most important film producer in the country. In 1980 a second adaptation of *Whitey* followed, directed by a more leftist critical filmmaker. Once again, Claes' novel proved to be the basis of commercial success. Robbe De Hert's *De Witte van Zichem* (*Whitey of Zichem*) broke all domestic box-office records, while a re-print of the novel became a best-seller.

Beyond the release of the film, it is important to see how *Whitey* and its meanings have been linked to later contexts and ideologies, especially in relation to issues of wartime collaboration, right-wing sympathies and the ideal of 'healthy' folk cinema. At the time, Claes' novel was a softly controversial work, whose critical layers were masked by humour, mostly remaining out of sight of the average reader. The criticism in the novel resided not so much in recalcitrant gags by the protagonist and his gang, but rather in an ambiguous atmosphere that surrounded Whitey. While joyful and funny through small acts of naughtiness, he also embodied rebellion and resistance against different forms of authority. Among those authorities were the church (in the figure of the community priest), educational bodies (the schoolteacher) and patriarchal system generally (represented by his father and elderly brothers).

The rebelliousness of Whitey could also be read as the resistance, bravery and courage of the 'Flemish people'. Whitey also stands for youth and the search for freedom, railing against repression and institutionalism.

Such a critique is all but absent from Vanderheyden's and Kiel's adaptation, partly a result of commercial imperatives and external pressures. Rather, *Whitey* the film shows, more than the novel, a consensual, highly conservative view of Flemish society. Contextual information, and the hegemonic nature of *Whitey*, go some way to accounting for this. We now know what happened to the main participants over the following two decades and these individual, political and ideological trajectories have irreparably influenced responses to the film. Against the background of these individual stories there is the development of a substantial part of the Flemish nationalist movement in Belgium, which closely associated it with extreme right-wing ideologies and wartime collaboration with the German occupier.

A most controversial figure, Jan Vanderheyden was, during the occupation, the chairman of the Belgian Chamber for Cinematography (Chambre Syndicale Belge de la Cinématographie/ Belgische Syndicale Kamer van de Kinematografie). At the end of World War Two, after Vanderheyden fled to Berlin with his partner, seditious articles began to appear, describing him as the 'Fuhrer' of Belgian cinema, while Kiel was seen as a Nazi spy. Three years later he was arrested and imprisoned. Released in 1951, he began producing again, mainly cheap popular comedies written and directed by Kiel. Even today, it is not entirely clear how far Vanderheyden's collaboration was inspired by ideology (including Flemish-nationalist sympathies) or opportunism. The latter might be more important given Vanderheyden's pre-war commercial drive in general. However it is clear that Vanderheyden's dubious past has cast its shadow over *Whitey*.

A similar story can be told of Claes. After the War the novelist was arrested on the basis of a relatively small file (for example, having written for the extreme right-wing and Flemish-nationalist newspaper *Volk en Staat*). A well-publicised trial ensued, but Claes was soon released and he achieved popularity again. More recently, incriminating evidence surfaced linking Claes to more serious pro-Nazi beliefs, which at one point he wrote about for a foreign newspaper. Archive material shows that he was a silent, but important supporter of the leading collaborating Flemish nationalist party VNV.

The KFA also had a troubled and controversial history. Some people within the KFA were engaged in various debates around the 'New Order' and Flemish national autonomy, basing itself on a Catholic worldview. An interesting example was the film critic Jeanne De Bruyn who first worked as a propagandist and writer for the KFA but later wrote for *Volk en Staat*, known for its crude support for Flemish nationalist aspirations and the 'New Order' policy. De Bruyn tried to integrate aesthetic and ethical arguments into her criticism, the latter being inspired by a Catholic and conservative ideology. For De Bruyn, who became an influential critic in Catholic newspapers and magazines, Vanderheyden and his films were artistically weak. However, through Vanderheyden's work she found the perfect platform to expound on her idea of *de volksfilm* ('folk cinema'), as opposed to 'intellectual cinema'. She soon developed an anti-intellectualist position, combined with a distrust of international, cosmopolitan modern art. In an ideal form, 'folk cinema' was characterised both by technical and creative genius, but moreover by extra-filmic elements. Here she referred to the intense relation between cinema and the people, the use of 'folk' themes (*volkscheigen themas*) and other concepts, echoing contemporary German ideas about the ideal of folk (*völkisch*) culture. These ideas on intellectualism, internationalism, modern art and folk cinema, however, whether inspired or not by German writings, were also present in Vanderheyden's discussions on the type of films he intended to make. His ideal was 'to produce films which coincide with folk nature'.

As a result of this, it becomes tentative to read Vanderheyden's and Kiel's *Whitey* in a rather biased manner. It includes the danger of not seeing the openness and the different layers in the film. It might sound strange, but this highly suspicious view is in complete contrast with the general audience's view of *Whitey*. The public image of the movie is one of innocent pleasure and entertainment, of a nostalgic and primitive expression of authentic popular Flemish cinema. This means that we should acknowledge the textual openness of the film, which probably explains to a great extent its long-term success among various social groups. Also, we have to be careful in interpreting references to folk art within the Belgian political and cultural context of the 1930s, where the abstract notion of 'community' had close ties with the concept of 'the people'.

Still, it is important to acknowledge *Whitey*'s clearly conservative worldview. It is not difficult to see how the film is about a nostalgic view upon traditional society, pitted against the unarticulated fear for urbanity and modernity. Although the film starts as an ode to Flanders with images of different Flemish cities, the city remains out of sight in the rest of the film. The lyrical introduction expresses nationalism, defined on the basis of medieval history and the old richness of Flanders. But at the same time, *Whitey* ignores urban realities such as the social disorder and unrest at the end of the nineteenth century. The film concentrates on a hermetically sealed local community with a clear social order, hierarchy, and respect for church and power.

It concentrates on innocent childish evils, not on the big evils and social conflicts in and around the cities, often associated with a lack of respect for power and peace.

Comparing the novel with the film, it is clear that some rather critical scenes were left out. Besides commercial imperatives by the filmmakers, external pressures did hold some influence. Vanderheyden gave in to concerns expressed by Claes and members of the KFA over certain changes. Morlion, for instance, openly wrote how Claes (seen as the script advisor) 'radically left out what could in one or another sense be disturbing'. And he continued with the example that 'we will not see how Whitey confesses other boys' sins, or how the priest jumps out of the confessional box to catch one of the boys who had stolen apples'. These and other examples show that the film will be 'healthy', ultimately illustrating that 'our Flemish people overall are sound folks'.

Official censorship also played a role in shaping the final film. Since 1920 Belgium had a film classification law banning cinema attendance for children under 16 for all films, unless approved by a state film classification board. Even in as small a country as Belgium, with practically no local production, the board had a wide influence over what kind of films were shown. Similar to other European countries and the USA, the Belgian censorship/classification board received wide criticism in the 1930s, mainly because of its severe decisions. From an economic point of view, it was crucial for distributors and producers to have their films passed for children. This will also have been the case with Vanderheyden, who as a distributor must have known perfectly well the many taboos and sensitivities of the classification board. But even when he made this joyful, 'healthy' picture, the board decided that one short scene – where pupils, led by Whitey, place a needle under the schoolmaster's cushion – had to be cut in order for it to be open for consumption by children and young adolescents; for the classification board this scene made a fool of the schoolmaster, eventually undermining his respect and authority.

Many critical accounts view *Whitey* as a milestone in the development of Flemish and Belgian popular cinema in the interwar period. It is seen as the innocent beginning of a popular regional cinema, resulting from the public's need to consume films in their own language. The long-time success of the film among diverse audiences obscured the fact that it carried a conservative, hegemonic view of Flemish society. *Whitey* was, more than any other Flemish movie before it, a cult event exposed to severe external pressures. What makes it so interesting is that their influence has been so blatantly clear and effective.

This ideological struggle over the film, combined with the fear for a commercial disaster, made the adaptation a near-perfect example of Antonio Gramsci's classic idea about a successful hegemonic culture. We could say that *Whitey* features challenges to authority, yet at the same time it ensures the ideology of the ruling classes as natural. Various systems of pressure and control regulated what could be shown and what was to be left out. Nearly half a century later, with the remake of *Whitey*, many things had changed, but mechanisms were still in place, trying to control what was to be seen on the screen as well as what was not.

Daniel Biltereyst and Sofie Van Bauwel

KOMEDIE OM GELD THE TROUBLE WITH MONEY

MAX OPHÜLS, THE NETHERLANDS, 1936

Komedie om geld (*The Trouble with Money*, Max Ophüls) was, in 1936, the most expensive film ever produced in the Netherlands despite only costing about 150,000 guilders (£25,000), half the sum of money that the main character, Brand, loses in the film. This was insignificant when compared to average Hollywood or German (UFA) productions, which had budgets averaging 900,000 guilders. The film earned only 10,000 guilders, failing, as it did, to appeal to Dutch audiences. This paradox of the inexpensive and yet very expensive 'Comedy about money' (as the Dutch title goes), played a crucial role in the film's subsequent reputation.

The Trouble with Money is a parable about the symbolic magic of money in a capitalist society focused on credit and credibility. The episodes are knitted together by a 'master of ceremonies', or barker, (Edwin Gubbins Doorenbos) who directly addresses us from a virtual fairground stage. In the prologue he lures us into witnessing the main protagonist: the bank clerk Brand who loses 300,000 guilders.

In the first scene, Brand's brother-in-law Ferdinand (Matthieu van Eysden), performs his 'dog trick'. He sells his dog to a middle-aged couple. Walking out of sight of the couple, Ferdinand whistles for the dog, who returns to him. Aware they have been duped, the couple call for the police, who search for the con man. Meanwhile Ferdinand and his dog walk out of town along the river, where they find Brand (Herman Bouber) fishing. Brand agrees to hideFerdinand, but scolds him for his bad behaviour.

Back at work at the 'CB' (Central Bank), in a sequence that highlights the hierarchy between employer and employee through the use of lightning and camera movements, Brand's boss forces him to sign a statement that he will break all contact with Ferdinand. Left with no choice, Brand agrees. Crosscut with this scene is a sequence where Ferdinand is refused entry to the bank. Ferdinand shows his good nature by preventing a hungry boy from stealing. In return for delivering a note to Brand, he gives him some money for food. Brand is not in his office, but his colleague tells the boy to sit aside and wait, watching on as he eats some of his lunch, before disposing of the rest. Finding a knife on the desk, when Brand's colleague leaves the room, the boy attempts to open the desk drawers in search of food. Brand is still busy at the cashier, collecting the 300,000 guilders he has to deliver at the Neptune bank. When he returns to his office, the boy has gone, leaving Ferdinand's note on the desk. With the money in a purse chained to his wrist, Brand leaves for a meeting with Ferdinand at the Groenburgwal, a small canal in the centre of Amsterdam, on his way to the Neptune bank. Ferdinand needs money to pay his dog taxes. Brand lectures him again while tapping, in close up, on his moneybag to emphasise his words. They split up and Brand arrives at the cashier of the Neptune bank where he finds out that the money is gone, showing the hole in the base of the bag by putting his hand through it.

The next scene introduces Willy (Rini Otte), Brand's daughter. She has just passed her exams as an exercise teacher and breaks her news to Ferdinand, who is waiting for Brand in front of her home. He stays outside with his dog while Willy runs upstairs to meet her father, but finds the little apartment crowded with policemen.

Brand is released by the police because of a lack of evidence, but his negligence loses him his job. He is told that keeping him on would hurt the bank's reputation. In a rapid montage of images and voice-over, Brand's life is seen to fall apart. He is evicted and his daughter is tarred by association and fired from her job. Neither seems able to find a job anywhere. Their name, Brand (fire), is on everybody's lips, shown in extreme close-ups. Both are expelled from the life they used to live and hide their humiliation from each other, promising that tomorrow things will improve. When Brand finds a job at a bowling alley, he discovers that Willy lied to him about her new job. A drunk gentleman talks proudly about how he prevented his wife from hiring her. This stuns Brand, conveyed by a bowling ball that thunders towards his head.

He returns home drunk and wakes Willy, who expresses her concern for him. He becomes hell-bent on suicide. In the fade out to black, we hear a solemn request for one minute of silence, not for Brand, but for the director of the International Finance Institute (IFI) whose suicide has left the IFI bankrupt. The managing director, Moorman (Cor Ruys), continues his speech in a spacious room, standing at the end of a very long table, as he suggests his final solution. The scene is crosscut with Brand trying to gas himself. When Moorman pays Brand a visit, he is still alive and accompanies Moorman back to the IFI.

At the IFI building, a virtual modernist building where literally everything appears out of proportion with the world outside, Moorman appoints Brand to the position new director of IFI. Moorman's speech about credit, credibility and the illusion of money and the social aspects of Brands job, convinces him to take the job. At this point the barker enters the conversation, singing: 'Saying yes at the right moment is all that matters.'

In the next scene Brand is barely recognisible in his new suit, entering the elevator and telling the operator to take him 'up, all the way up'. In his huge office he attends his first meeting, about a housing project for the lower classes. Immediately he starts improving the plan: windows are enlarged, children's rooms directed to the south, a fishing pond in the neighbourhood is added and gas lighting is replaced by electricity. 'I don't have good memories of gas,' Brand murmurs. He barks his orders, confusing the criminal builders, who leave his office to complain to the real man in charge, Moorman. 'Let him play director for a while,' he comforts them, while ordering them to get rid of the street organ that plays continuously below him. Ferdinand appears on the street, as a doorman is given the order to dismiss the street musician. He refuses, referring to his old life: 'I'll never send anyone away', and goes up to see Brand. Brand likes the music but when he hears that Moorman ordered to send the organ away, he agrees, patronising Ferdinand with a speech about big business and important works. In contrast to their earlier conversation, Ferdinand lectures Brand on moral standards, telling him, 'it starts with giving in'. Nevertheless, Brand shouts his orders at Ferdinand who leaves the office disappointed.

Brand accompanies Willy to the aiport and a plane that will take her to Switzerland, where she is enrolled on a college course. On the way, she speaks of her suspicions about their change in circumstances. However, his concerns are fogotten when, in Switzerland, she falls in love with a German refugee who works in a tank station. Brand is furious when he hears the news and orders her to come home. At home, Brand receives business associates in his library and has a butler (Hans van Meerten) who barely hides his contempt for his *nouveau riche* employer. He confesses to Willy, who appears dwarfed within the confines of the enormous lounge, that he let Moorman believe the lost money is in his possession, saying that he did everything for her sake. Willy chides him and he leaves her to meet the builders woking in another part of the house.

The next day, Brand resigns as director at Moorman's office. Moorman agrees but demands that the money remains at the IFI in spite of Brands protests of not having the money. Brand orders the elevator 'down, all the way down' and leaves the IFI building as a broken man. Ferdinand follows and they get drunk in a pub. When they leave later that night, they stop at the point where Brand's troubles began: the Groenburgwal. There Ferdinand repeats Brands lecture, tapping on a virtual money bag. Drunk, he falls through a drain. Looking for Ferdinand, Brand and the dog find the lost money.

The next morning, Brand returns the money to the Neptune bank, where they refuse to take it claiming, 'painful, painful, it is a business of the insurance'. They turn him over to the police. Brand is condemned for theft because he cannot tell the court why there was a hole in his bag. The barker, in the film's *deus ex machina* climax, enters the story again, to clear everything up. He tells of the hungry little boy who, in his search for food, cut a hole in the bottom of Brand's moneybag. Brand is found inocent and is free to return to his life, his reputation unblemished.

For Max Ophüls, the offer to direct a film in Amsterdam was perfect timing. When he received the offer he and his family had just returned to Paris from Moscow, with no projects on the horizon. It must have been strange for Ophüls, coming to Amsterdam just after his Moscow experience. As Helmut Asper wrote in his biography of the director, before traveling to the Soviet Union with his family, there was some hope of a longer contract there, perhaps even two years, but disappointed by standards of living and aware of signs of political repression, wisely chose not to stay, returning instead to Paris.

In Moscow he wrote an 'open letter' to his German exile colleague Gustav von Wangenheim, praising his film *Der Kämpfer* (*The Struggle*, 1936) and his view of a people divided under National Socialism: 'Nothing in the picture is shown in sheer black and white. No matter how grim the subject matter – imprisonment, concentration camps, assault, blood purges – the figures of the other side are never overdrawn, never caricatured or depicted with blind hate. Often there is a residue of humanity shown, which may lead them back, someday, where they belong, on the other side.' The letter was published twice in 1936, in the German-language exile magazine *Das Wort* and the American magazine *New Theatre and Film*, edited by Herbert Kline, who would become an important friend to the Ophüls family. The American version was published in October 1936, the same month that *The Trouble with Money* premiered. Ophüls's anti-Nazi stance was always clear and not just because he was Jewish. A more urgent reason was that he wrote the letter to support Von Wangenheim in and outside Moscow, because the film was under suspicion of the Soviet regime and was in danger of being shelved. This grim climate for German exiles was not particularly inviting for intelligent humanists like Ophüls.

In the Netherlands, however, this certainly was not the reason why Tuschinski employed Ophüls and *The Trouble with Money* does not directly refer to the actual political situation in Germany. It would have never been allowed by the producers who only wanted light-hearted amusement, by the Nederlandsche Bioscoop Bond (NBB) who feared every political involvement, and definitely not by the Dutch government which cherished its neutral position.

The offer to make a film in the Netherlands was, for financial reasons, more than welcome. Never secure of work and income, life in exile was hard. Ophüls left his family and his almost completed film *La tendre ennemie* (*The Tender Enemy*, 1936) behind in Paris, travelling to Amsterdam alone. He stayed there from mid-May to the beginning of September, paid by the day. Katinka Dittrich stated in her dissertation on German exiled filmmakers in the Netherlands, that Ophüls did not have the chance to incorporate himself within the Dutch film industry because, like every foreign filmmaker, he had to leave the country as soon as he had finished his film. Ophüls was unlikely to have wanted to stay any longer. He had a film to finish in Paris, which was eventually released a week before *The Trouble with Money*, on 24 October, and he already complained that making films in the Netherlands took him much longer than in France, due to the primitive working conditions and poor technical equipment available. He was not like Kurt Gerron or Ludwig Berger, who really wanted to stay and work in the Netherlands but were refused, under the strict governmental laws and the protective policy of the NBB.

The Trouble with Money was meant to be the jewel in the crown of the Tuschinski family: designed to celebrate the fifteenth anniversary of the prestigious Tuschinski Theatre in Amsterdam. According to his biographer, Henk van Gelder, Abraham Tuschinski had finally been officially recognised as a valued member of the Netherland's cultural sphere, and a committee of officials was set up to organise the festivities. The crisis in the 1930s had been hard for the Tuschinski cinemas and they had high hopes the jubilee would turn the tide for them. Abraham's only child, Will Tuschinski, who had some experience as a producer after working at the Paramount studios in Hollywood, was appointed producer of the film that was regarded as the 'triumph of the Dutch film industry' before shooting had even begun. He had contacted Max Ophüls' agent in Paris and had arranged, by Dutch standards, solid financial backing.

Contrary to some assertions, *The Trouble with Money* was not based on an original story by Ophüls, but on an idea of Walter Schlee, another German-Jewish exile who had adapted an article from a magazine. Will Tuschinski's best friend, Alex de Haas, as a writer of scenario's and songs, directed his attention on Schlee's story. According to Asper, Ophüls reworked this story together with Schlee and De Haas, and may have added the introduction with the dog trick. Actress and writer Christine van Meeteren translated the dialogues into Dutch.

Ophüls behaved like a prima donna during his time amongst the small Dutch film community: he demanded costly set renovations and enraged Will Tuschinski when he did not appear on the set because he stayed in bed to think. These anecdotes are repeated in almost every reference to the film. His philosophy about spending large sums of money was that it was all for the sake of the film: if it was a success, it would earn its investments back in no time, if it was a flop nobody cared about some extra thousands anyway. The actors had to work hard, repeating the same lines endlessly, but in the end all were grateful for the results.

After seeing the film in a rather late stage of production, the elder Tuschinski feared that his audience would not understand the experiment and accused his son and Ophüls of forgetting that they were working in the amusement industry. Nevertheless, this did nothing to dampen the celebrations when the film premiered on 30 October 1936, be it with its director absent. The programme opened with a *Betty Boop* cartoon, followed by a performance by the dance group *Tamarina and Her Gentlemen* and various speeches, singing the praises of Tuschinski and Dutch film culture, ending with the Dutch national anthem and the screening of *The Trouble with Money*. However, the celebrations were not enough to convince the general public who were less than enthusiastic, resulting in its disappearance from cinema programmes in Amsterdam and Rotterdam after only a week.

The Trouble with Money is seen as Ophüls' only film that is neither a romantic comedy nor melodrama. Although there is the minor love story featuring Willy, it remains peripheral throughout, merely offering Ophüls the opportunity for a wonderfully sweet moment, when Willy sees her lover through a car windscreen as it is being cleaned.

It is difficult to locate *The Trouble with Money* within a specific genre or style. The first part features mostly realistic sequences, shot on location in Amsterdam: at the Berlage bridge, on a fishing pond, in a pub, at the Groenburgwal, in a small apartment and the luxurious villa outside town. In the second part, when Brand is suddenly made director, the visual style shifts dramatically. In the place of everyday locations, Ophüls employs a subtle expressionistic approach to the modernist architecture and designs, magnifying the impact of the trappings of wealth. The sets consist of elaborate designs by Heinz Fenschel, combined with effects produced by cameraman Eugen Schüfftan. Prefiguring Charles Foster Kane's 'Xanadu', Brand's fireplace is a remarkable creation.

Some film scholars see a clear analogy between National Socialist politics and the ideology of the International Finance Institute (IFI), comparing Moorman's speeches to those of Goebbels. Pushing this line of thought a little further, one can see a link in the first half of the film between the poverty-stricken Brand and the old Germany, and in the second, between the corporate Brand and the New Order representing the politics of aesthetics. These aesthetics consist of indoctrinating words, spectacular architecture and dress code, or as Willy states in the film, *alles uiterlijkheden* ('all appearances'). Unrealistically realistic in story as well as in its images, the film has an ambiguous cinematic touch that was very unusual for Dutch films.

Hitherto those had been either adapted popular novels or plays, the so-called Jordaanfilms, or documentaries without much of a story. The theatrical structure, emphasising the staged character of the play and compromising the spectators in their role of audience directly addressed by the barker, fits well in the Dutch tradition of film adaptations of staged revues of the much-despised Jordaanfilm.

When the film was released, critics compared it with Pabst and Brecht's *Dreigroschenoper* (*The Threepenny Opera*, 1931) because of its abstract references to the world of money and the structure of the story organised around a lecturer who emphasises the moral. In the eyes of the critics it was not enough 'film' for that reason. Their Film Liga education with its emphasis on film as a visual art, made the theatricality of the film the hardest part to swallow; they were used to condemning everything relating to the stage as bad cinema. However, most impressed by the sets of Heinz Fenschel and the lighting and camera movements of Eugen Schüfftan, critics also praised the intention and admitted that the artistic quality was unusually high for a Dutch film. Moreover, Ophüls had worked miracles with the actors, who with the exception of Cor Ruys and Rini Otten had long careers in popular theatre. Bouber in particular was unrecognisable in his acting compared to his normal roles in Jordaanfilms.

Despite the good notices, no one was totally impressed by the film. D. C. van der Poel in *De Groene Amsterdammer* summarised its weaknesses due to its scenario and tempo as follows: 'Thus … unreality did not become unreal, reality not real, the play not playful and the irony not sharp enough.' Except for a negative reference to it as 'industriefilm' and to compare it to smaller productions, like Max de Haas' *Ballade van den hoogen hoed* (1934), the most radical and critical film magazine in the Netherlands remained silent about the film. The Catholic magazine *Filmfront* was not particularly happy with the German-Jewish refugees working in the Dutch film industry, especially when they were backed by migrant Jews from Poland, like Tuschinski. *Filmfront* seemed more keen to support the films of the Dutch former avant-garde.

Will Tuschinski would never produce a film again. Months after the release of the film, creditors kept visiting his office, prompting a running gag amongst his personnel: 'Komme die om geld?' ('Do they come for money?'). Before recovering financially, he became ill with cancer and died in 1939, leaving his parents devastated. In 1942 they were killed in Auschwitz. Max Ophüls, who in 1936 already wrote about concentration camps, managed in 1940 to escape with his family to the United States where they continued their life in exile.

Ansje Van Beusekom

GLAS GLASS

BERT HAANSTRA, THE NETHERLANDS, 1958

In 1960 Bert Haanstra became the first Dutch filmmaker to be awarded an Academy Award. He received the honour for his sublime documentary short film *Glas* (*Glass*), made in 1958. The Academy Award was not the only prize Haanstra received for the film; it was distributed worldwide and awarded at least 13 other prizes, including a Silver Bear in Berlin. According to Haanstra himself, *Glass* became his international breakthrough film. Even now, almost fifty years on, the film is still considered to be one of the most influential documentary shorts of Low Countries cinema. But who was Haanstra, and what made *Glass* such a special film?

In its entirety, *Glass* is only 10 minutes and 30 seconds long. This short duration certainly adds to the film's reputation, making it a perfect example to watch and rewatch, especially in film classes. Yet *Glass* is not a didactic film, as is often argued, nor a critical analysis. Rather, it is an atmospheric film on the subject of glassblowing in the Netherlands of the late 1950s.

Before embarking on the production of *Glass*, Haanstra had made another film on the same subject. Commissioned by the glass factory 'NV Koninklijke Nederlandsche Glasfabriek te Leerdam', *Over glas gesproken* (*Talking About Glass*, 1958) was a 25-minute instruction and advertising film in which every effort was made to satisfy the client, and in which Haanstra, almost playfully, creates a portrait of the company and its products. Through the preparations for *Talking About Glass* Haanstra discovered the visual beauty inherent in the traditional craft of glassblowing. A tragi-comic accident Haanstra witnessed during pre-production also made him aware of how automatisation was introduced, and the effect it could have. A bottle with a broken neck caused an automated pair of pincers, which was supposed to pick it up, to miss its target, and all subsequent bottles fell from the conveyor belt until a worker manually removed the broken bottle. The seconds during which the broken bottle blocked the way, the automated pincers kept pincing air, evoking the image of a mindless jack. With more emphasis on the opposition between man and machine, implying the larger cultural conflict between industrialisation and tradition, this incident was to become one of the most discussed and celebrated scenes in *Glass*. The incident itself prompted Haanstra to apply for a grant from the Ministery of Education, Culture and Science to make another film on glassblowing, to be shot back to back with *Talking*

About Glass, but shorter, and in colour instead of black-and-white. Whereas *Talking About Glass* was made to promote the firm and its products, *Glass* became what Haanstra called an 'experimental film poem', from which all advertising elements were banned.

Judging from the images in *Glass*, it is clear that Haanstra was fascinated by the glassblowers: men who made simple bottles as well as sophisticated glass designs, with nothing more than sand, fire and air. *Glass* not only showed the viewer the remarkable diversity of glass being crafted, in all sizes, variations and colours, but also the men making it. Against the smoke of the ovens, Haanstra focused on the chubby cheeks of the blowers and their hand movements on the blow pipes, calling to mind dancing movements, with each movement producing different shapes and designs. The reference to dancing is reinforced by a jazz score, by the Pim Jacobs Quartet, which Haanstra edited over the images. The combination of horn and trumpet sounds coinciding with images of men blowing glass also leads to a slightly amusing, humouristic tone.

In contrast to his affection for the traditional craft, Haanstra presents the automated part of the production process more analytically. The images appearing on the conveyor belt are much colder (blue instead of red), and the jazz music is replaced by a monotonous mechanical counting machine, processing the number of bottles passing by. During this part of the film, Haanstra also recreated the incident he observed earlier, turning *Glass* into a comment on work and industrial practices in modern times. By repeating the same number – 5336 – over and over again, in an increasingly alarming tone, when the automated pincer continuously fails to remove the broken bottle, Haanstra even introduces drama in the film. When a worker manually corrects the failure, the count resumes, in a much calmer tone. Yet there is still humour here, in the mechanical sounds and robotic movements of the bottles on the conveyor belt. This humour, balancing the contrast between criticism and love, imbues *Glass* with an elegant overtone, and the fast tempo (influenced by Russian montage style) turned it into a hugely enjoyable film.

Taking into account the limitations of the format, the reception of *Glass* was highly positive. 'Haanstra's pleasure is clearly visible in every image of this robust and funny symphony of scenes' wrote Dutch film critic Gerdin Linthorst. She continues: 'from the noble handcraft of the glassblower until the conveyor belt where, through a technical failure, one milk bottle after the other falls to pieces. [It is] accompanied by the only human sound in the film, that of the filmmaker himself, which continues to count in a dry comical way – 5333, 5334, 5335, 5336, 5336, 5336, 5336, hey watch out!, 5336, 5337, 5338. Haanstra's warm, funny approach of the subject and the editing rhythm, which so perfectly fits the rhythm within each shot, have significantly contributed to the success of *Glass*.'

Glass was not only praised in the 1950s. Almost half a century after it was made, *Glass* is still being shown in practically every Dutch and Belgian film school (as well as in American film academies), year after year, to new generations of filmmakers who still seem to enjoy the film, even (or perhaps especially) in times of MTV-style editing. For that matter, the film has a very 'televisual' and modern look, with its fast montage, many close ups and overall breezy style.

Aside of its textual qualities, one of the reasons that *Glass* is so special is that it is a perfect example of the relationship of its maker with the so called Dutch Documentary School. Haanstra's opinion of the school cannot be overestimated. The Dutch documentary tradition had for some time lacked any formal organisation. It centered around a couple of individuals, of whom Haanstra was one of the most important. Even Paul Verhoeven, leading the next generation of filmmakers, recognised the crucial role of Haanstra. In Robbe De Hert's and Willum Thijssen's Belgian documentary *Op de fiets naar Hollywood* (*On the Bike to Hollywood*, 1994) Verhoeven stated that 'my favourite Dutch films remain influenced by my youthful admiration for Dutch documentaries. Especially filmmakers like Ivens, Haanstra and Herman Van der Horst have influenced me more, and have given me a much more profound love for film, than any other Dutch fiction filmmaker'. And Verhoeven is not alone. For a long time, with scandal-successes like *Turks Fruit* (*Turkish Delight*, Verhoeven, 1973) notwithstanding, Dutch cinema was associated with documentary filmmaking. In 1994, *Halliwell's Filmgoers Companion* devoted two sentences to Dutch cinema: 'Holland has produced two major documentarists: Joris Ivens and Bert Haanstra. Fiction films have not been the country's forte, though Fons Rademakers has his adherents.'

So it should be no surprise that the documentary is still considered the Netherlands' strongest contribution to international filmmaking. As far back as the early 1930s, Joris Ivens' films like *De Brug* (*The Bridge*, 1928), *Regen* (*Rain*, 1929) and *Zuiderzee* (1930–33) had established a reputation for Dutch documentaries, along with the widespread movement of the combative social documentary, like the union films *Triomf* (*Triumph*) and *Stalen Knuisten* (*Fists of Steel*), two Polygoon productions from 1930. After World War Two, Dutch documentary saw a remarkable revival, with the work of Van der Horst and, somewhat later, Haanstra. The quiet Haanstra (1916–1997) was very much the opposite of the revolutionary Joris Ivens. Whereas Ivens tried to change the world with his documentaries, Haanstra was merely attempting to observe Dutch society from a distance, in all its shapes. Without ever becoming polemic or controversial, the suggestiveness and associational structure of Haanstra's work often offers a view of Dutch society that Gerdin Linthorst calls a 'cosy, secure haven of somewhat snuggish, well-meaning but naive, good citizens', which the Netherlands were in Haanstra's time.

Besides the three figureheads, Ivens, Van der Horst and Haanstra, the post-World War Two era saw a great deal of activity from less well-kown documentary makers, like Charles Huguenot van der Linden, Hattum Hoving, Jan Wiegel and cameraman John Fernhout (who collaborated with Ivens on *Sky over Holland* in 1967 and which won a Palme d'Or at Cannes). Still later, Johan Van der Keuken would attract worldwide attention with his documentaries. These individuals transformed the Dutch Documentary School into an internationally appreciated notion, even if there was, like in neighbouring Belgium, not so much an organised school as a collective of talented individuals. Regardless of their differences, the School had, according to Linthorst, some common characteristics: 'thorough craftsmanship, a poetic view on nature and society, a certain nostalgia for a rich past, and a mild, sometimes lightly chauvinistic view of national cultural identity'. It is a description that certainly fits Haanstra's work.

Many of Haanstra's films carry one predominant theme, that of the continuity of life, no matter what changes take place in society. This is most strikingly presented in *Rembrandt, Schilder van de mens* (*Rembrandt, Painter of People*, 1957), the film he made before starting to work on the 'glass' films. The film ends with a series of superimpositions of Rembrandt self-portraits. Haanstra shows the portraits through match cuts on the eyes; the eyes remain the same and around them, the face of the painter changes, from a young, ambitious person to an old, tormented man. According to Linthorst, this series of images shows how Haanstra's preoccupations flawlessly flow over each other; his compassion for humankind, his preference for portraits, his careful use of the technical possibilities of the medium, and his habit of dramatising reality through montage.

Haanstra was well in his thirties before he began making films. His first was *De Muiderkring Herleeft* (*The Muiderkring Lives Again*, 1948), followed by *Spiegel van Holland* (*Mirror of Holland*, 1950), which introduced his observational style and his fascination with the unique relationship between Dutch society and the struggle to tame the forces of nature, especially water; a struggle that shaped the country and its inhabitants. The film showed the Netherlands as mirrored in lakes, rivers and pools of water. It earned Haanstra a Palme d'Or at Cannes and it attracted large audiences at home. According to Haanstra's biographer Jo Daems, *Mirror of Holland* should be seen less as a document, and more as a monument: 'It doesn't get more filmic than this: a pure rhythmic stream of images, uninterrupted by commentary, but supported instead by an exquisite musical score.' *Mirror of Holland* established Haanstra's reputation as an art filmmaker. His next film, *Panta Rhei* (*Alles Vloeit/Everything Flows*, 1951), was a short film poem in which he sketched the ever-flowing movement of nature in the Netherlands. Both *Mirror of Holland* and *Everything Flows* were seen by Haanstra as simple exercises, although Daems calls this 'an overly modest description' and that 'the latent presence of a pure poetic feeling, and an unusual craftsmanship make them much more than exercises'.

From the beginning of the 1950s, Haanstra began making commisioned films for, amongst others, the Dutch oil company Shell (*Verkenningsboring/Trial Drilling* and *De opsporing van aardolie/The Search for Oil*, both 1954). Yet his fascination for the relationship between Dutch society and water never disappeared. In 1955 he made *En de Zee was niet meer* (*And the Sea Was No More*), a historical documentary detailing the Dutch effort to dam the Zuiderzee and reclaim land from the sea, in which special emphasis was placed on the disappearing folklore around the Zuiderzee. The film also showed the sharp contrast with Ivens, who had also made a film on the Zuiderzee works, but had stressed the industrial scale of the labour instead of the underlying nostalgia of lost history. The sea is also a central feature in *Delta Phase I* (1961–62), a 20-minute prize-winning documentary commissioned by the Dutch government portraying the large damming works that would protect the South Netherlands from massive regular floodings, like the one in 1953, in which several thousand people died. Haanstra's most elaborate 'water' film, *Stem van het Water* (*The Voice of The Water*), co-written by the popular writer Simon Carmiggelt, was released in 1966. Internationally acclaimed, and awarded several prizes, it sums up the fascination for, fear of, and struggle against water which has shaped Dutch cultural identity.

But Haanstra was more than a director of water films. From the 1960s he also began focusing on humans as a strange breed of animals, comparing human and animal behaviour, and introducing anthropoligical concerns in his work. *Zoo* (1962) displays a mildly humorous view of people watching animals in a zoo. Rhythmically structured, the film made use of a then new technique – candid camera to observe people without them noticing it. Haanstra used the technique again in his next film, the feature length *Alleman* (*Everybody*, 1963), which focused on the oddities of human behaviour and which once again earned him many accolades. Throughout *Everybody*, Haanstra maintained a humanist perspective. As Fred Bredschneyder wrote: 'although observing them without their knowledge, Haanstra refrains from sharp criticism of the people he films – he is not a voyeur. He tries to catch people in their most natural, unguarded moments, but without trying to film acts that they would deliberatley try to keep secret.' Bredschneyder thus described a view many Dutch had of Haanstra at the time, as being 'too nice, too kind' to people. Haanstra did become more critical in his best-known film on human behaviour, the feature-length *Bij de beesten af* (*Ape and Super-Ape*, 1972), which compared human and animal behaviour from a purely anthropological point of view. Haanstra spent three years preparing the film, and it caused a huge controversy because of its main thesis (that overpopulation leads to agressive behaviour). Today, *Ape and Super-Ape* seems outdated, partly because the theories on the relationships between animal and human behaviour have changed considerably since, and partly because the general theme of the film, as well as its look, has been copied (and improved), for instance in the documentaries of Desmond Morris. In 1984, Morris would collaborate with Haanstra by introducing *Chimps* for the BBC, and for doing the English language commentary for it.

After *Ape and Super-Ape*, Haanstra gradually shifted his focus towards observing animals. In 1978 he directed a commissioned film on the National Parcs in the Netherlands (*Nationale Parken*), and in the 1980s he concentrated on filming the behaviour of apes, with the award-winning *Chimps*, and *Monument voor een gorilla* (*Monument for a Gorilla*, 1986–87), for which, at the age of 70, he went to film the animals in their natural habitat in Cameroon, after having initially studies their rituals in Dutch zoos.

The success of his documentaries enabled Haanstra to direct fiction films. Of these, *Fanfare* (1958), telling the story of rivalry in a local brass band, is probably the one for which he is best remembered. Like his documentaries, the film portrays simple folk in their natural behaviour, with emphasis on the tragi-comic aspects of daily life. Yet despite the fact that it was a huge success in the Netherlands, it became increasingly difficult for Haanstra to get his fiction projects financed. Drawing a comparison with Giuseppe Tornatore's remarks that 'a director dies between two films, and his audience does not even know it', biographer Daems explains how this period was difficult for Haanstra, with this next two attempts to make a fiction film (including a parody of *The Flying Dutchman*) failing to attract financing. His next film, *De zaak M.P.* (*The Mannekin Pis Case*, 1960), centered around Brussels' most famous statuette, was not well received and was, for most critics, an artistic failure. After that, Haanstra concentrated on documentaries, until the mid-1970s when he directed *Dokter Pulder zaait Papavers* (*When the Poppies Bloom Again*, 1975). One of his most ambitious films, *When the Poppies Bloom Again* turned its attention back to smalltown life. The local doctor receives a visit from his former study-friend, who turns out to be a junkie trying to steal the doctor's morphine and other drugs. Although the film is seen today as a well-meant, humouristic take on liberal values in the Netherlands of the 1970s, the reactions to the film at the time were mixed, with some critics seeing it as too naïve and simplistic. The commercial failure of Haanstra's next fiction film, *Een pak slaag* (*Mr Slotter's Jubilee*, 1979), which may have contributed to a heart attack and ensuing depression, put him off making fiction films for good. He only briefly returned to docu-drama in 1983 to film *Vroeger kon je lachen* (*We Used to Laugh*), a series of everyday life sketches set in Amsterdam, and a homage to both his friend and former collaborator Carmiggelt, as well as the city of Amsterdam.

Haanstra's last films again showed his interest in plain people. The briskly edited 16-minute commisioned film *Nederland* (*The Netherlands*, 1982–83), which sketched an all-round image of the nation, and which Haanstra shot for the Ministry of Foreign Affairs, is, like most of his other documentaries, a sharp observation of everyday life in the Netherlands. And his final film, *Kinderen van Ghana* (*Children of Ghana*, 1988), a pilot for a Unicef series, demonstrated how his interest was in no way limited to his native country.

Throughout his career, Haanstra and his films have always remained popular. In 1993 two of his documentaries, *Everybody* and *Ape and Super-Ape* still featured in a 'top 20' of most succesful Dutch films, alongside more commercial films like *Turkish Delight* and *Flodder* (Dick Maas, 1986). According to film historian Bert Hogenkamp, 'it is ironic that Haanstra's documentaries, which were once discarded as old-fashioned, are now seen as hugely relevant. They are lessons in the art of editing. It is beyond doubt that Haanstra was a craftsman who mastered his profession in detail. In a time, now, in which we regularly hear the claim that many Dutch documentaries have become too Dutch in subject, and hence impossible to sell abroad, there is much to be learned from his films, which were, at the same time, very Dutch, yet still attracted foreign sales.'

Haanstra's popular appeal can largely be attributed to the fact that his films portray recognisable people, in situations that allow them to show themselves as humans. The symphony of faces and hand movements of the glassblowers in *Glass*, and the possibility to show how human intervention overcomes mechanical failure, demonstrate this. Even if the viewer does not know these people, they are very much real and they can be sympathised with. In the larger context of the industry of glassblowing, *Glass* also shows how these people are part of how societies and cultures are shaped. Like the struggle against water in *The Voice of Water*, and like the unguarded mannerisms, exposed in *Everybody*, the glassblowers in *Glass* are part of a culture of which Haanstra shows us its most human face.

Jan-Pieter Everaerts

DE MAN DIE ZIJN HAAR KORT LIET KNIPPEN

THE MAN WHO HAD HIS HAIR CUT SHORT

ANDRÉ DELVAUX, BELGIUM, 1965

André Delvaux's first feature, *De man die zijn haar kort liet knippen* (*The Man Who Had His Hair Cut Short*, 1965), put modern Belgian cinema on the international map. Its success also spurred the planned state support of film production via subsidy grants administered by the two main linguistic communities, French and Flemish, in Belgium. The film marked the beginning of Delvaux's lengthy exploration of magic realism in cinema, informed in each instance by an aesthetic of formal rigour, of studied interiority, and of immersion in the multiple cultures of his native land. By the time of his death in 2002 he had become one of the best-known figures in Belgian cinema.

The Man Who Had His Hair Cut Short tells the story of Govert Miereveld (Senne Rouffaer), a lawyer and father of two, who also teaches at a Flemish girls' school. He falls desperately in love with one of his graduating students, Fran Veenman (Beata Tyszkiewicz). After visiting a barbers, Govert misses Fran on the final day of school and can only wander the building in search of memories of her presence. Several years pass. Govert, forlorn and unable to cope with his professional duties, becomes a court clerk. By chance, he meets Professor Mato (Hector Camerlynck), an eminent legal pathologist, who invites Govert to accompany him to a rural autopsy. His sudden confrontation with death disturbs Govert profoundly. Overcome by the heat and unsettled by his experience, Govert enters a village café, presumably to vomit or to order a stiff drink. A fastidious individual, who likes to keep cool and whose life, by necessity, is always organised, becomes deranged. Unable to excuse himself from the company of Mato and his assistant Verbruggen, Govert accompanies them to a smalltown hotel near the Dutch border where Mato has arranged to meet another colleague. In the car, Govert's discomfort grows as the pathologists calmly describe the details of their work and express their sense of beauty in the idea of the human body transformed by death into another state. He unexpectedly encounters Fran, now a renowned actress, on the hotel staircase. Later that evening, he goes to Fran's room to declare his love. At first Fran reciprocates, but as dawn breaks she confesses that far from being his ideal of beauty incarnate she has led a sad, worldly existence. She reveals an affair, the first of many, with Govert's predecessor at the school, Judge Brantink, and her father's consequent rejection of her. Disillusioned and disoriented, Govert takes a gun she has shown him and shoots her. The pathologists enter the room to find Govert in a state of shock. Time passes again; Govert lives in a psychiatric institution, working in its garden and carpentry shop. Astonished to see an interview with Fran in a newsreel, he now believes that he did not kill her and rushes to the director of the institution, who seems to confirm it. His guilty burden lifted, Govert contemplates the merits of the reclusive life he leads: humility, faith in 'God's peace' (his full name is Godefried), and simple manual work.

The Man Who Had His Hair Cut Short is based on a 1947 novel by Johan Daisne, a leading Flemish exponent of magic realism. Having already made several short films and become head of the film department at the newly-established state higher educational institution in Brussels (RITS), Delvaux was invited by Flemish public television (BRT) to make a feature film. In a nation notorious for its bicultural tensions, it is remarkable that Delvaux did not make the film in Flemish rather than French for any ideological reason (he considered himself a non-political filmmaker, touching only occasionally on political issues) but simply because BRT gave him an opportunity. Having long admired Daisne's novel, Delvaux unhesitatingly chose it as his first project. It was a bold but prudent choice. The support he would otherwise almost certainly have received from the Flemish ministry was as yet unavailable, since the production of the film preceded implementation of the policy of linguistic community grants to Belgian film-makers. Yet he also knew that as a first-time feature director he could not expect commercial film sector production support either to adapt such an unconventional text or to propose an original subject.

The film received a small budget from BRT and the National Education Ministry, which under the guidance of Paul Louyet had been involved in supporting film projects in Belgium since the late 1940s. The production was therefore determined largely by available funds. In an interview with this author, Delvaux explained the consequent effect on form and style: 'There was no money to build sets. Out of necessity we had to use the reality around us. Moreover, we made it in black-and-white as there was no money for colour. But that was our prefer-ence anyway, since we had learned much from the great black-and-white tradition in cinema. We also worked with unknown actors, with subjects that could be set up easily and shot very quickly. A rapid technique was required, so we shot mainly in long takes and with very little movement because when you work without movement the shots can be lengthened – and the dialogue grows longer. ... It means that the development of the production leads to the aes-thetic transformation of the conditions under which you write your scripts and under which you shoot them. It's an important consideration, because you realise that *homo cinematographicus* is conditioned as much by money as by anything else.'

After Daisne declined to write the screenplay, Delvaux assumed that task in collaboration with Anna De Pagter. He shot directly from the screenplay, his construction of the film in three clearly defined sequence blocks permitting him to dispense with the detail of a shooting script. While he followed Daisne's novel quite closely, the literary narrative took the form of a first-person retrospective confession by Govert written in the psychiatric institution. Wary of the cinematic limitations of subjective viewpoint and flashback, Delvaux opted for a chronological story in three distinct time periods, separated by two ellipses. He created a plausible and suspenseful plot that followed Govert's slow decline into madness, filming in a way that allowed the viewer to identify as far as possible with his protagonist's inner turmoil.

Belgian critics largely derided the film following its Brussels premiere in late 1965, but foreign critics were more enthusiastic. Amongst many others, French critic Michel Ciment praised it in his *Positif* review in 1966. The film began to draw attention on the festival circuit. Selected for London and New York, it soon won prizes at the Hyères Young Cinema Festival in France, at Mannheim and at Pesaro (where it was lauded by Jean-Luc Godard). It won the British Film Institute's award as the 'most original and imaginative film' of the year. On its brief reappearance in Brussels in 1967, a number of Belgian critics admitted that they had misunderstood it and had dismissed it partly out of habit, doubting the possibility of such an accomplished Belgian film. On the strength of its international reception Delvaux obtained generous French commercial sector production support as well as the services of two stars, Yves Montand and Anouk Aimée, for his next film, *Un Soir, un train* (*One Night ... a Train*, 1968). Yet even this film failed to gain Belgian ministerial support, only because its story unfolded amid linguistic conflict between French and Flemish speakers, an issue so volatile that it brought down the Belgian government in that same year.

One Night ... a Train took Delvaux's magic-realist mode to another stage, as did his next two features, *Rendezvous à Bray* (*Rendezvous at Bray*, 1970), set in France, and *Belle* (1973), set in Wallonia. Another film with magic-realist overtones, *Benvenuta* (1983), reverted in part to a Flemish setting. Apart from *The Man Who Had His Hair Cut Short*, his only other feature in Flemish was *Een vrouw tussen hond en wolf* (*Woman in a Twilight Garden*, 1979), a provocative domestic drama set in and around Antwerp during World War Two. In *L'Oeuvre au noir* (*The Abyss*, 1988) as well as in two unconventional documentaries, *With Dieric Bouts* (1975) and *Babel Opera* (1985), Delvaux subtly elaborated his vision of Flemish history, life and landscape.

In these three films, as throughout his career, Delvaux found reasons both to celebrate and to question the complexities of Belgian culture and identity.

As a Belgian raised speaking Flemish and educated in French, Delvaux saw identity as a major problem: 'the problem of identity forms the basis of the execution of my films insofar as the characters are induced to ask themselves the fundamental question, "Who am I?" ("What am I?" as a matter of fact). This question is asked in a completely ambiguous way in *The Man Who Had His Hair Cut Short*, since that character ends up growing aware of his own schizophrenia, which is a multiple form of identity. Faced with this ambiguity, he asks himself the fundamental question. At the end of the film, when he has gone through all the ups and downs of his story, he says, finally, "I am another." It's possible that this situation reflects that of someone who belongs to two cultures at the same time, perhaps to several cultures at the same time, who is never wholly in one or the other because by defining himself in terms of the one, he excludes the other, disavows the other in a way, is unfaithful to the other.'

The Man Who Had His Hair Cut Short also addresses the themes of love, beauty and death. Displaying the artistic control and formal unity that became a hallmark of his cinema, Delvaux constructs the film around the three major sequence blocks (home and school, autopsy, hotel) followed by a brief coda (psychiatric institution). He establishes a dialectic between the ideal of love and beauty and the reality of death and decay. The three blocks depend on a highly interiorised realism that conveys the various stages of Govert's increasing emotional and physical disturbance. Delvaux's film style invites the viewer to identify with these stages. He resists the master shot, preferring to offer partial views of the action and glimpses of its setting. Whether in over-the-shoulder shots, tracking shots, or close-ups, Delvaux's camera focuses on Govert most of the time, suggesting his point of view, exploring his sense of space, and showing his reaction to events taking place around him.

The coda brings Govert some hope. In an echo of Rimbaud, his assertions that 'I am another' and 'I always see the truth in two or three different guises' confirms his schizoid personality. But in the light of the newsreel and the director's reassurance that he did not kill Fran, he is able at least to accept a distinction between the real and imaginary. The first word of the film is his wistful utterance of Fran's name. Recalling their fateful reunion, he now speaks it again with an air of detachment. The last word of the film, which he utters lovingly, is 'Cora', the name of his wife.

A director not given to impulse or improvisation, Delvaux's effective interpretation of his subjects always depended on meticulous planning, economy of sound and image, and tight control of the resources at his disposal. He was also known also for his sympathetic and constructive work with actors, technical directors and crews. His attention to detail and avoidance of melodrama set a tone for the performances of his actors, notably that of Senne Rouffaer, whose portrayal of Govert has been described as almost Bressonian in its intense restraint.

Classically trained and experienced in accompanying silent film screenings at the Cinema Museum in Brussels, Delvaux considered music to be so important to *The Man Who Had His Hair Cut Short* that he began working with his composer, Frédéric Devreese, whom he described as 'intuitive', before writing the screenplay. Dreamy and romantic in the first part, ominous in the second, a blend in the third and poignant at the end, Devreese's score is more than incidental. It weaves itself into the fabric of the film in meaningful counterpoint to images and themes. The only diegetic music occurs in the school scene: an anthem accompanied by piano, a girls' chorus and 'The Ballad of Real Life', performed by Fran. Its lyrics, composed by Delvaux, refer to 'three kings [who] suffered shipwreck for me', a cryptic reference to the parts played in Fran's destiny by her father, Judge Brantink, and Govert. In later films Delvaux introduced similar songs and rhymes that also function as semantic riddles, but his development of the potential of musical structures in film proceeded so rapidly that already by 1971 *Rendezvous at Bray* was based on sonata form.

Delvaux used sounds in an equally allusive way, filtering them through Govert's uneasy mind. In the autopsy scene, for instance, Delvaux increases the revulsion we share with Govert by maintaining a distance from the coffin while allowing us to see and hear the pathologists at work with their tools. The contrast between the procedures of the autopsy, the idyllic rural setting, and the sounds of birdsong, church bells and a distant choir imparts a gruesome irony to the scene.

This suggestive rather than descriptive use of image and sound identifies Delvaux as the cinematic heir to Symbolism (well represented among Belgian artists and poets), alert to the possibilities of synesthetic effects, of eerie symmetries, of intricate correspondences, rhythms and rhymes. Some examples in the film: long, empty corridors of school, hotel and institution; the confusion of pleasure and pain between barber's and pathologist's tools; the sense of oppressive heat pervading the film (as in Bergman's *The Silence*, 1963); bells and voices waking or summoning Govert at various times. In a subtle play of correspondences, the institution garden and the graveyard resemble each other as sunny and peaceful locations, but activities there concern death, the diggers exhuming a decomposed body on which Mato works with his tools, Govert digging in search of something rotten beneath the earth. After the revelation of the newsreel changes his understanding of things, Govert looks instead to the future, wishing to plant flowers in the garden. Indoors he works with tools, like Mato, but uses them on inorganic matter to fashion useful objects such as a wooden stool for his wife, 'a silent contribution to my home'.

A key scene, part of the third major block of the film, takes place in Fran's hotel room. Govert wakes during the evening to the sound of voices and bells, reprising the opening scene of the film at home when his daughter wakes him from a dream or reverie of Fran. He goes immediately to Fran's room and knocks on her door. Fran admits him silently and they drink a glass of wine, but this dreamlike mood of erotic pleasure gives way to awkwardness as Govert bluntly pours out his heart. He and Fran circle one another, even lie on a bed together, but do not touch. Nor do they truly converse; one monologue follows the other. During Fran's confession Delvaux's camera focuses mainly on an increasingly agitated Govert. At first her response seems to confirm his hopes and dreams, but then she reveals her sordid past. As dawn breaks, Govert draws back the curtains, but his long night of truth is not yet over. Further revelations intensify his shock. The body in the autopsy was that of Fran's father, apparently killed in a riverside accident. She produces three keepsakes representing each of her 'kingly' victims: a book Govert gave her via an intermediary at the school-leaving ceremony; a gun her father gave her on disowning her; and a hand of justice presented by the school to Brantink, whom Govert learns had been forced to resign his teaching position on account of his liaison with Fran. Also visible in the room are two other objects, both viewed longingly by Govert at the school: Fran's class photo and her coat hook label.

'This is my sunrise', says Fran; the femme fatale, the vampire-woman must now face her fate (Delvaux expressed his admiration for F. W. Murnau's *Nosferatu*, 1922). Asking Govert to carry out her father's will by committing an act she dare not, he picks up the gun and shoots her. Several rapid close-ups of Fran after the shooting culminate in an identical image to the one preceding Govert's awakening at the beginning of the film. After a reaction shot of Govert, Delvaux cuts to a high-angle long-shot of him in the same position with Mato and Verbruggen appearing at the door. This short take, restricted in its framing, prevents the viewer from ascertaining the entire disposition of objects and persons in the room. The viewer does not see Fran – dead or alive – only a traumatised Govert falling before the men in the doorway and shouting 'Don't dissect her', as if autopsy and death have indelibly fused in his disintegrating mind. The newsreel subsequently casts more doubt on the precise nature of what occurred in the room, particularly the consequence of the shooting. Did he fire the gun at all? Did he miss or merely injure Fran? So strange is the scene that the viewer may even be tempted to speculate that he did not go to her room at all, or that he knocked on her door to no avail, dreaming the rest of the scene as an ultimate and tortured projection of his desire. The true awakening into madness perhaps occurs off-screen. The only certainty at the end of the scene is that, consciously or not, he believes he has killed her.

While the entire film until this scene has an uneasy quality, a growing sense of slippage, it remains grounded nonetheless in a steadily paced realism. Delvaux's sudden change of mood and tempo in this scene, his defamiliarising of it, helps to represent Govert's feverish mental state, his growing confusion between real and imaginary. As Govert's instability increases following his apparent murder of Fran, Delvaux alters his slow cutting rhythm for the only time in the film, introducing a series of jump cuts. He has described how, in the film's climactic moments, he dealt with the rest of the scene by shifting the focal lengths of his camera lens dramatically from 40mm to 32mm, 100mm, and finally to 18mm, when the shot is fired. As Delvaux builds to this climax we hear what sounds like a mixture of metallic blows and tolling bells, comparable in effect if not in volume, suddenness or duration, to Bernard Herrmann's discordant notes for the shower scene in Hitchcock's *Psycho* (1960). Like that scene, a brief and bewildering montage depicts an act in excess of all reason.

Most early approaches to *The Man Who Had His Hair Cut Short* focused on Delvaux's precocious mastery of film form and technique, as well as his adoption of magical realism. This mode corresponds not only to his literary influences, but also to a tradition in Low Countries art from the Renaissance, through to Symbolism and Surrealism, wherein the ordinary and extraordinary, the real and imaginary, the beautiful and ugly, coexist in a variety of fantastic ways. In Delvaux's films the spirit of Bosch and Brueghel lingers behind the more direct Surrealist influence of Paul Delvaux and René Magritte. Two instances in *The Man Who Had His Hair Cut Short* recall the predilection of those Surrealists for mysterious places, frozen moments and strange juxtapositions of object and idea. One, a rear shot, as momentarily uncanny as it is mundane, shows the dark-suited pathologists staring at a watery landscape. In the other, a prelude to the hotel room scene, Delvaux transforms the ordinariness of Govert's errand to replace his soiled shoes by filming him in dark, empty streets to the accompaniment of a haunting musical theme.

While Delvaux's major literary and artistic reference points are this native pictorial tradition and German Romanticism, he also absorbed influences from the history of cinema. *The Man Who Had His Hair Cut Short* inserts Delvaux into an evolving canon of

European art cinema, particularly in the wake of the French New Wave. His admiration for Alain Resnais' meditations on time, memory and subjectivity (certain moments in the hotel recall *Last Year at Marienbad*, 1961) attracted him to the serious, philosophical side of that movement. In rejecting theatrical adaptations, lavish productions and escapist illusions, he gestures equally toward the New Wave's rejuvenated cinema based on neorealist principles and a direct filming style.

Later critical approaches to *The Man Who Had His Hair Cut Short* have continued to recognise its qualities, offering occasional fresh insights. Jacques Aumont praised its originality, its shades of Buñuel and of French New Novel narrative techniques, and Delvaux's evocation of a peculiar Flemish obsession with mud and rot. The work of Laure Borgomano and Adolphe Nysenholc also deserves attention. While each has written separately on diverse aspects of Delvaux's career, together they reviewed Delvaux's formal procedures in relation to his magic-realist mode. One of these procedures was the circulation of objects. Borgomano observed that in *The Man Who Had His Hair Cut Short* the simultaneous appearance of the five objects in the hotel room, while plausible in the circumstances, has 'something a little excessive in its coincidence', inviting the suspicion that Govert 'could be hallucinating them' or even the entire scene. Drawing on Simone Vierne's studies of initiation in literary narrative, Borgomano added a new analytical element in keeping with the narrative form of much magic-realist fiction, including that of Daisne: the initiatory journey of the protagonist. She identifies this deep structure in the screenplays of six films (including *The Abyss*) that she and Nysenholc consider to be Delvaux's magic-realist oeuvre. The three main phases of this ritual are preparatory crisis, the journey itself and death overcome. In *The Man Who Had His Hair Cut Short* the crisis of Govert's fruitless pursuit of Fran leads to his unforeseen journey northward with Mato as initiator and to confrontations with death, first at the autopsy, then in the hotel room. The epilogue follows the pattern by suggesting a reaffirmation of life.

There is substantial writing on Delvaux in French, Dutch and Italian, including several interviews with the director, invariably marked by his gracious and thoughtful responses. Significantly less criticism exists in English. John Wakeman's criticism remains the most extensive. Surveying Delvaux's career in the context of francophone cinemas, Lieve Spaas has summarised the main points of *The Man Who Had His Hair Cut Short*. Readers may also wish to consult Richard Roud's review of the film in *Sight and Sound*. In the same magazine Tom Milne's article on *Rendezvous at Bray* and Dan Yakir's interview with Delvaux also review his earlier work. In my own history of Belgian cinema I include an interview with Delvaux that centred on conditions of production. Elsewhere I have discussed his musical structures in the context of *Rendezvous at Bray*, and his adaptations of literary texts.

The Man Who Had His Hair Cut Short rewards repeated viewing for the emotional force of its story, the profundity of its philosophical themes, and its director's mastery of form and technique. Delvaux's imaginative response to the challenge of making his first feature film set a high standard that he maintained throughout his distinguished career.

Philip Mosley

MIRA, OF DE TELEURGANG VAN DE WATERHOEK MIRA

FONS RADEMAKERS, BELGIUM/THE NETHERLANDS, 1971

On 4 March 1971, the day *Mira, of de teleurgang van de waterhoek* (*Mira*) began its theatrical run at Cinema Twins in Brussels, the cinema owner's wife was in a panic. Mrs Weis dialed the office of Kunst en Kino (Art & Cinema), *Mira*'s production company and spoke with its head, Jan Van Raemdonck: 'I remember she called me at three o'clock in the afternoon. "Jan", she cried, "there are five hundred people lining up here. I don't know what to do!" At the eight o'clock screening, the same thing happened. People wanted to smash the window of the ticket booth. "We want to see this film!" they shouted. So an extra screening was organised after midnight … [and] even more people showed up. And so it went on, the same story when the film was [screened] in the Netherlands.'

Mira was not only Jan Van Raemdonck's first major hit, it was the first Flemish film to find a large audience for some time. And it took its producer by complete surprise. Before *Mira*, domestic cinema had never experienced this kind of popularity. There had been the immense success of *De Witte* (*Whitey*) in 1934, a film based on the work of popular novelist Ernest Claes and directed by Jan Vanderheyden, with the help of Edith Kiel. Both of them directed a number of popular comedies after this first success, but their appeal was limited to local audiences.

Flemish film had fallen out of favour with its home audience in the 1960s. Since 1964, Flanders had a government support strategy for Dutch-language film, which had generated a number of interesting films such as *Monsieur Hawarden* (Harry Kümel, 1968), *Het afscheid* (*Farewells*, Roland Verhavert, 1966), and *The Man Who Had His Hair Cut Short* (André Delvaux, 1965), but audiences rarely saw or cared for them. This kind of cultural cinema was, after all, very different to the popular films like the ones directed by Kiel or Jef Bruyninckx (the boy who became famous as 'Whitey' in the 1934 film, and who later on turned to directing). According to Jan Van Raemdonck, few distributors were interested in screening *Mira*. Except, that was, for André Weis, head of Cinevog distribution and owner of Cinema Twins. 'But that was only because Cinema Twins was performing very poorly at the time, and was in no position to attract high-profile titles', commented Raemdonck. 'There is no explanation for the immense success. It was a Flemish film, with actors who were completely unknown, about some old-fashioned book nobody cared for.' However, *Mira* made Van Raemdonck one of Belgium's leading producers. It also established a genre, or rather a formula, from which many later Kunst en Kino films were indebted: the adaptation of classic Flemish literature, or 'heimat' novels – period dramas set in the countryside during the late nineteenth century. As a result, Van Raemdonck was often criticised for his conservatism when it came to film production. Although there may have been grounds for this, he deserves credit for succeeding in bringing audiences back into the cinema to see film from the Low Countries.

In addition to Van Raemdonck, there were four other figures instrumental in *Mira's* success. They were director Fons Rademakers, screenwriter Hugo Claus, novelist Stijn Streuvels and the film's star, Willeke van Ammelrooy.

It is part of the paradox that surrounds the Flemish success of this film that *Mira* is actually directed by a Dutch filmmaker, who was not even fashionable amongst audiences. Rademakers had started out in the theatre, as an actor, prior to World War Two. He turned to directing after the war and his first feature, *Dorp aan de Rivier* (*Village on the River*, 1958) was an instant success. The film was awarded the Silver Bear at the Berlin Film Festival the following year, and in 1960 it was nominated for an Academy Award. The film was influenced by neo-realism, which gave it a realist edge that appealed to Rademakers and audiences at the time. The story of anarchist Dr Van Taek, it was based on the novels of Anton Coolen, with a screenplay written by Belgian novelist Hugo Claus.

Rademakers was had been an admirer of Claus' theatre work: 'He was the first author in my time, who had a real dramatical talent.' Claus and Rademakers became friends and they would work on numerous projects over the years, including *Het Mes* (*The Knife*, 1961), *Dans van de Reiger* (*The Dance of the Heron*, 1966) and *Mira*.

In general, Dutch films have never been popular in Flanders, but *Mira* proved to be the exception. To a large extent this was because the audience hardly perceived the film as being Dutch. The novel by Stijn Streuvels, on which the film was based, was Flemish, as were the locations and most of the actors. The main actress may have been Dutch, but her voice was dubbed into Flemish. Moreover, the director was only 'half a foreigner'. Rademakers was born in Roosendaal, close to the Belgian border, and spent an important part of his youth in Antwerp. 'So I felt myself half a Fleming, perhaps even up to 75 per cent', commented Rademakers.

Claus was a crucial component in the genesis of the production. He was the link between Rademakers and Van Raemdonck. His contribution in building the Dutch/Flemish co-production structure was considerable. Half of the budget (the total budget was less than 400,000 euro) was Flemish, provided by Flemish Television, the Ministry of Culture, and to a lesser extent by Van Raemdonck's Kunst en Kino. The remaining half of the funding came from the Netherlands in the form of contributions from the Dutch productions fund, Dutch television and Rademakers' own production company. Belgium's part in the production outnumbered that of the Netherlands by a small percentage, so when *Mira* was selected for Cannes, it was registered as a Belgian film.

It is no coincidence that *Mira* was released in 1971. It was the hundredth anniversary of the birth of Stijn Streuvels. To celebrate it, a number of cultural events had been organised and it was decided a film would be produced, based on one of his novels. One of the people behind the idea was the then head of BRT, the Dutch-language Belgian television, Paul Vandenbussche. He appeared to have contacted Streuvels, and apparently, Streuvels himself asked Vandenbussche to put the matter into the hands of Hugo Claus. This was not to the liking of the dominant Catholic lobby in Flanders, since Claus was perceived as a fairly avant-garde author, known for his anti-clerical profile. Streuvels' choice of Claus was not illogical. He was an artistic polymath whose work by that point encompassed novels, poems, plays, painting and even filmmaking. In 1968 he made a low-budget feature called *De vijanden* (*The Enemies*). It was a story set against the 'Battle of the Bulge', the World War Two battle in the Ardennes, and which featured Rademakers in one of the lead roles. The film also included the American actor Del Negro, and future *enfant terrible* Robbe De Hert, the founder of the film collective, Fugitive Cinema, and in 1980 director of the famous *Whitey* remake. One year later, in 1969, Rademakers had a part in *Friday*, a play by Hugo Claus, which proved to be an immense success, especially in the Netherlands. As Rademakers remembered: 'It wasn't at all what I had expected. Sometimes the Dutch can react very negatively against that "Flemish stuff", but not this time.' 'I like the primitive aspect in Hugo's work', Rademakers expressed in more than one interview, 'I prefer it to a more sophisticated kind of writing.' Apparently Rademakers was not alone in this.

So, with the blessing of Streuvels, Claus finally chose *De teleurgang van de waterhoek* (*The Decline of the Waterhoek*), a novel from 1927. His Dutch friend Fons Rademakers would direct the film: 'He was by far the most appropriate man for the job because, as you know, he is half a Fleming.' In the novel, Streuvels described events that took place over twenty years earlier. In 1905, a bridge was built over the river Scheldt, near Avelgem, the town where the author worked as a baker at the time. From the marshes of the Scheldt, Streuvels was able to observe the construction. The novel is an account of what happened at the time. It portrays the opposition of the local community to the bridge, the murder of a surveyor and his servant, the love affair of the head engineer with a local girl, and finally the inauguration of the bridge on 9 September 1906. Literary historians have identified a number of characters in the book as people who lived near Avelgem at that time. The character of Mira, for instance, is based on Marie-Virginie Vermeeren, who models for the female protagonist. The engineer's name is Maurice Mostaert. In real life, the two got married (only to divorce soon afterwards). In a later stage of his life, around 1924, Streuvels appeared to renew his acquaintance with the girl. According to Streuvels' biographer, Hedwig Speliers, he fell in love with the woman, 'with the girl that was twenty and danced with him in Avelgem'. And for a period of three years they kept in close contact. During these years, he wrote *The Decline of the Waterhoek*.

Why would a writer like Claus, who was associated with the literary avant-garde, concern himself with this kind of literature, which is often linked to 'heimat' (folk) culture and with a conservative attitude towards life, particularly in the heavily politicised atmosphere of the 1970s? In a television interview at the time, Claus offered his reasons: 'There is something very modern in this book. It shows how modern technology gets a grip on the countryside, where you could lead an idyllic, heathen life. These things happen increasingly around us. This grip becomes more and more oppressive, day by day. That's why I chose this book, because it's recognisable. It's full of situations we go through every day.'

The basic theme of both novel and film is the conflict between tradition and modernity. The bridge will, so to speak, connect the Middle Ages with modern life. It will also bring foreign influence into a community which had until then been cut off from the twentieth century. The Waterhoek was a very closed and primitive society, governed by its own rules. Men preferred to marry women from their own surroundings. There was even an element of incest linked to the community. In the first part of the film, Uncle Lander comes home. He is a good looking young man (played by Jan Decleir, a who has since become the very face of Flemish (and Dutch) cinema). His father is a ferryman, the gatekeeper of the community, and an authoritarian. Lander falls in love with his niece, Mira. She is the opposite of his father, representing freedom of spirit, modernity and desiring a break with old traditions. Mira (played by another newcomer, Willeke van Ammelrooy), ignores the rules the community imposes on her. Though attracted to her, Lander's desire to free himself from the shackles of the values held dear by his father's generation is mixed with trepidation. He does oppose his father's authority by having a love affair with young girl, but on the other hand he is also drawn into his father's political struggle against the building of the bridge. He joins the conservative side and kills a surveyor and his servant. Soon after the murder, Lander is caught by the police and sentenced to life imprisonment. His exit takes place at the middlepoint of the film and the vacancy left by his departure is filled by Maurice, the urban, shy, inexperienced engineer, and clearly the character Streuvels most identified with. Maurice becomes Mira's new love. However, Maurice believes he will gain control over Mira by marrying her. But for her, marriage is a convention of the past. The day after the marriage feast, Mira is gone. She gives up the past for the future. This uncompromising ending strengthened the film considerably, as it works so strongly against audience expectations. At one moment during the production, Rademakers and Claus considered bringing Lander back into the story at some point, perhaps to soften the blow of the ending. But fortunately they decided to stay with the original, bleak end.

However relevant the central theme of the conflict between old and new may have been at the time *Mira* was released, ensuring it appealed to modern audiences was hardly an easy job for Claus: 'The book was a kind of antique drama situated in Flanders of the time. There is no dramatic potential. You have a lot of filmic descriptions, there is information about the characters, but there are no scenes, there is no drive. The power comes basically from the language which, even now, if you take away all the particularisms, is still very powerful. So I had to write a story that lasts one hour and a half, in dialogues, but there were no dialogues. I had to invent everything.'

In his adaptation, Mira becomes the central character. In the novel, the reader is closer to Maurice, Streuvels' alter ego, because he shares his thoughts with us. Claus remains true to the idea, the spirit and even to the structure of the book. Streuvels would most likely have been pleased with the film, but did not live long enough to see it. He died on 15 August 1969, and his funeral was attended by thousands of people. In the spring of 1970, Claus wrote the final draft of his script. In the meantime, Elly Claus and Fons Rademakers supervised the casting. Rademakers had discovered his leading actress some time earlier, at the Studio theatre in Amsterdam; Van Ammelrooy had a part in *Le Jardin des délices*, by Fernando Arrabal. For the part of Lander, Rademakers chose young actor Jan Decleir: 'When I met Jan Decleir, I asked him to walk towards me; as simple as that. For the first time I saw an actor in the Netherlands and Belgium who could be a cowboy, like an American actor. He could walk through the scenery ... Maybe, I thought, he will be able to play a gentleman, but he most certainly can be a cowboy.' Carlos van Lanckere played Dean Broeke, Landers' father; Roger Bolders his son-in-law, Sieper; and French-speaking Luc Ponette was cast as the unfortunate engineer. Among the smaller roles were Charles Janssens, famous from the popular comedies of Edith Kiel and Jef Bruyninckx, and Romain De Coninck, the surveyor who will be killed, and who came from the same background as Janssens. Rademakers himself had to stand in as a notary. The actor who was originally meant to play the part dropped out in the last minute, apparently because he did not feel comfortable about having to perform a scene in his underwear.

At the beginning of August 1970 shooting started in Berlare. Lili Rademakers, joined by Peter Simons, assisted the director. In the 1980s she went on to make two fascinating films herself: *Menuet* (1982), based on Louis-Paul Boon's novel, and *Dagboek van een oude dwaas* (*Diary of a Mad Old Man*, 1987). Hugo Claus wrote the screenplay for both. The scenes on the main street were filmed in Nevele. Powerlines and television antennas were dismantled, and a recently asphalted road was covered with sand. The scenes on the Kluisberg were filmed in the Sonian Forest. The final scene, which included 350 extras, was shot at the old bridge in Hamme. In September, the interiors were filmed at the Cinetone studios in Amsterdam.

On 2 March 1971, *Mira* received its premiere at the Palais des Beaux Arts in Brussels. The event was presented as the *vernissage* to the international intercultural exhibition Europalia, devoted to the Netherlands. It was also the twenty-fifth anniversary of the Belgian-Dutch cultural agreement and, as previously mentioned, the hundredth anniversary of Stijn Streuvels.

The critical response was mixed, with all reviewers agreeing on only one aspect of the film: its look. As the film's director of photography, Edouard Van der Enden, commented: 'My first impression when I arrived at the place of shooting, was the greenness. It was a lovely summer that year. For us cameramen, green was the most difficult colour in those days. We didn't like the idea of having everything in green. But in the end, it was great. To create a contrast with the bright colours outside, we used a lot of sepia filters for the indoor shooting which turned everything into ochre.'

There was also an enthusiastic response to the young leads (Van Ammelrooy and Decleir). According to the euphoric critic of *Le Soir*, Hugues Vehenne, Van Ammelrooy's screen appearance generated a sense of drunkenness in the audience. He compared her presence to 'hot bread' and 'wild menthos'. In Wallonia and in the Netherlands the reception was more positive than in Flanders, partly because Flemish critics found difficulty with the kind of language that is spoken, described as artificial and lifeless. The debate concerning the kind of Dutch dialect or standard language that characters ought to speak in a Flemish film still haunts domestic cinema even today. In Wallonia and Holland, language was less of an issue. Georges Delerue's score was also dismissed by some critics. As was the lack of, according to certain reviewers, narrative structure. According to others, the film had a poetic directness, precisely because there was little logic to it.

The audience, however, loved *Mira*. With its 642,400 tickets sold, the film still features in the Flemish all-time box-office top ten (at the time of writing it holds its ground in sixth place). As a result of its success, numerous films were made in an attempt to profit from it. Van Raemdonck and Verhavert combined forces to further develop the genre of the rural film. They made *De Loteling* (*The Conscript*, 1973) then *Pallieter* (1975). 'They often say I made too many rural films', says Van Raemdonck, 'I agree, but was Brueghel a farmer? The western *Stagecoach* is also about cowboys, farmers. Is that a rural film? It's not my problem, you see? To me, quality is all that matters. It doesn't matter if it's about the countryside or the city, as long as the film is good. Some people in Flanders wanted modern contemporary films, like the ones you have in America. But then you have to compete, and you can't compete, if you have 50 million [Belgian francs] and they have 2 billion. You don't stand a chance.'

Van Ammelrooy connected *Mira* with fundamental aspects of the hippie culture of the time. Rademakers and Claus were fifty and forty at the time and the make-love-not-war generation and the hippie-culture was something they could not care less about. It was the playground for spoilt youngsters, not for them. Theirs was a different generation: they grew up in the ruins of World War Two and built their art from there, turning *Mira* into a fairly classical, even somewhat timeless, literary adaptation. There was even some social criticism (against poverty and working-class exploitation, and also against a society dominated by a French-speaking elite). But above all, it featured Willeke van Ammelrooy. When Rademakers signed up Van Ammelrooy, she was just back in the country after a three months stay in Morocco, where she had been living in communes. One was populated with theatre addicts, and in the other sex was the binding element. From that angle it seems quite obvious that Mira was the symbol, or rather the embodiment, of free love, void of all sense of guilt.

Van Ammelrooy, and particularly the portrayal of her body, appears to be the enduring memory of the film for many. Very often they have forgotten all the rest. Not because Van Ammelrooy is naked throughout – nudity was hardly new in Flemish films – but in the case of *Mira*, the nudity appeared in a culturally respectable film, a Flemish classic. The amount of nudity in *Mira* is limited, but it addressed an attitude that 'I do with my body what I want, and not what my father or the Church tell me to do'. And by choosing this image, the filmmakers explicitly referred to a younger generation, to the 1970s hippie culture. 'I came back from Morocco as a hippie' says Van Ammelrooy, 'with long skirts and wild hair. When Rademakers came to visit me a few months later, he saw me standing at the top of the stairs, wearing my long dress. He looked at me and said "You read the script?"' By putting a hippie at the centre of his adaptation, Rademakers gave the film a particular relevance for the early 1970s. And it is no minor accomplishment that in dealing with two distinct periods (1900 and 1970) the film, and particularly its two central characters, retain a remarkable freshness even today.

Erik Martens

* All the interviews to which this article refers were made during the production of my documentary *The Mira Archives*. This documentary is part of the DVD project 'History of Flemish Cinema' which is set up by the Royal Belgian Filmarchive to release eleven digitally restored Flemish classics from the period 1955–90.

LES LÈVRES ROUGES DAUGHTERS OF DARKNESS

HARRY KÜMEL, BELGIUM, 1971

Of all the Belgian films of the early 1970s, a boom period in Belgian cinema culture, *Les lèvres rouges* (*Daughters of Darkness*, 1971) is probably the most talked about, yet least known. Although it still stands as one of most commercially successful and academically referenced Belgian films, it is hardly screened today, and even its DVD and video distribution has been hampered by a series of difficulties, ranging from legal to aesthetic objections. This dual status is perhaps the most typical characteristic of the film, being both a high-profile example of Belgian cinema at its most international, and a consciously ignored part of a nation's film heritage. This chapter will highlight the making of the film as an attempt to combine aesthetic and exploitation elements in one film. It will discuss its most important aesthetic features and place the film within its national cultural context, including an analysis of the career of director Harry Kümel and an overview of its reception. In so doing, it will show how much *Daughters of Darkness* is, by chance or design, if not one of the oddest then certainly one of the most (dis)reputable films in Belgian film history.

Belgian film culture of the early 1970s can best be described as both dynamic and dualist. The introduction, in the mid-1960s, of direct state support for the production of films, and a greater permissiveness within global film culture, helped boost national film production, facilitating a new wave of Belgian film. Within this new wave, a distinction arose between commercial/exploitation cinema and auteurist/culturally relevant cinema. The latter, modelled on *nouvelle vague* and modernist European cinema quickly became the norm (or according to some, the requirement) for state-supported productions, whereas the former used genre cinema and B-films as sources of inspiration, making no secrets of their commercial goals. As a result, most Belgian films produced between 1965 and 1975 fall within one of the categories of this dual framework. But only one side of the spectrum received official attention. Virtually every single film commentator of the time showed a preference for the more 'refined' auteurist/culturally relevant model, consistently dismissing commercial cinema as pulp, exploitation or trash. Hence, Belgian film culture found itself in the curious situation of having a significant output of commercially inspired film, but no discourse to validate it.

Unsurprisingly then, Belgian permissive commercial cinema of the late 1960s and early 1970s was often equaled with trash because of it showed 'a lack of moral concern'. Because of the sheer quantity of such films, it is worth pausing for a moment, to consider some of them. Films addressing explicit sexuality, like Paul Collet & Pierre Drouot's groundbreaking *Cash? Cash!* (1967) and *L'etreinte* (*The Embrace*, 1968) were condemned for their 'excessive brazenness.' Similarly, films like *Psychédélissimo* (*Rhythm of Love*, Christian Mesnil, 1968), *Pandore* (*Pandora*, Guy Nys, 1969), *Princess* (Herman Wuyts, 1969), *Nathalie apres l'amour* (*Nathalie After Love*, Boris Szulzinger, 1969), the short films of Jean-Louis Van Belle (*Le sadigue aux dents rouges/The Red Toothed Artist*, 1970; *Pervertissima*, 1971), *In Love with Death* and *The Naked D* (both Guy Nys, 1970), *Brigade Anti-Sex* (*Anti-Sex Brigade*) and *Et ma soeur ne pense qu'à ça* (*Take Me Or Rape Me*) (both Henri Xhonneux, 1970), *Ontbijt voor twee* (*Breakfast for Two*, Rob Van Eyck, 1972), *Au Service du Diable* (*The Devil's Nightmare*, Jean Brismée, 1972), *Le Nosferat* (*Nosferatus*, Maurice Rabinowicz, 1974) and the animated *Tarzoon, Shame of the Jungle* (Picha & Boris Szulzinger, 1975) were derided by critics. Belgian/foreign co-productions by Jean Rollin and Jess Franco (including Rollin's *Les demoniaques*, 1973; and Franco's *Eyes of the Night*, *Female Vampire*, *Exorcism* and *Shining Sex*) which made up a significant part of the country's film production and which were, as Philip Mosley puts it, 'among the few export successes of Belgian cinema', also received fierce negative reviews. Only when critics could ascribe pseudo-aesthetic motivations to a film would the tone of evaluation change, although still expressing unease with the explicit subject matter. The reputation of Roland Lethem, director of notorious shorts such as *La Fée sanguinaire* (*The Bloodthirsty Fairy*, 1968) and *Le sexe enrage* (*The Crazed Sex*, 1969) as an 'experimental' artist 'exploring provocative, uncompromising approaches' synthesises how critics generally discussed these films.

Only few filmmakers and films with subject matter that included explicit sex and/or violence escaped from this disdain. The naughtiness of *Mira* (Fons Rademakers, 1971) seemed to escape criticism, because of the literary kudos of those who made the film. Two other notable examples are *Les tueurs fous* (*The Lonely Killers*, Boris Szulzinger), and *S/J Fossiléa* (Jean Mulders) which both premiered in 1972, the same year as *Daughters of Darkness* (at least in Belgium). It remains unclear why these two films were much more favourably received than others. In the case of *S/J Fossiléa*, general opinions were probably far less outspoken because the film fell outside every category. Its director, Jean Mulders, was unknown, and its narrative was far too hermetic to be compared to any other commercial film. Yet its explicit references to sex and the fantastic prevented it from coming under the auteurist framework. In fact, the lack of information prevents any categorisation (even the Belgian Royal Film Archive has little or nothing on the film). In the case of *The Lonely Killers* there was enough information to place the film within the commercial/exploitation framework, since the director, Boris Szulzinger, had already directed the soft-sex film *Nathalie After Love*. The violent subject matter of *The Lonely Killers* (two serial killers on the rampage) only supported this categorisation. Yet in this particular case, several critics and commentators decided to praise the 'raw realism' of the film (probably because it was based on real-life events), and refrained from condemning it morally. Though many still disliked the film, it was not as rudely (or ironically) dismissed as films such as *Overdrive* (David McNeil, 1970).

The above comments correctly suggest the crucial importance of film critics and commentators in Belgian cinema. Many, if not most, Belgian films of the time were closely scrutinised by the critical establishment before, during and after production. It led to outrageous reactions from filmmakers, and Harry Kümel's position as a critic of these practices has been well-documented. Throughout his career he objected to this form of complaint-culture, and his oeuvre demonstrates his desire to rise above the dual framework of Belgian cinema. Ironically, the early years of his career seem to suggest an adherence to the auteurist framework. Even when still a teenager, Kümel (born in Antwerp in 1940) joined SCM, the Small Film Club in Mortsel. He started making short films in 1953 and by the end of the 1950s had directed a series of seven shorts. In 1958 he co-founded, with Rik Kuypers, 'Film '58', a collective that set out to renew Belgian cinema. Kümel never attended film school, but from 1959 on he began to write screenplays for other directors (Rik Kuypers and Herman Wuyts), and directed more professional shorts. Of these, *Anna la Bonne* (1959), based on a poem by Jean Cocteau, and *Pandora* (1960), co-directed with Herman Wuyts, are still regarded as some of the most mature and promising shorts in Belgian cinema history. Between 1961 and 1965 Kümel mainly worked for the public broadcast service BRT, directing for the film review show, *Premiere*. Among the reports he directed were portraits of John Huston, Roman Polanski and Vincente Minelli. He also directed a number of short documentaries and a short film, *De grafbewaker* (*The Cemetery Guard*, 1965), based on a play by Kafka. He also wrote for film magazines *Film & Televisie* and *Skoop*.

By the time Kümel made his feature debut in 1968 he was regarded as the *jeune premier* of Belgian/Flemish cinema, undoubtedly the most promising of a generation of film auteurs. Kümel's first feature, *Monsieur Hawarden*, based on novels by Filip De Pillecijn and Henry Pierre Faffin, cemented his reputation. It opens with a dedication to Joseph Von Sternberg, and its black-and-white aestheticism clearly linked it to the *nouvelle vague*. Structurally and stylistically, the film fitted in with the new 'Belgian film style' of magical realism. According to Adolphe Nysenholc, magical realism in Belgian film is typified by 'an interest in the representation of the split between the real and the imaginary, or a dialectic between life and illusion', akin to surrealism. At the time, the style was most famously employed by André Delvaux. Conforming with new practices for artistic films, most of the picture was financed through state-support funding. The story of *Monsieur Hawarden* however was more risqué than most Belgian films, telling the tale of a woman (played by Ellen Vogel) pretending to be a man and trying to escape her murderous past. When released, the film was not a great commercial success, although it received many accolades, including prizes at festivals in Chicago, Edinburgh and Hyeres, making it into Peter Cowie's 'ten best films of the year' as listed in the *International Film Guide*. It was praised not just for its 'Sternbergian atmosphere' and its 'use of chiaroscuro', but was also appreciated, much to Kümel's anger, for its 'Freudian symbolism', its restrained 'ambiguous sexual implications', and its generation of a new sensual sensitivity, inviting comparisons to contemporary horror styles and themes.

These comments already indicated a shift in Kümel's position as an auteur, which was further confirmed by his subsequent productions. His appointment as a lecturer in the Netherlands, and his profile of Joseph Von Sternberg for the BRT, still suggested a strong authorial position, as did a documentary report on censorship that he shot. But his involvement with films like *De blanke Slavin* (*The White Slave*, Rene Daalder, 1969) and the cult film *Princess* showed that his interest in exploitation cinema was becoming as important as his auteurist ambitions. Kümel's next film, *Daughters of Darkness*, deepened the gap between his auteurist reputation and commercial and stylistic opportunism even more.

The troubled reception of *Monsieur Hawarden*, and the fact that it fell between two frameworks of appreciation, inspired Kümel for his subsequent project. It made him look for a way to address both frames simultaneously, thus challenging the norms of Belgian film interpretation. The next project had to be exploitative and artistic at the same time. Looking back on *Daughters of Darkness* in David Soren's book, Kümel identified his intentions: 'I was so angry about *Monsieur Hawarden* being so badly received here and my next project *Malpertuis* [1974] was too expensive so I said "we are going to do something nasty".'

Kümel eventually decided to base his film on the legend of the bloodthirsty vampire-like aristocrat Elizabeth Bathory. He wrote a contemporary version of it, together with French veteran screenwriter Jean Ferry and co-producer Pierre Drouot, asking his co-writers to bear in mind 'that it would be undignified trash'. Drouot's company, Showking Films, became the initial producer. Drouot had set up Showking Films with Paul Collet after the success of their commercial exploitation films *Cash? Cash!* and *The Embrace*. They used it primarily as a basis for co-productions. Although Collet and Drouot had recently benefited from state support for *Louisa, een woord van liefde* (*Louisa, A Word of Love*, 1972), it was decided that the subject matter of *Daughters of Darkness* was on the one hand probably too risqué to receive state funding, and on the other commercially viable enough to be able to find co-producers, especially after French film star Delphine Seyrig (famous for her role in *Last Year in Marienbad*, Alain Resnais, 1961) became involved in the project. According to Kümel, the decision not to apply for state funding was a very conscious one. In an interview with Gilbert Verschooten he claimed, 'of course, I wanted to show these people that I didn't need them'. However, a little later he insisted the film was in no way a 'revenge' on the film commission, but a trashy joke: 'All we knew was that we intended to make a commercial picture, with erotic as well as violent scenes, and that we wanted Delphine Seyrig for the lead role … It was just a question of getting a young and beautiful couple to fuck as much as possible, with a maximum of bloody scenes in between. A real commercial machine! But we thought that wasn't enough, so we also decided to include erotic and chic elements. In that respect we were the predecessors of *Emmanuelle*.'

With Seyrig attached to the project, Showking Films managed to find several other production companies to invest: Cinevog (Belgium), Maya Films (France), Gemini Pictures International (US), Roxy Films (Germany) and Mediterranea (Italy), making it the most international Belgian production at that point. Inevitably, each of these producers wanted to have their say over the material, prompting numerous disputes. Shooting began on location in Ostend and Bruges, in May 1970, although the story was set in winter. Kümel later produced three different language versions (English, French and Dutch), and found himself in conflict over the final cut of the film, resulting in two different versions (one English-language version of 87 minutes, and a French-language version of 96 minutes). At the instigation of one of the co-producers, Maya Films, the initial title, *Le rouge aux lèvres*, was dropped in favor of *Les lèvres rouges*. This title was subsequently translated/transformed into various local versions. The most recurrent title, and chronologically the first to be released to the public, was *Daughters of Darkness*, the US title. Eventually, no less than 14 different titles are used, ranging from the clearly exploitative, like the Italian title *Vestala di Satane* (*Satan's Virgins*), through the more soft-sex oriented *The Promise of Red Lips* (alternative UK title) and literal translations like *Blut an den Lippen* (German title) and *Dorst naar bloed* (Dutch title), to ambiguous titles as

Erzebeth, Blood Love/Blood on her Lips (UK title) and *Children of the Night*. Kümel also became dissatisfied with the pressure under which he had had to work, from both budget restrictions (resulting in several last-minute script changes – for instance the final scene in which Seyrig is impaled) and Seyrig's attitude (according to Kümel, she was 'reluctant', 'self-destructive' and 'difficult'). Finally, Kümel disassociated himself from the film entirely, prior to its premiere, in May 1971.

Daughters of Darkness tells the story of a vampire countess and her female servant, in seducing a newly-wed American couple on their honeymoon in a hotel in Ostend. When Stefan (John Karlen) and Valerie (Danielle Ouimet, Miss Quebec 1966) arrive at the Thermes Hotel their initial plan is to stop only for a night or two, so that Stefan can call his mother and inform her of the fact that he got married (the two were married quickly and secretively). But Stefan soon finds himself strangely attracted to two other guests in the hotel, Countess Elizabeth Bathory (Seyrig), and her servant, Ilona (Andrea Rau). After Stefan becomes excited after seeing a corpse drained of blood, Elizabeth tells him the story of the female vampire, Countess Bathory, slowly luring him into her trap. Valerie, on the other hand, is frightened of Elizabeth and Ilona (who appears naked on her balcony). Stefan tries to comfort Valerie, but while they make love, they are secretly watched by Elizabeth and Ilona. After finally phoning his mother, the relationship between Stefan and Valerie quickly deteriorates. He beats her with a belt, and when she tries to leave she is stopped at the train station by Elizabeth. The Countess then turns her attention to Valerie and tells her of her love for her. Although Valerie is disgusted, she also finds herself strangely drawn to Elizabeth. Meanwhile Ilona, acting upon instructions from Elizabeth, seduces Stefan. But after they struggle in the shower – it is not clear if Stefan tries to force her into making love or is trying to resist her – she falls on a razor blade and dies. When Stefan looks up from Ilona's naked body, he sees Elizabeth and Valerie looking at him.

After the death of Ilona, Elizabeth takes control. She forces Valerie and Stefan to help her bury Ilona and kill a detective who had become suspicious after the first murder reminded him of similar events that took place thirty years earlier. She also sets Valerie against her husband and they end up sleeping together. By the next day, it becomes clear that Valerie is now replacing Ilona. She is ordered by Elizabeth to kiss Stefan and, though repulsed, she obeys. When he resists, both women attack and kill him, and then drink his blood. After burying Stefan, Elizabeth and Valerie drive away from Ostend, anxious about their newfound happiness. But when the morning sun blinds them, they crash the car and Elizabeth is impaled on the branch of a tree. In an epilogue we see a young couple at a seaside resort talk with a strange woman. She tells them how great their friendship will be. It is Valerie, with Elizabeth's voice.

From this summary it is clear that *Daughters of Darkness* lacks a conventional story-line. There is no plausible chain of events, and much of the interaction between the four main characters occurs through suggestion rather than any utterance of their desires for each other. Evidently, both Stefan and Valerie and Elizabeth and Ilona long for lasting love, but the way they express that longing does not relate to traditions of storytelling. Rather, their respective longings form a centre around which several clashes and sudden outbursts between them (Stefan beating Valerie, Ilona falling to her death) as well as subtle games of desire, attraction and repulsion, are played out. Thus, the unevenness in the respective relationships also affects the narrative, transforming it into an uneven, odd tale of want. It has been pointed out by several critics that this unevenness was the result of the concessions Kümel had to make when writing the script. No less than three other writers were involved, with Jean Ferry, Drouot and J. J. Amiel (of American distributor Gemini) all adding their own touch, and with shooting circumstances requiring last-minute rewrites.

But the story still remains very different from similar exploitation horror films, in that it evokes a feeling and atmosphere of longing that is, at the same time, sexual/sensual and philosophical. Probably the most bizarre scene in the film takes place when Stefan finally makes a telephone call to his mother (his wife having urged him to get in touch with her). But his 'mother' turns out to be an elderly, bored and decadent male, suggesting a macabre sort of sadomasochistic and homosexual relationship between the two. Played by Dutch director Fons Rademakers, with visible pleasure, the 'mother' figure only appears in that scene. But via the few times she is referred to it is clear that she determines Stefan's actions, and through him, those of his wife too. This sense of being driven by forces out of their control governs all characters. It gives them their sexual motivation, but it also adds an almost academic expression of issues of power and control that inform the entire narrative. The surreal settings and lighting in the film strengthen the impression of distanced observation. Edouard Van der Enden's photography captures the loneliness of the characters, but at the same time connects them to the desolation of the Thermes Hotel and medieval Bruges, turning the shots themselves into postcards of paintings, inviting not only evident comparisons with René Magritte and Paul Delvaux, but also with James Ensor and Leon Spilliaert, both resident artists in Ostend.

The duality between its exploitation elements and the academic coolness prevented *Daughters of Darkness* from becoming the exploitation hit it was designed to be. Most pre-

premiere publicity materials provided by the producers of the film attempted to emphasise the eroticism and violence, tying it to a trend of similar films, thus inviting a specific reception. But through that emphasis, most artistic pretexts of the film were lost. It is perhaps understandable that there is no reference to Kümel's reputation as an auteur, since the producers probably aimed for a release as exploitation cinema *tout court*. Similarly, there is hardly any emphasis on Delphine Seyrig, who was supposed to be the 'artistic passport'. More remarkably, no mention is made of Kümel's reputation as the *enfant terrible* of Belgian cinema, a reputation that had been widely publicised during the shooting of the film, and to which Kümel himself often referred (especially in his clashes with the film commission). Equally, no mention was made of Kümel's previous film, *Monsieur Hawarden*, not even references to 'the sexual tone' of that film. Nor were there any references to sensational production stories (the fact that Kümel initially wanted '700 to 800 virgins' in the film, or that it featured Miss Quebec, 1966).

Most critical accounts of the time did not consider *Daughters of Darkness* to be a masterpiece. Aside of the *New York Times* review by Howard Thomson, celebrating the film as the best artistic vampire movie ever, and some French reviews which referred to the film's artistic pretensions, most reviewers struggled with its duality: too raunchy to be art, but too chic to be exploitation. However, this did not prevent the film from becoming a commercial success. Within weeks of its release on three screens in New York on 28 May 1971, it became a huge hit, drawing $46,667 in its first ten days (setting a house record at the New Embassy cinema, with $7,680 on a Sunday), ensuring its place in *Variety*'s list of 50 top-grossing films of 9 June. Frédéric Sojcher called the film's box-office results in Paris 'unsurpassed by any other Belgian film up until now'. It was not a huge hit in its home territories, but considering the competition, with major directors like Fons Rademakers (who played 'mother'), Delvaux, and Collet and Drouot releasing films like *Mira*, *Belle* and *Louisa*, it fared averagely well. Unfortunately, its public visibility lasted only weeks and, like other exploitation material, it was quickly forgotten.

It still remains unclear whether *Daughters of Darkness* would have made a bigger impact at the time if all-encompassing slogans like 'It's lesbian time in Transylvania!' or 'A group-sex round, with Miss Seyrig's chum seducing the boy honeymooner while she takes over the bride', would have been balanced by attention to some of the more artistic elements in the film. But in the end, *Daughters of Darkness* did gain a respectable reputation. It became an underground cult hit within a couple of years. Legal battles over ownership made prints scarce; its appearance at university campuses led to the first aesthetic considerations of it (even leading to a book on Kümel by critic David Soren, in 1979). By the beginning of the 1980s, it received small but significant praise on the art-house circuit, being shown in film archives in New York, London and Brussels. In that context, *Daughters of Darkness* finally received the kind of interpretation its narrative called for, with an article by Bonnie Zimmerman in the left-wing academic journal *Jump Cut* discussing its treatment of gender issues in relation to elements of power and control, and labeling it a 'feminist film'. Since then, *Daughters of Darkness* has become a regular at Gay and Lesbian Festivals, and still attracts academic attention.

For Harry Kümel, *Daughters of Darkness*, together with his next feature, *Malpertuis*, on which he had already begun working by the time *Daughters of Darkness* was released in the Low Countries, proved to be the height of his career. In *Malpertuis* he continued to explore power relationships and their connection with issues of gender and sexuality, while building on different source (a well-known book by Jean Ray) and adopting a more baroque style. Even more than *Daughters of Darkness*, *Malpertuis* expressed duality and unevenness in almost every shot of the crooked Malpertuis mansion, perhaps most famously encapsulated in the massive, but immobile, on-screen presence of a bed-ridden Orson Welles in the lead role. Symptomatically, the production circumstances of *Malpertuis* were very similar to those of *Daughters of Darkness*, including the struggle over the final cut and the release of three different versions, and a more troubled reception. Recently, screenings of *Malpertuis* in London and New York seem to suggest a similar re-evaluation to the one that took place with *Daughters of Darkness*, awarding it the admiration it deserves.

Since then, the career of Kümel has been largely confined to the Low Countries. He continues to teach in the Netherlands and work for television in Belgium. His subsequent films, *De Komst van Joachim Stiller* (*The Arrival of Joachim Stiller*, 1976 – originally a television miniseries) and *Het Verloren Paradijs* (*Paradise Lost*, 1978), suffered from bad reviews and the increasing unease of Kümel within his environment (both artistically and financially). The difficulties prevented him from making another film until the mid-1980s when he directed *Secrets of Love* (1986) much in the same tradition as *Daughters of Darkness*. Kümel's last feature, *Eline Vere* (1991), based on the work of Louis Couperus, and fittingly a Dutch/Belgian co-production, again illustrated his difficulties with producers, who often refer to him as 'arrogant and impossible'. Although the film was reasonably well received, Kümel insisted on producing a 160-minute director's cut to show how different the film would have been had he been given complete artistic control. Regardless of the production troubles, *Eline Vere* also demonstrated, in its visual flair and Kümel's ability to evoke tragic and censored sexuality in his characters, his mastery over visual style.

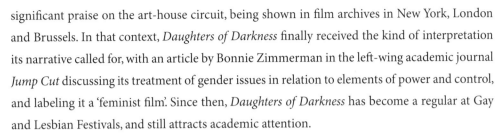

In his many encounters (often clashes) with different aspects of Low Countries film culture, Kümel always remained the outsider. His flamboyance and his insistence on pursuing his own vision made him one of Belgium's most unwanted directors. But at the same time no one disputed Kümel's talent and ability to turn even the most formulaic traditions, like vampire films, into art. Duality and unevenness were always Kümel's trademarks. They expressed what lay at the heart of his oeuvre, and point to the potential that every film has to become, at the same time, more and less than it aspires.

Ernest Mathijs

TURKS FRUIT TURKISH DELIGHT

PAUL VERHOEVEN, THE NETHERLANDS, 1973

Paul Verhoeven's *Turks Fruit* (*Turkish Delight*, 1973) is a film that deserves credit as one of the most intriguing and compelling studies of desire and decay produced during the 1970s. *Turkish Delight* is, at the same time, extreme and typical. Its typicality lies in how well it fits in with trends in 1970s cinema. For lovers of celluloid sin and followers of filmed forbidden flesh, the 1970s was *the* undisputed period of 'porn-chic', and *Turkish Delight*'s success can certainly be attributed to the fact that people went to see such movies. Its extremeness lies in how the film deals with sexuality, the human body in its context and, strangely, the film's place in the perhaps lesser-known – by comparison with certain other European countries, at least – Dutch film culture.

During the 1970s, erotic experimentation challenged both prevalent sexual values as well as affecting the boundaries of artistic expression. It saw the emergence of a new wave of explicit American hard-core narratives, which managed to make the journey from the grind-house to the mainstream movie theatre and into the hearts and loins of middle-class audiences via their 'feel good' message about copulation. In a far darker vein, the 1970s also saw many European art-house auteurs beginning to dabble with semi-explicit imagery as part of a wider political agenda. *Turkish Delight* is perhaps the most exemplary of these. It stands at the forefront of a wave of films not just from the Low Countries but from a far wider context.

The emphasis in these films was not on sexual liberation, but on the ways in which exaggerated displays of desire epitomised the destructive workings of male/female relations as well as the psychic, social and historical conditions that have predetermined these drives. With their focus on the links between desire, death and decay, films like *Turkish Delight* offered rich explanations of what made their dysfunctional and oversexed protagonists 'tick'. In contradiction to the feel-good policy of American porn, these European productions were far more nihilistic in their recodification of scenarios of sexual pleasure into extended scenes of alienation, suffering and death. For instance, Liliana Cavani's notorious 1974 film *The Night Porter* used the backdrop of fascism to explore the sado-masochistic practices between a former SS guard and his psychologically-damaged lover. A similar conflation of explicit sexual politics and power was raised in Pier Paolo Pasolini's *Salo* (1975), which adapted the Marquis de Sade's writings on sexual liberation to question Italy's most shameful historical past. Bernardo Bertolucci delivered a powerful film about desire and mourning that helped to redefine Marlon Brando's 'dangerous' persona beyond the Hollywood machine with *Last Tango in Paris* (1972).

The fact that many of the European porn avant-garde directors of the 1970s were Italian is more than just coincidence. Although post-war Italian filmmakers have long held a reputation for transgressing the limits of taste and decency, their dominance in an era when larger quarters of Europe were seen as leading the way in representing sexual liberation raises important questions about wider issues of cinema, dominance and national identity. It also leads to questions concerning the international visibility of other countries' films addressing explicit sexuality. Specifically, the idea that only certain areas of European film production 'sexed up the 1970s' has relevance for those nations traditionally classified as the Low Countries. As Matthew Ross has argued, cinema in countries such as the Netherlands have frequently suffered from a position of double exclusion, whereby domestic audiences shun home-grown productions in favour of foreign (primarily American) imports, while these very same productions also enjoy very little foreign exposure. Remarkably, this is even true for porn-chic productions, which failed to make an international impact, even though they were hugely successful (and relevant) within their own borders. This is made more explicit in the case of 'big name' Dutch directors such as Paul Verhoeven, whose reputations are often only latterly secured via their work on big-budget Hollywood productions such as *Basic Instinct* (1992) and *Starship Troopers* (1998), rather than their early, home-grown productions.

Much of this problem is theoretical. As Ross notes, 'European cinema' as a concept tends to be unfairly focused on relatively well-funded, high-profile players such as Britain, France and Germany, who set the standard by which filmmaking culture in this domain is judged. As a result, the films produced in other European countries are frequently seen as an addendum to these major nations, while a lack of appropriate state funding and a resultant need for cross-cultural collaboration all add to the perception that these regions and countries lack their own legitimate, national cinema. Quoting the work of Ginette Vincendeau, Ross notes that beyond the dominance of countries such as Britain, France and the Soviet Union: 'The rest of Europe tends to be considered in regions – Central Europe, Northern Europe – while "minor" countries remain in isolation if not oblivion: Belgium, Holland, Greece, Portugal, Austria, Switzerland.'

Turkish Delight is a perfect example of this problem. Although it explores a number of themes similar to the morbid tales of lust depicted in films such as *Last Tango in Paris*, its reception has been far more uneven, particularly outside of its native Holland. For instance, John Coleman's review of *Turkish Delight* summed up the views of many foreign commentators, who saw it as a cynical attempt to establish an international focus for Dutch smut. As Coleman unsympathetically stated: 'Paul Verhoeven's *Turkish Delight*, painfully extracted from a Netherlands best-seller by one Jan Wolkers, is so clearly there to put Clogland on the international map that I hearby award it a merited Dutch cap.' Coleman's statement is both strange and revealing. As a phenomenon, *Turkish Delight* remains one of the director's most powerful early films, and one which casts clear allusions to the cynical and nihilistic examination of love and desire found in later Hollywood epics such as *Basic Instinct* and *Showgirls* (1995). While *Turkish Delight* was also one of Holland's most celebrated movies the film's largely positive domestic reviews have not been evenly matched outside of its European context. For Ross and others, this can be linked to the so-called invisibility of the Low Countries, which has meant that the film has belatedly been re-appraised outside of its native context.

It is this position of perceived cultural invisibility and European contexts that sets the background to an analysis of Verhoeven's *Turkish Delight*. Its content needs to be understood not just against the context of Dutch film culture, but internationally as well. A comparison with *Last Tango in Paris* will show why and how.

Adapted from the novel by Jan Wolkers, *Turkish Delight* explores the tempestuous relations between the young bohemian artist Erik Vonk (Rutger Hauer) and his psychologically immature lover Olga (Monique van de Ven). Its taboo-breaking images of copulation as well as its underlying tone of youthful rebellion managed to capture the mood of sexual anarchy that was spreading across parts of Europe during the 1970s. Writing in Verhoeven's biography Rob van Scheers has concluded that the film remains the most successful Dutch film of all time, attracting an audience of 3,334,044 as well as providing 'an accurate portrayal of Amsterdam during the 1970s that was presented via a complex art-house structure'.

While Verhoeven has himself commented on the film's presentation of desire and loss through a complex series of multi-layered flashbacks that remain essentially anti-Hollywood in their construction, it was not so much the film style as its content that perturbed many contemporary American reviewers; in particular, its constant equation of sexual desire with extreme states of physiological decay and disgust. While writers such as Coleman argued that a 'sense of tumour' was needed to enjoy the film's grisly delights, another commentator connected the film's commercial success to 'the assault audiences will put up with for the sake of a little titillation.' It is also worth noting terms like 'repellent' and 'garbage' used by other reviewers who commented upon, 'Verhoeven's view of man as unloving and unloved. He sets out to paint a repellent picture; and succeeds perfectly', and 'The quickest way of out of this week's dilemma – how to say something gleamingly witty and useful about the garbage before us – is probably marked EXIT'.

What these reviewers found disturbing was Erik's insistence on using extremes of sexual activity to break down the conservative and superficial moral barriers that surround him. From his disgust at the conservative dignitaries who censor his explicit work before a royal visit, to his derision of the sexual repression encountered in the family unit, Erik's libido embodies a nihilistic rage rather than a mere quest for physical gratification. It is the protagonist's intention to shock and deprave that brings him into direct conflict with Olga's overbearing mother, who repeatedly attempts to thwart the couple's union, having rejecting the young artist's actions as irresponsible. Although the narrative does begin by detailing the protagonist's cavalier attitude to life, his prolonged relationship with Olga reveals a more sensitive side. This is confirmed in the latter part of the movie when Erik nurses Olga through a traumatic bout of brain cancer, from which she eventually dies.

With its emphasis on a relationship cut short by illness, as well as its theme of a love constrained by class and cultural differences, *Turkish Delight* has been unfavourably compared with *Love Story* (1970) by some foreign critics. For instance, one American reviewer defined Verhoeven's film as 'the other face of *Love Story*', before outlining what he saw as the film's unsavoury qualities: 'Whereas *Love Story* was romantic and aseptic and bland, here the story is told in terms of the most unsparing realism. Sickness is hideous and foul to the nose; sex is clumsy and graceless (but fun); people have bowels and bladders which never stop plaguing them and everyone else'. As this quotation indicates, it is not so much the film's depiction of sexuality that provokes unease, as its constant equation of these acts with disgust and decay.

In the words of Rob Van Scheers, *Turkish Delight* is a narrative in which 'death constantly shows itself in apocalyptic visions and images of decay'. The film's macabre view of sexuality is indicated by its opening fantasy scene, when Erik imagines bludgeoning Olga's new middle-class boyfriend to death with one of his art objects before shooting his former lover with a pistol. Although this scene is later revealed as dream sequence, it establishes a connection between sexuality and death that permeates relations between the couple.

Indeed, the extended flashback scenes that follow (detailing the couple's history as well as the social pressures that provoked their separation) are constantly littered with references to decay and the impending doom that befalls the couple. For instance, the film reveals how the pair met after Erik has been ejected from an archaeological dig because of his unruly behaviour. After hitchhiking at the side of the road, he is picked up by Olga, whom he instantly tries to seduce while she is driving. However, this brief bout of copulation is violently interrupted when Erik finds his penis caught in the zipper of his flared jeans and the pair are forced to seek the help of strangers. When Erik later tries to show his affection to his new-found partner by offering her a coat he has stolen, Olga becomes distracted and loses control of the car they are travelling in, seriously injuring them both.

This violent encounter (which is intimated as one possible cause of the heroine's future brain cancer) is only one example of how the film endlessly defers the couple's erotic thrills via the trait of impending death and suffering. This effect is confirmed later in the film when Erik attempts to court the recovering Olga, much against the wishes of her mother. As a result, the pair meet in secret at a fairground before Erik attempts intercourse with her at his studio workshop. However, the protagonist's sexual desires are thwarted when the heroine falls asleep on his bed amid the elaborate array of candles that Erik has arranged as part of his seduction. As a result, Olga's naked body (which Verhoeven depicts in an overhead shot via a series of mirror reflections) appears corpse-like, part of some bizarre funeral display.

This uncanny effect is returned to later in the film, after Erik has received a commission to create a monument for a new hospital wing. Using Olga as a muse for his inspiration the pair break from their artistic endeavours to share an intimate moment together. Here, Erik decorates his lover's body with an arrangement of flowers he has stolen from a local garden. Olga's inanimate pose in the scene once again give the appearance of death, arranged in a semi-erotic display. The overtones of decay in the scene are confirmed when Erik removes the flowers from her body, Olga's breasts and stomach are covered with maggots and insects. Similar overtones of decay and disease are also present in a scene where Erik forces a red rose between Olga's buttocks, before spanking her rear in an act of unmotivated foreplay. The force of the character's hand against the flower gives the appearance of Olga's backside being covered in blood, once again reiterating the connection between sexuality and disease.

As the above examples indicate, *Turkish Delight* is a film that equates sexual desire with death and imminent decay, or else defers sexual gratification via the spectre of loss and mourning. In this respect, Verhoeven's film bears some similarity to the more celebrated European vision of the porno-macabre, *Last Tango in Paris*. As the *Los Angeles Times* commented upon the American release of Verhoeven's film, this comparison can be justified on the basis that both films present 'an all-out assault on our bourgeois sensibilities'.

Whereas *Turkish Delight* focuses on the bourgeois forces that disrupt Erik's relationship with Olga, Bertolucci's film details the coupling between a young woman, Jeanne (Maria Schneider), and two men. Her boyfriend, Tom (Jean-Pierre Leaud), is an idealistic filmmaker who dreams of marrying her. However, their relationship is complicated by Jeanne's sexual involvement with the significantly older Paul (Marlon Brando). It is revealed that Paul, the owner of a seedy hotel in Paris enters into the relationship with Jeanne in order to resolve his guilt over his involvement in his wife's recent suicide.

The construction of these two male love objects sets up a number of important polarities within the narrative. While Tom's activities as a documentary filmmaker make him an intrusive character, his visual activities also link him to the concept of life: his obsession with filming Jeanne gives her instant celluloid immortality. By contrast, her relationship with Brando is marked by an overwhelming sense of regression, death and decay. Most obviously this link is established by virtue of the couple's relationship evolving from the suicide of Paul's wife. Beyond this, Brando's connection with death and decay is confirmed by his ownership of a dank, crumbling Parisian hotel.

From Bertolucci's acknowledged interest in the links between eroticism and the unconscious, the polarisation of life and death between these two male suitors translates into a distinction between mature (post-Oedipal) sexuality and unresolved infantile desire. This libidinal reading of Paul and Jeanne's relationship is confirmed by the lack of speech that accompanies their sexual activity. According to psychoanalysts such as Jacques Lacan and Julia Kristeva, the child's entry into language occurs upon resolution of the infant's initial desires and attractions. The lack of language in the couple's relationship is established by Paul's insistence that they do not disclose their names or any information about their former identities. This policy of retarding the role of speech stands in sharp contrast to Jeanne's relationship with Tom, which is dialogue-led. This is demonstrated by his obsession with adding a running voice-over to her actions as he films Jeanne's every move.

Beyond their respective relationships with life and death, the other important distinction between Jeanne's two male love objects is provided by their differing relationship to issues of the self and bodily hygiene. Reflecting his obsessions with genitalia and the sex act, Brando's character wallows in a fascination with the body and its waste matter. This preoccupation initially takes the form of memory, when Paul narrates how his big high school date was ruined because his clothes were covered in cow's excrement from working on his father's farm. Later in the film Paul's obsession with filth and waste matter becomes defined through his violent and excessive exploration of Jeanne's body in a series of acts which replicate the infant's fascination with the body and its associated products such as excrement, urine and saliva.

While Bertolucci's dalliance with bodily matter earned *Last Tango in Paris* notoriety, its visceral elements pale against *Turkish Delight*. Here, the camera explores every aspect of the body's bi-products from semen, saliva and blood to excrement, vomit, snot and urine. For many, the physiological focus of the narrative can be seen as reflecting the supposed 'earthiness' of Jan Wolker's source material. Yet this unsavoury imagery also adds to the fascination of the flesh, death and decay at the heart of the movie. Indeed, for psychoanalysts such as Kristeva, our duel fascination and revulsion with waste matter and the abject can be traced to the unresolved pleasures of the body and the flesh that preoccupied us during our infancy. Although in adulthood the so-called 'pleasures of play' that relate to the body and its waste products evoke a sense of guilt and disgust, they also signal an unresolved regression to an infantile world without shame or morality.

It is exactly this same universe that is evoked in both Wolker's source material and Verhoeven's film rendition of *Turkish Delight*. Here, Erik and Olga's actions are rendered abject via the narrative's constant equation of the sex act with bodily fluids and waste matter. As one critic has noted, abjection so dominates Wolker's novel that 'because of its stench, his work should be sold in a fishmongers'. In Verhoeven's adaptation, the viewer is treated with a visual onslaught of abject matter, which firmly connects copulation with body matter and the disgust it provokes. In particular, the film repeatedly equates intercourse with excrement in a manner that highlights a theme of near-infantile regression. For instance, the opening scene of the movie shows Erik asleep in his filth-ridden workshop following the breakdown of his relationship with Olga. As he awakes, his first action is to masturbate before a photograph of his former lover. His repeated comments of 'You shit on me, I'm coming now' present the first instance of the film's connection between copulation and anality.

This strategy is later reinforced by the infamous scene in which the couple's lovemaking is interrupted after Olga finds blood in her excrement. In response to his partner's unease Erik examines the waste matter with both hands before determining the substance to be the remains of beetroot she had previously consumed. The link between excrement, sexuality and decay implicit in the heroine's fears are later confirmed when the pair have to abandon their lovemaking after receiving information that Olga's father is dying of stomach cancer. The patriarch's death scene underscores the film's balance of tragedy and humour. Here, the group of family members gathered to say their final goodbyes to the dying elder have to restrain themselves from retching at the smell of his uncontrollable bowel movements. (This feeling of nausea is arguably shared by the viewer thanks to Verhoeven's inclusion of a shot of the patient's excrement seeping through the bottom of his stained mattress.) Once again, this disturbing scene carries connections to the sexual as Erik tries to console the grieving Olga with an enforced act of anal intercourse before her mother intervenes.

The unsettling focus on excrement in *Turkish Delight* represents just one possible category of abjection that Kristeva has identified as a threat to our adult sexual identity. Under the general label of 'waste matter', this bodily product can be seen as provoking unease in its viewer, not because of any intrinsically disgusting qualities, but because it references an archaic period of our infancy that adult, civilised society seeks to repress. Its existence in Verhoeven's film is supplemented by several other categories of depiction that can classified as abject.

For instance, Kristeva, in *The Powers of Horror*, has identified the concept of food loathing as central to the feeling of unease that certain substances evoke in us. In particular, food that is decaying or lacks a specific form is liable to provoke disgust because it connotes the primary drive towards excessive orality that defined the pleasures of infant's world. It is a similar state of excess and loathing that haunts Verhoeven's film, which from its opening images of Erik shovelling decaying food stocks down the lavatory makes clear a series of unsavoury connections between oral consumption, waste matter and the regression from adult behaviour.

Rather than being a source of nourishment, the menus on offer in the film provoke not only physiological unease, but also frequent bouts of nausea. This strategy is initiated in an early scene, when Erik discovers a sheep's eye staring at him from his dinner plate at an archaeological dig. It continues in a later segment when the overly spicy food fed to Erik by Olga's family leads to him vomiting over the assembled middle-class diners. If these examples indicate that food loathing in the film links extreme states of orality to regression and decay, then this particular variant of the abject reaches its natural conclusions with the final scenes of Olga's decline. Lying in a hospital bed, she imagines that her illness has caused her teeth to weaken and as a result she displays trauma at being unable to consume the Turkish Delight sweets that Erik has brought to her. Once these fears have been dispelled, she devours them in an infantile manner, leaving her partner to clean her afterwards, in a scene that indicates the film's drive towards regression is complete.

While these final images can be seen as further evidence of the abject at work, the film also draws a parity with psychoanalytic accounts through its depiction of maternal agents as smothering and overbearing figures. The figure of the mother retains an ambivalent status within adult, civilised society, because of her close associations with the primary period of the child's development. These close connections with the child's universe of filth and waste matter mean that the mother is often viewed as abject by association and as a result is often viewed with a sense of horror and dread in adult life. Frequently, abject associations of motherhood are seen when these figures appear as threatening and disgusting rather than nourishing characters, who threaten the autonomy of those under their charge.

From the outset, Verhoeven's film reproduces the notion of the abject mother in a number of guises. For instance, in one early brief scene, Erik is accosted by an ageing and overweight matronly figure who tries to force her sexual attentions on him with the statement 'Give mama a kiss.' If this unsavoury come-on establishes a connection between motherhood and the abject it is also confirmed by one of *Turkish Delight*'s most controversial scenes. Here, Erik and Olga attend a mass civic wedding service to consummate their relationship only to find the ceremony disrupted when a heavily pregnant wife-to-be goes into labour. With the film's characteristic focus on the body and its waste products, Verhoeven's camera dwells on a shot of the woman's water's breaking and flooding the chair on which she is seated, before a pet dog appears to lap up the fluids her body has produced.

Arguably, the film's most visible depiction of monstrous motherhood belongs to Olga's mother, who represents a literal threat to the couple's security. However, as the narrative reveals, her body is also cast as a source of disgust. In one scene, Erik finds one of the character's padded bras in the family home and parades himself in the garment before Olga, in a display that mocks what he sees as femininity. It is only then that the heroine reveals that her mother had to have her breast removed after childbirth. This leads to Olga to confide in Erik that as a child she was made to feel responsible for this illness after having been told that she may have bitten too hard on her mother's nipples when being breast fed. This revelation indicates yet another example of the film's recodification of the mother's status from a figure of comfort to a source of threat and disgust. These constructions fit well with a narrative, directed as they are towards the translation of desire into abjection and decay.

As the brief comparison with *Last Tango in Paris* shows, the themes present in *Turkish Delight* are not untypical for European cinema. They are certainly not abnormal for Low Countries cinema. An emphasis on European cinema ignoring the Low Countries has so far prevented any appraisal of these themes in critical writing. Only after Paul Verhoeven's move into the arena of American film production, and after he finally achieved an international level of popularity and visibility unmatched by any other figure from the Dutch film industry, have critics started to note them. As the director has even confessed, this level of exposure remains impossible within the limits of cultural invisibility imposed on his native Netherlands: 'In most countries people know my name now. I never achieved that just with my Dutch work, that's just the way it goes. Even English-language spoken Dutch films never manage to cross the border. European countries don't buy each other's films and they don't want to see each other's films.'

With his acquisition of an international status, Verhoeven's American successes have also prompted a frenzied interest in his earlier, non-English-language works. *Turkish Delight* is central to this early body of work, and remains a controversial and challenging examination of lust in the Low Countries. As argued above, it is also time to re-evaluate the position of this film in a cultural context. Much remains to be said about how *Turkish Delight* reflects Low Countries culture, but that it does, both as a celebration of sexuality and an attack on bourgeois sensibilities, is beyond doubt.

Xavier Mendik

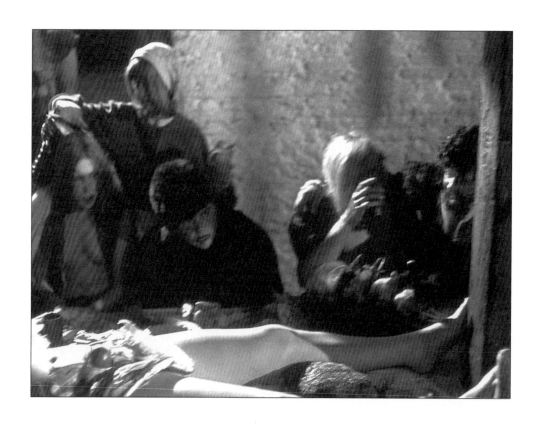

MARIKEN VAN NIEUMEGHEN MARIKEN

JOS STELLING, THE NETHERLANDS, 1974

The impact of a film marks its cultural importance. After the release of *Mariken van Nieumeghen* (*Mariken*, Jos Stelling, 1974) *Elsevier* magazine wrote: 'this is a Dutch film not trying gaspingly to follow fashionably foreign trends. A film that (despite its technical imperfection) feels so bog-ore Dutch, that one amazingly wonders what other native filmmakers have been doing up until now.' This suggests that the film marks a turning point in Dutch cinema and this chapter focuses on the cultural impact of the film by looking at its production, reception and the director responsible for it.

Mariken is based on a sixteenth-century Dutch miracle play. Miracle plays are religious plays in which a miracle happens by intervention of Maria or another saint. Here, a young girl, Mariken, is seduced by the devil, embodied as a human called Moenen. She is his mistress for seven years, but she repents on seeing a 'wagon' play in which the devil's henchman is defeated by Christ in the battle for man's soul. The film focuses on the relationship between Mariken and Moenen. The plot starts when the plague has erupted in Antwerp. People believe it is caused by the devil, who is disguised as a strolling player with a patch over his eye. As a result, the town's people organise a witch hunt for Moenen and Mariken. The latter escapes town, hidden under a shroud. Lying among the corpses of the plague victims, she reconstructs her dreadful fate.

Her story starts when her uncle sends her to the market at Nieumeghen, where she is to stay at her aunts. On the way Mariken sees a group of strolling actors rehearsing a miracle play in the woods. At Nieumeghen's busy marketplace she meets them again. A one-eyed young actor, playing the devil, catches her eye. When arriving at her aunt's house, she finds her aunt has hung herself. Mariken flees the house and wanders in fear until she meets the one-eyed actor again. He offers his help. They clamber over the town walls and together they set off in his wagon for Den Bosch and Antwerp.

Wherever this Moenen goes, upheavals break out and people start killing each other, yet he remains a bystander. When the whore Berthe warns Mariken of him, it is too late. Moenen has secured Mariken's devotion and as a result is no longer interested in her. From then on, he disappears for days at a time. The drama reaches a climax when four men rape Mariken, and then kill their leader in fear when Moenen suddenly returns. They carry the dead man to a swamp and dump him. Rats swarm out to devour the body, the plague breaks out and Moenen vanishes as mysteriously as he came. Consequently the villagers are trying to find Mariken and Moenen, and in the meanwhile they convict Berthe of being a witch and an associate of Moenen. While Berthe is being burned at the stake, Mariken escapes from the burial pit and rushes off to freedom. In the woods the players are still rehearsing their miracle play. The devil is among them uttering his lines. Mariken's will to live has saved her. The players move on to another town. The wheel has come to full circle, and the game will start again.

Jos Stelling was only 25 when he began an ambitious plan to turn this miracle play into a film. He was born and raised in Utrecht. An autodidact, he learned his skills by making six feature films on 8mm and 16mm, *Tim Linch* (1965), *Een Stenen druppel* (*A Drop of Stone*, 1966), *Zij, mij en ik* (*She, Me and I*, 1966), *Recital* (1967), *Mijn Barbaar* (*My Barbarian*, 1967) and *Essay* (1968). In 1969 he was commissioned by his hometown to make a documentary about its history up to the Reformation.

Stelling was more oriented towards the visual arts, such as drawing and photography. The Catholic boarding school he attended, run by French Jezuit priests, also had a great influence on him, especially as one of his teachers loved the cinema. He organised screenings on Sundays and taught his pupils the principles of cinematography and editing by instructing them to tell a story using slides. As fellow students told different stories based on the same set of slides, Stelling found himself drawn to the various narrative possibilities of the images. After his school years he had several jobs before he began making films. Although he already developed ideas for a feature film about *Mariken* in 1966, it was the documentary about Utrecht that made it possible to hire an office, gather a crew and begin planning the film. By 1970, 300 people were already involved in the production and a plan to complete the film by March 1974 was agreed.

Although the author of *Mariken* is unknown, it is the best-known miracle play of the sixteenth century. Crucial to the plot is the repentance of Mariken. After she sees the play 'Masscheroen' in which the devil is defeated, she realises what she has done. Moenen tries to kill her, but fails. Mariken travels to the Pope in Rome and is forgiven after carrying out penance in a convent for seven years.

Stelling argued that the repentance, from a dramatic point of view, was useless for film. As he stated in an interview, what interested him in the original play was the simple opposition of good and evil, or life and death. Therefore the relationship between Mariken and Moenen interested him for what it has to say about learning to come to terms with life and death. He did this with disregard for the religiosity and emotions of the medieval period. Instead, the film showed the miracle play from a humanist perspective. Its theme is universal: a virgin becomes a woman. Yet Stelling wanted it to be situated in the Middle Ages for its alienation from contemporary society. This was motivated by the idea that people still have a need for mysticism, like medieval people, for which there is no place within contemporary society. Two of his other films, *Elckerlyc* (1975) and *De Vliegende Hollander* (*The Flying Dutchman*, 1995) are also set in the Middle Ages. The first one was based on a medieval morality play and filmed during the post-production of *Mariken*. To earn a living, Stelling gave lectures at schools about the Middle Ages. *The Flying Dutchman* was an original story, inspired by the famous legend.

Although research had been carried out and academics were consulted in the early stages of preparation, Stelling argued that it was simple to visualise the Middle Ages. The period had no fashion, for medieval people clothes or materials just had to be effective. As Stelling recalls in an interview with Anton Haakman, the film's motto was: 'If it's dirty and brown it looks authentic.' The film aimed at authenticity. The sets were built on location, mostly in the small city of Buren, in the province of Gelderland, and the market scenes in Nieumeghen were shot at the 'Buurkerk' in Utrecht. The sets were built out of wood. Costumes were not washed. Stelling even preferred his actors not to wash for weeks, to have them as filthy as possible on the set. Prostitutes were hired for the sex scenes.

Shooting *Mariken* proved difficult. Without any roots within the Dutch film scene, Stelling was isolated. He rejected Dutch films that were imitating Hollywood, for instance gangster films situated in Amsterdam. He wanted to create something typically Dutch and was convinced that a historical film offered that peculiarity. From the beginning, his plans were not taken seriously. Financing such a film as an unknown, self-educated director was difficult. Stelling demonstrated his organising skills and perseverance by his unique – self-developed – financing system of participations (shares) and 'points'. Between 1970 and 1973 gatherings were organised, selling participations of at least 100 guilders. During those encounters, the project was outlined and, whenever possible, illustrated by rushes from a recent shoot. The money was used to pay for film material and equipment. During the production no salaries were paid. All crew members earned points per hour. Eventually, participants and investors would get 40 per cent of the profits. In total 100,000 guilders was invested by 152 participants, many of whom were crew members. Leaflets informed them about the progress, always urging to find more participants. As such, the shooting of *Mariken*, which only cost 146,000 Guilders, was a test case for the production of low-budget feature films. The production cost of an average

Dutch film at the time was about two million guilders. It was a special case, not only in terms of its budget, but also with regards to the Dutch film industry's possible independence from state funding.

Cast and crew consisted of amateurs. As most of them had daytime jobs, the film was mostly shot over weekends, from April 1972 until the end of 1973. Stelling hated the term amateur, because it usually indicated a lack of professionalism of the filmmaking process. He argued that cast and crew were all committed, working towards fulfilling their mutual dream. All he did was organise it. As a director, he preferred working with amateur actors because they were spontaneous and enthusiastic. *Mariken* shows his inate talent for casting. Ronnie Montaigne, who had studied pedagogy, played Mariken. The one-eyed Moenen was played by Sander Bais, a young physicist. After shooting this film they both went to the United States to complete their doctorate degrees at Stanford University, California, and never acted again. Montaigne's performance in particular was convincing. About 800 extras were used, many of them inhabitants from Utrecht and Buren. They represented a collection of oddities: toothless, deformed, crippled or otherwise out of the ordinary in some way. In adverts for auditions, all sorts of supporting actors were asked to attend, 'especially people who are not beautiful, but old, young, fat, thin, long and short'.

A detailed design and careful use of camera are the most important elements in Stelling's films. He considered himself to be a camera director, partly due to the fact that he worked with non-professional actors. He was not interested in actors or characters, but in situations that created drama. This was achieved by a subjective camera, occupying a space in-between the characters. The actor became unimportant; it was the situation that mattered. The camera in *Mariken* was often hand-held, literally taking the point of view of a character. When the position of the camera changed in the next shot, it meant a change of perspective occured. For instance, when Mariken and Moenen see each other for the first time at the marketplace in Nieumeghen, Moenen is on stage and notices her in the audience. Mariken looks at him. By changing the perspective from one character to the other, the camera shows the tension between them. In another situation, when Mariken and Moenen enter the inn, the subjective camera continually changes perspective. By reflecting the vivid and chaotic atmosphere of the inn, it is suggested by the camera that the audience is amongst the characters. Obviously a subjective camera is extremely voyeuristic. The explicit sex scenes underlined this. The first time Mariken and Moenen make love at the inn, people gather to observe. To startle and punish the voyeurs, or perhaps the film audience, Moenen sticks a knife through one of the holes and gouges someone's eye. However, the others keep watching. As the lovemaking becomes more intense, the observers themselves tear at each other's clothes, descending into an orgy that is only interupted when Mariken removes Moenen's eye-patch, yells in fear and a peeping Tom at the window falls back in shock, landing on a spear. The next shot shows people taking his body away the next morning.

The limited use of light in this film, due to a lack of resources, also accentuated Stelling's attention to setting. The contrast of light and dark was carefully designed and made what remained invisible as exciting as what was visible. Focusing on the situation instead of the story is a style that can be described as the art of omission. Because the psychological motivations of characters are not relevant, it is harder to identify with characters. This expressive, thematic rather than narrative, film depends on the engagement of the audience, the willingness to associate with the pictures and arrange and connect them thematically. It is probably one of the reasons why Stelling's work has always been received with ambivalence and interpretations of his films differ so much.

The two years of shooting resulted in seven hours of useful material. But in the editing process Stelling became frustrated with his lack of progress and needed an experienced producer to finish the film. Rob du Mee, producer of successful films such as *De Inbreker* (*The Burglar*, 1972) and *Naakt over de Schutting* (*Naked Across the Fence*, 1973) by Frans Weisz and *The Family* (1974) by Lodewijk de Boer, was impressed by the material, and consequently took care of all post-production and the release of the film. The Production Fund agreed to subsidise the post-production, which eventually pushed the cost of the film to 400,000 guilders. Jan Bosdriesz, who had worked on *Turks Fruit* (*Turkish Delight*, Paul Verhoeven, 1973) and *The Family*, and who was considered one of the best editors at the time, took charge of editing. Because he wanted the audience to be curious about the events that led Mariken to her faith, he edited the film within a flashback structure. Bosdriesz thus arranged the mosaic that Stelling wanted. Because the film was shot without sound, author Mies Bouwhuis wrote a dialogue. Her texts deal with the religious intentions of the miracle play, particularly in the lines recited by the rehearsing actors that Mariken meets: 'Ah my child, when I look at humans I would beg it to pass. That there is nothing. That every time again it could be repeated like it was at the beginning.' Then followed by God's lines: 'they will die of disease, grief and death. All that one man can do to the other will be their part once more.' In the dubbing process a Flemish accent was spoken, to create an authentic, or perhaps more Catholic, sound. The score was by a young composer, Ruud Bos. His music, with fierce drums and horns often resembles a dead march. For the festive scenes, traditional pieces, played on flute and guitar, were used.

In December 1974 the major distributor Tuschinski released *Mariken* on seven prints. The film and its director impressed and attracted much attention from the press. Moreover, it was a commercial success, selling over 300,000 tickets, finally accruing a domestic box-office total of 25.7 million tickets by the end of 1974. Although the film's style received praise, critics were less enamoured with its narrative structure. Some reviews stated that 'The events are hardly interesting', and 'Stelling is not capable of telling drama ... his filming is reckless'. The most severe criticism was written by Herman Pleij, who argued that Stelling's depiction of the Middle Ages was over-simplified. The characters were too passionate for food, drink and sex, and at the same time too devoted. Stelling was seen to have abused the original play by ignoring its spiritual and political context, for it is the complexity of events and themes of this play that contradicts the simple view of the Middle Ages. Generally, the film was praised for the colourful, unromanticised images of medieval life. A number of critics compared the imagery of *Mariken* to the films of Pier Paolo Pasolini or to Ingmar Bergman's *Seventh Seal* (1956), while the excess was seen by some as influenced by Federico Fellini and the use of light and colours and the composition to the paintings of Brueghel and Bosch.

In March 1975 *Mariken* became the first Dutch film to be selected for competition at the Cannes Film Festival. Other films in competition attracted more attention, such as Martin Scorsese's *Alice Doesn't Live Here Anymore*, Bob Fosse's *Lenny*, Werner Herzog's *Jeder für sich und Gott gegen alle* (*The Enigma of Kaspar Hauser*), which was awarded three prizes, and Palme d'Or-winner *Chronique des années de braise* (*Chronicle of the Years of Fire*) by Algerian Mohammed Lakhdar-Hamina. For the Dutch film industry it was important to have a film in competition, in order to be internationally recognised. Although initially eager to go to Cannes, Stelling experienced the festival as a media circus that did not appeal to him, and the reception of the film was ambivalent. Most French newspapers disliked it, arguing that it was old fashioned (*Le Monde*), too bloody and cruel (*France Soir*) and a very sad film (*Le Figaro*). One Dutch newspaper reported that the film recieved damning reviews, whereas others reported a mildly positive reception. The press conference was dominated by Ronnie Montaigne, considered by some to be a new Brigitte Bardot. She was flown from the United States with Sander Bais, by invitation of the Dutch Ministry of Culture. Belgian critic Marc Turfkruyer, who was furious about the depiction of the Middle Ages, started the debate at the festival: 'our ancestors also did other things than eat, drink and have sex', he argued. The director and cast replied that they had not deliberately looked for the violence, but had found it in their research of the Middle Ages.

Although the film was not a festival hit, it did become an international success. It was shown at other festivals and was sold to many countries. Responses to the film depended on each country's cultural backgrounds. In Spain, there were difficulties with censorship because of its explicit sex scenes. In Italy the film was renamed *Mariken from Hell* and was compared to Faust. The function of the film's reference to Flemish painting was analysed, arguing that it was not just a pictorial reference, but 'also its implicit reference to social and cultural relations, to violence and aggressiveness: all properties of that style of painting, with results that are perhaps too realistic, violent and expressed'. At the festival in San Francisco one critic considered it existentialist, another was wondering what the film was about and did not understand why feminists did not protest against it.

Although it was Du Mee who saved the project and some claim that it was Bosdriesz's editing that made it a feature film, *Mariken* established Stelling's position as an independent filmmaker. Except for this debut and *The Illusionist* (1983), his films have not been successful in the Netherlands. Yet internationally he remains one of the most popular Dutch film directors, especially in Italy, Germany and Eastern Europe. A possible reason for that, according to Stelling, is that film is a Catholic medium; it is about symbols, adoration for pictures and illusion. The Dutch however, are contemplators and readers; the iconoclasm of 1568 has destroyed the adoration for visual culture.

In twenty-five years Stelling has made eight very different feature films. As critic Ab Van Ieperen noted, 'However indefinite in time and space, they are all very Dutch in their visual design, between jocular and refined, made with passion that withdraws from the current Dutch Calvinism.' This visual style and Stelling's views on the medium are already evident in *Mariken*. With a few other directors, Alex van Warmerdam among them, he has been considered a representative of a Dutch School; referring to films of the 1980s with an identifiable 'Dutch' style: an acting style inspired by *commedia dell arte* rather than nineteenth-century naturalistic theatre, and themes dealing with boys who will not grow up, who have ambiguous sexual identities and whose lives are disrupted by the arrival of a strange woman. Stelling always builds his dramatic conflict around polarities, confronting characters with themselves. In *Mariken*, it is life and death as good and evil. In his forthcoming production, *Duska*, a man called Duska from Eastern Europe visits a man in Western Europe. In this film the East is synonymous with the day-dreamer, present and spiritual, the West with the workaholic, future-minded and materialistic.

The spiritual Duska proves elusive for the materialist Western character Bob. Stelling imagines this film as a poetic anthem to nihilism. The stories in his films are usually structured in cycles such as birth, life and death or spring, summer, autumn and winter. The scenes are arranged similar to arias in opera.

Stelling's first four films were produced in a similar fashion to *Mariken*. His fourth film, *The Pretenders* (1981), displayed a hitherto unseen maturity. For the first time it had no historical setting, instead taking place in a cafeteria in Utrecht, over the weekend of 5–6 August 1962, when Marilyn Monroe took her life. It is a very personal and intimate film; a miniaturist masterpiece. Since *The Illusionist*, Stelling has worked with professional crews and reasonable budgets. That film was based on a show by comedian Freek de Jonge, with whom Stelling wrote the script and who is the main character in the film. The imaginative power of the fantasy world of two brothers is created without any dialogues and filmed in a baroque or even surrealist style. The film shows the technical and visual development of Stelling's style. *De Wisselwachter* (*The Pointsman*, 1986) is arguably Stelling's best film, featuring the perfect synthesis of theme and style.

The international success of his films has enabled him to co-produce films and work with actors like Nino Manfredi and Oscar-winning composer Nicola Piovani. Despite this success and the awards he has received for his films over the years, Stelling remains something of an oddity in the Netherlands. Often working with the same crew, Stelling is a visionary, always demanding absolute control, and by turns persuasive and pernicious. For him, making films is a passion rather than a profession. Film is creating a dream, with each participant bringing a special skill to the production. One of his skills is in organising a team which he has used to great effect as a gallery owner. He opened his café and Springhaver cinema in 1978 and will open a centre for visual culture, the Louis Hartlooper Complex in 2004. He was also founder of the Dutch Film Days in 1981 (originally 'De Nederlandse Filmdagen', but renamed in 1994 as 'Nederlands Filmfestival'). The festival is a meeting place for filmmakers, yearly awarding the best productions with Golden Calves.

There are various reasons for the impact of *Mariken*. In short, it is the remarkable debut of a self-educated director, made over a period of seven years, with amateurs as cast and crew, a stunning depiction of the Middle Ages and uniquely financed. Jos Stelling changed Dutch film culture not only by his production method, but also as a film auteur and as founder of the Dutch Film Days.

Bas Agterberg

JEANNE DIELMAN 23 QUAI DU COMMERCE 1080 BRUXELLES
JEANNE DIELMAN

CHANTAL AKERMAN, BELGIUM, 1975

When *Jeanne Dielman 23 Quai du commerce 1080 Bruxelles* (*Jeanne Dielman*, Chantal Akerman) played in the directors' fortnight at Cannes in 1975, it was not only the longest Belgian film ever to have solicited international attention, it was also the first selected by Cannes to have been made by a Belgian woman. Whilst Belgian women filmmakers had existed before Akerman, their work had either been lost (Aimee Navarra), largely unseen (Claude Misonne) or the source of critical approbation (Edith Kiel). Later in her career, Akerman's 'Belgian-ness' would be elided as her work was measured alongside European art cinema, feminist or independent models. However for this first moment, the Belgian origin of the film was held up alongside its length and Akerman's gender as markers of its uniqueness. James Monaco's film encyclopedia notes that 'This 200-minute, minimally plotted film scrutinised three days in the life of a woman … who adheres to a regimented schedule of cleaning, cooking and caring for her teenage son. Every day she also takes in one male caller to make ends meet. On the third day her schedule is interrupted, and she later experiences an orgasm with her male caller. Her response to these unfathomable alterations in her routine is to thrust a pair of scissors into the man's throat.' John Coleman stated that 'the film's time-span covers a Tuesday (stew and potatoes), Wednesday (wiener schnitzel) and heady Thursday (meat loaf and Jeanne has an orgasm and kills her client with a pair of scissors). This orgasm bit is bound to strike the serious-minded as an unfortunate blow to crass commercialism.'

As the reviews above suggest, *Jeanne Dielman* takes place over three days of the heroine's life, beginning late afternoon on Tuesday and ending at a similar time on Thursday. The film's length of 3 hours and 20 minutes is often exaggerated, as is the use of 'real time' throughout. Obviously as the time span of roughly three days has to be fitted into 200 minutes, there are only a few actions (largely preparation of food) filmed in real time. However, the acute impact of these actions when viewed can be judged by the fact that, as Coleman's review shows, they become central to most reviews. This reversal of attention, where housework and cooking are emphasised over the killing of the man, proves the success of Akerman's sustained project to shift the hierarchies of importance that suggest that, say, a kiss would be shown over someone cleaning their shoes.

The film is structured in order to emphasise the daily routines and the repetitiveness of Jeanne's existence. Her days largely consist of getting her 15-year-old son, Sylvain, to school, preparing their evening meal and sometimes shopping, receiving male callers in the afternoon, then serving Sylvain his meal and spending time with him (reading or going for a brief walk), before going to bed. This day emerges only gradually, as we begin and end the film in the afternoons of days one and three, and day two, which should have been the most complete day, is also when the first disturbance of her routine occurs. Jeanne's routine emerges, then, only in retrospect. As a result it is difficult to get an overview of the film and this would perhaps explain critics' fetishisation of the details.

Alongside this extraordinary content, Ackerman presented a restrained style, although the modest international success of the film, as well as her subsequent films, placed Akerman alongside André Delvaux as one of Belgium's bankable auteurs. Ironically, *Jeanne Dielman* can be said to offer a direct challenge to the conception of the skilled authorial voice and to bourgeois norms of consumption, through its stubborn assertion of itself as a deliberately flawed product. This is established thanks to a cinematically primitive style that deletes the usual range of devices through which a film can be said to interpret the surface of the world and inflect it with levels of significance. There are no point of view shots to promote identification with character, no close-ups or zooms to highlight a significant piece of narrative information or to shift the narration into a register of heightened emotional intensity, no camera angles or camera movements to comment on the characters or the situation, and a fixity of camera throughout.

Akerman's style was frequently compared to that of Michelangelo Antonioni – in its restraint and in the way she holds her shots beyond the exit of all human content – and to Robert Bresson in the use she made of her actors. With *Jeanne Dielman*, though, Akerman's explanation of this style has centred on the respect she wished to indicate for her subject: 'It was the only way to shoot that film – to avoid cutting the woman into a hundred pieces, to avoid cutting the action into a hundred pieces, to look carefully and to be respectful.' A specific dynamic is indicated between subject and director which, when compared to Antonioni and Bresson, renders their respective styles dry and emotionless in the face of Akerman's passionate detachment from her characters. The effect of Akerman's style is to offer a different way of representing character as robbed of the means to inflect meaning; *Jeanne Dielman* forces us to experience through an immersion in the accumulation of details. Significance is present, but not 'pointed out'.

It is possible to read *Jeanne Dielman* purely from an independent or feminist position, and we shall consider this below. However, before doing so it is worth exploring the lesser-known Belgian connections which, along with the film's title, situate it formally and aesthetically within a Belgian context.

Accounts of Akerman's early days as an ingénue filmmaker tend to paint her as some kind of ciné-innocent, largely unaware of the filmmaking world and wanting to be a writer. However, the trajectory that led to *Jeanne Dielman* contains connections to Belgian film culture that she would never lose. Legend has it that her first short film, *Saute ma ville* (*Blow Up My Town*, 1968), was shown on Flemish television and reviewed by André Delvaux who helped her apply for subsidies for her next project (though this was ultimately turned down by the Ministry). Early colleagues here include Boris Lehman and Eric De Kuyper with whom she was to co-write the script for her Proust adaptation *La Captive* (*The Captive*, 2001). Influences at this time were Jean-Luc Godard (with *Pierrot le fou*, 1966) and, on crossing the Atlantic to New York, filmmakers such as Michael Snow. No Belgian directors are mentioned and Akerman does not seem to have seen herself as part of any Belgian movement . Akerman was never emotionally attached to Belgium, leaving the country for Paris and New York and embracing the cult for women filmmakers and auteur discourses, both of which placed her in international rather than national contexts.

One of the most concrete connections to Belgian cinema, which has often been overlooked, is the presence of the Grandfather of Belgian cinema, Henri Storck, in the opening scene of *Jeanne Dielman*. The film begins with a shot of Jeanne's hallway as she answers the door. She lets in a man, takes off his coat then they go into her bedroom. The 'real time' legend of the film is broken here as there is a moment of ellipsis, then the couple exit the room, she hands him his coat and hat and turns to the front door. He gives her some money then squeezes her hand and says 'à la semaine prochaine/see you next week' and smiles. Within the narrative of *Jeanne Dielman* this is a rare and fleeting moment of connection between Jeanne and another human being, though it is perhaps indicative of its difference to the rest of the film that it is largely overlooked (or even forgotten, overshadowed by the extended duration of the rest of the film). We might also read Storck's gesture of benevolence here extra-textually as an encouragement for the rookie Akerman from, at that time, Belgium's most experienced and long-serving director. Storck's gentle squeeze of hand effectively passes the baton from one generation to the next.

As well as the location within a Belgian scene – though she may not agree with this herself – there is a real sense in which Akerman's work can be situated thematically within several Belgian traditions. First, she echoes many of Storck's concerns: the attention to the day-to-day details of people's lives that we find in his series *Symphonie Paysanne* (*Peasant Symphony*, 1944) as well as in the structure of films such as *Images d'Ostend* (*Images of Ostend*, 1929), *Trois Vies et une Corde* (*Three Lives and a Rope*, 1933) and *Idylle à la plage* (*Romance at the Beach*, 1931). Also, *Toute une nuit* (*All Night Long*, 1982) and even *Nuit et jour* (*Night and Day*, 1991) seem to follow André Delvaux' depiction of the 'magical realism' of city spaces, largely captured at night and owing much to the painter Paul Delvaux.

Perhaps the place where we might most productively read across from Belgian cinema to Akerman's work is in her softening of the boundary between documentary and fiction. In her early work, Akerman mixed the two registers. In *Hotel Monterey* (1972) she created the rhythm and tension associated with narrative through the way in which she frames and edits a non-fiction space. Later, observing New York City from a distance in *News from Home* (1977) she accompanied these images with a soundtrack of her reading letters her mother had sent her while she was staying in the city. Though the image track is unmarked in terms of person, and therefore assumes an observational tone, the soundtrack allows us to create Akerman as a character, the daughter reading (to herself and, in the film, aloud) the mother's letters. Follow-ing these early moments where, significantly, it is possible to discern Belgian characteristics, Akerman moves firmly away from Brussels, physically, formally and aesthetically. *Les Rendez-vous d'Anna* (*The Meetings of Anna*, 1978), the film that followed *Jeanne Dielman*, was Aker-man's first European co-production and though she would return to Belgium for her smaller-scale 'home movie' *All Night Long* and film *The Eighties* (1983), she has most recently lived and worked in Paris, where she has enjoyed better access to finance and production facilities.

For Marsha Kinder, '*Jeanne Dielman* [is] the most important film to première at this year's Filmex and the best feature that I have ever seen made by women'. A testament to the fact that the film is most frequently interpreted along feminist lines. 'Feminist' is, however, a label Akerman herself has resisted, for instance by stating that 'I'm not making women's films, I'm making Chantal Akerman's films'. The article from which Marsha Kinder's words are drawn was just one of several which placed *Jeanne Dielman* at the centre of debates around such terms as 'women and cinema', 'women's cinema' and 'feminist film practice'.

Jeanne Dielman's importance goes beyond its contextual connections however, and it will be used here for its particular polemical power. The film manages to combine two dominant yet opposing schools of film feminism. First, through its content it adheres to many essentialist tenets, such as the promotion of a 'women-only' space in the cinema. In its earliest application, 'women's cinema' should be read as 'cinema from the women's movement'. Such a classification refers us to the fact that these films were made by those 'moved', as Jan Rosenberg notes, 'by social and political not aesthetic impulses'. Wanting to create a space for women to emerge from their imposed position of invisibility, silence and absence, these women seized the visibility and the voice that the medium of film allowed.

Secondly, through its form, *Jeanne Dielman* engages directly with a more theoretically committed impulse, which is interested in the articulation of the female; as a result it becomes a test-case for the conflicts inherent in the notions of, firstly, a 'feminist film practice' (opposing the above collectivity and women's cinema with independence and auteur cinema) and, secondly, feminist film theory, where documentary, *cinéma vérité* and 'truth' are rejected in favour of narrative and 'demystification'. Let us examine these two tendencies further.

In using an all-women crew, *Jeanne Dielman* answers demands for a cinema made 'by' a collective of women. Although the film addresses narrative and not documentary forms, and although Akerman is ultimately still 'in charge' of *Jeanne Dielman*, the chosen subject (a housewife) and the methods of production mean that the sense of the film as 'female' necessarily widens. Through its focus on housework, the film also shares some of the 'authenticating' or essentialising aspects of the women's movement films. Despite these few coincidences between the women's cinema inspired by the women's movement and that practiced by Chantal Akerman, as we can see from the Kinder and Akerman juxtaposition, the relationship between Akerman and the women's movement is not so clear-cut. She has said: 'I'm not interested in working collectively in the sense that word is usually used. In collaboration, yes. At the time of *Jeanne Dielman* … there were many things against women in films, so I wanted to show that you could make a movie with only women.'

Generally, 'women's cinema' is created as, among other things, an opposition to 'auteur cinema' and the fact that such an opposition suggests that women's cinema should not be an auteur cinema may provide one reason why Akerman rejects women's cinema; to consider the rift between Akerman and the women's movement further we can turn to Jayne Loader's article in the journal *Jump Cut*, which expresses some of the complexity of the reception of the film. She writes that 'the sections of *Jeanne Dielman* which examine in minute detail the function and practice of housework and the role of the traditional mother within the repressive structure of the nuclear family are among the finest examples of feminist cinema yet'. The representation of women's work, and the portrayal of the female condition are therefore praised. However, Loader continues: 'I only wish Akerman had been content with this magnificent and unique achievement rather than succumbing to the demands of the traditional narrative film form that requires a bang-up ending and the culture that requires a neatly packaged and thoroughly acceptable message. In this case: killing is good for you.' If in its content *Jeanne Dielman* appealed to those advocating a female, feminine 'women's cinema', in its form it alienated them; by contrast it was precisely its form which appealed to feminist film theory, to which we now briefly turn.

Perhaps the full impact of *Jeanne Dielman* can be felt through the juxtaposition of the following lines of reasoning expressed by two notable feminist critics: B. Ruby Rich states that 'according to Laura Mulvey, the woman is not visible in the audience which is perceived as male; according to Johnston, the woman is not visible on the screen … how does one formulate an understanding of a structure that insists on our absence even in the face of our presence?' She also claims that '[*Jeanne Dielman*] invents a new language capable of transmitting truths previously unspoken'. Teresa de Lauretis argues that '[*Jeanne Dielman*] defines all points of identification … as female, feminine or feminist'. If, in social, ideological, philosophical or psychoanalytic terms woman is figured only as a negative or absent other, then the quotes by de Lauretis ('female, feminine and feminist') or Rich's talk of 'a new language' imply that *Jeanne Dielman* enunciates the formerly silenced. *Jeanne Dielman* seemed to fulfill the desires of many as it countered, de-constructed, intervened, made present and visible, and not surprisingly it formed the focus of this early phase of feminist film theory. The difference of the film was noted by all then, from John Coleman's cynical review which treats the film as one extended cookery programme, through Jayne Loader's commendation of its rigorous depiction of a woman's routine, to B. Ruby Rich and others' recognition that it offered a corrective to the spectacular narratives so derided by feminist critics.

Clearly *Jeanne Dielman* affected and was effective. For many of the critics above part of the difference of *Jeanne Dielman* comes from the character of Jeanne herself. She is not 'attractive' in the conventional sense, being neither an erotic or seductive object, yet she is still central to both narrative and image and therefore attracts our attention. A closeness to her is implied through the film's taking place in her space and evolves, more or less, according to her sense of time. Furthermore the precarious structure of the film revolves around her since it is only through careful attention to her rituals and to the pattern that is revealed by them that the film's meaning emerges. In the absence of the meaning that we would usually find in the linear pattern of narrative, in character interaction or framing and camera movement, we are forced to turn to Jeanne and to see through her seductive blankness to a world in which, attaching her to her time and her space, a plenitude of meaning emerges.

We are immersed in Jeanne's world through a formal system, which seems intended to mimic the control she exhibits over her time and space, as well as her fear of change. This system, outlined below, is masterfully executed to the extent that, though the film uses no conventional modes of identification – such as eyeline or point-of-view shots, close-ups and camera angles – identification with Jeanne is implied and invited through a growing familiarity with Jeanne's routine.

Jeanne Dielman's structure hinges around repetition and ritual. While some elements of classical narrative do exist (there is a sense of cause and effect and ultimately a climax) the thrust of the film is not linear. In fact the system of repetition is such that rather than offering the progression of linear narrative, *Jeanne Dielman* is constructed to ensure no change. Jeanne's movements and the framing in each of the three sequences in which she shows in her clients can illustrate this system of stasis or 'reduction'. Jeanne's actions are as follows: the bell rings, Jeanne undoes her housecoat, walks from the kitchen to the hall, pulls her cardigan around her chest, walks through the hallway turning on the light, opens the door, stands facing the client and takes his hat/coat/scarf, pulls her cardigan once again, and walks to the bedroom followed by the client. Meanwhile the camera action and framing can be described as: Jeanne is framed in the kitchen area, the bell rings, as she walks forward to turn off the light so the spectator is presented with a beheaded body, the kitchen is held in darkness, we hear Jeanne's shoes walking outside, a door opening, then 'Bonjour'; a door shuts. We cut to the hallway. Jeanne is framed from the side in medium-close-up from neck to hips, the camera is static as she moves out of frame to hang up a coat, then re-enters the frame, to walk down the corridor to her bedroom.

This sequence, which is repeated for each of the three clients, reveals repetition and ritual as the main structures of the film. Yet it also portrays a 'reductive' pattern, hinged around a 'folded' action. Both the pattern and the action produce the stasis previously mentioned. The most important and apparent folding shots are those framing the sexual act. It should be evident that the movement from the front door to the bedroom, then from the bedroom to the front door offer mirror images. Thus, when the bedroom door is opened the actions of both Jeanne and the camera are repeated, but in reverse. The effect is such that the shot is almost divided, with the sexual act as a line in between, which vanishes into nothingness. A similar pattern is present in Jeanne and Sylvain's nocturnal walk around the block, filmed in a series of three shots, the first and third being exactly the same, only in reverse. Also, as Jeanne moves through space and moves things, she returns them almost immediately to their place. Finally, the end of the day mirrors the beginning. What emerges is a pattern of 'reduction'. Once the action is completed we return to where we started. This sense of stasis is in keeping with Jeanne's desire for fixity through ritual and repetition, as well as being a necessary condition in her construction and maintenance of her own time and space.

Having painstakingly constructed the strict rules and rituals of Jeanne's life and emphasised the need for control and stasis, Akerman involves us further in Jeanne's plight by using this sense of routine and our growing familiarity with it to underline its breakdown to such an extent that we almost become complicit in it. From the reductive system of its opening day *Jeanne Dielman* shifts to a system, which demands an act of recognition and remembrance from the spectator. Now familiar with how things 'should' be, the spectator is encouraged to notice the, at first subtle, differences. It is again through this attention to Jeanne's actions and those of the camera that meaning is made. Thus, on the second day, after the client's visit Jeanne moves not to the kitchen but back to the bedroom, prolonging our attention on this act. The next sequence showing her stripping the bed and bathing, which contains ellipses, emphasises a slippage in Jeanne's time plan caught perhaps by something unexpected during the sexual act. When we finally do return to the kitchen, the potatoes are burnt (the first obvious break in Jeanne's routine), and both her reactions and those of the camera combine to reinforce this break. First of all, Jeanne's entrance into the kitchen is framed from a new angle (the only time that such an angle is used), which reveals the formerly concealed fourth wall of the space – the position previously occupied by the camera. Second, the ritual of turning off the lights is broken, the potatoes are burnt and consequently Jeanne's automatic performance is shattered, as she wanders distractedly from room to room.

Through the course of the second and third days, the breakdown escalates, with Jeanne's loss of control indicated by a fragmentation of her sense of her own time and space. Previously, she moved with ease through her space. Yet, as the film proceeds, so Jeanne's occupancy of the flat is fragmented, and her sense of time is disrupted. On the first day her action consisted of economical and precise movements. With the second day, they become less precise. By the third day, she actually pauses and seems lost in her space. Her rooms seem to have moved from 'containers' suggesting ordered and functional zones, to 'vacuums' in which she is no longer sure of her place, relation or meaning.

The confidence and efficiency of Jeanne's actions on day one and her completion of everything started, suggests her control of the temporal axis of her days. The disintegration is initiated on the second day with an ellipsis, which could imply a hurrying on her part, fully manifest on the third day. Jeanne's day begins out of time: she gets up too early, and arrives at the post-office before it has opened. Then, on returning to the flat, she has difficulty filling her time, and makes constant trips to her alarm clock. Finally, on the third day, after a futile shopping trip trying to match a button, she is interrupted in her opening of a parcel by the arrival of a client.

The gradual breakdown of Jeanne's routine, a routine that had been established in the first third of the film, lends the film its structure. Without this careful attention to Jeanne's rituals the film would seem to build towards a climax. Once we do watch, as the film encourages us to, another world of space, movement, sounds and light opens up for analysis. Having drawn the spectator's attention through its systematic replaying of the rules and rituals that make up Jeanne's existence, the distance and attention of the camera's gaze produces an intimate and tactile vision. Through our constant exposure to this vision we become aware of spaces and their spatial properties, and the patterning of space and dimension provides an alternative, yet reinforcing narrative. Thus, Jeanne's heels announce her constant presence and we in turn are surrounded by the sounds that sustain her ritualised life: food boiling, doors shutting, water running, traffic outside or lights clicking on and off. The absence of facial or verbal expression seems to posit Jeanne's gestures as our only index to her self outside of the rules and rituals. As well as the clasping of her hands and pulling her cardigan around her, attention is drawn to her making the meat loaf, or peeling potatoes; through that she seems to vent her frustration or attempt to restore to her day the balance which was formerly present. The flip side of the film's 'lack' (of camera movement, angles, close-ups, conventions) is the abundance of meaning and expression provided if we take up the invitation of Akerman's *mise-en-scène*. This is an invitation to study Jeanne, her space, her time, her rituals and gestures with the loving patience expressed by Akerman's urge 'to look carefully and to be respectful'.

Jeanne Dielman was very much of its time. When P. Patterson and Manny Farber write that 'Chantal Akerman, a shrewd Belgian, is bridging the gap between the commercial film and the structural', they suggest that the film reacted to currents in independent filmmaking of the 1970s. It also offered an idea of a cinema which through its content explicitly addressed women and through its form avoided 'the strictures of voyeuristic definition', thus paving the way for a feminist film practice to develop. However, the legend of the film – whether because of its length, its form or content – has lasted to such an extent that in 2001, 26 years after *Jeanne Dielman*, Akerman chose to use the last ten minutes of the film as a video installation (entitled *Woman Sitting Down After Killing*) for the Venice Biennale.

Catherine Fowler

SOLDAAT VAN ORANJE SOLDIER OF ORANGE

PAUL VERHOEVEN, THE NETHERLANDS, 1977

Paul Verhoeven is one of the most provocative, daring, challenging and controversial contemporary filmmakers. His name has become a byword for controversy, and his films have frequently shocked moviegoers. The director of some of the most successful Dutch films ever made, he is now one of the most commercially successful expatriate filmmakers in Hollywood. In this he is like Louis Malle, Jan Troell, Alan Parker, Philip Noyce, Ridley Scott or Wolfgang Petersen – all of them directors whose talent Hollywood succeeded in 'buying in' from abroad. He has earned a reputation for films honest – and often brutal – in their presentation. From *Wat zien ik?* (*Business is Business*, 1971) to *Starship Troopers* (1998), Verhoeven draws attention to the individual, examining the dilemmas he or she must face when caught up in overwhelming events.

Provocation and individual responsibility lie at the heart of *Soldaat van oranje* (*Soldier of Orange*, 1977), a film that stands among the most renowned of Verhoeven's Dutch oeuvre. Together with the equally daring *Turks Fruit* (*Turkish Delight*, 1973), it is also one of the few that has attracted attention from international critics and scholars. This has, of course, much to do with the film's subject matter: the period of German occupation during World War Two. In his book on Dutch cinema, Peter Cowie names it an 'arduous undertaking, rendered doubly hazardous by the proximity of the drama to the hearts and memories of so many Dutch people'. Based on a book by Erik Hazelhoff Roelfzema, an aide to Queen Wilhelmina, Verhoeven's presentation of that period is not only a meticulously researched and executed project, it is also courageous. As Cowie states, 'not many filmmakers would have dared to show the anti-Jewish feelings that existed in Holland, or the quasi-Fascist initiation ceremonies among the university students in 1938 [sic], or the Dutch crowds pressing flowers into the hands of Nazi soldiers as they marched through the streets – an incident, says Verhoeven, that he based directly on newsreel footage'. The issue of the representation of war, and the Dutch reaction and sentiments towards it, make *Soldier of Orange* not just controversial, but transform it into one of the most important films addressing Dutch cultural identity of the time.

Verhoeven not only presented an era, he went to great lengths to present rounded individuals, and the way they intersected and related in such a repressive environment. The film follows the stories of half a dozen wealthy Dutch students who greet the imminence of war with the complacent words, 'a spot of war might be exciting'. It is an attitude that changes over the four years of German occupation during which they, like their country, must do whatever it takes to stay alive, each individual striking their own balance between idealism and pragmatism. Like their country, they are portrayed with moving realism, as Verhoeven depicts a microcosm every bit as vivid and poignant as a larger event of the war.

Central to the film is Erik Lanshof (Rutger Hauer). Initially, Erik pays little attention to the looming threat of war, being much too busy enjoying university life. After a humiliating initiation ritual for new students, during which he confronts, and is hit by, senior student Guus (Jeroen Krabbé), he develops a friendship with him. Other friends include Alex (Derek de Lint), Robby (Eddy Habbema), Jan (Huib Rooymans), Nico (Lex van Delden) and Robby's fiancée Esther (Belinda Meuldijk). When war breaks out, none of them is moved, believing the Netherlands will remain neutral (as they were in World War One). But soon after, following a few of the group's decision to enter military service (Erik is rejected on medical grounds – unsatisfactory eyesight), the Netherlands are attacked and German troops occupy the country. After the surrender, Erik enters the Resistance to illegally escape to England. Awaiting his transfer, he gets into trouble with the national militia (collaborating with Nazi Germany), for helping Jan. An attempt to get him to England fails, and Jan is captured. Later, Erik is arrested too (while Guus manages to escape). In jail, Erik learns that the person delivering them to the Germans, Van der Zanden, operates in London. Jan is executed shortly afterwards (a scene Cowie describes as unforgettable – 'the condemned man gazes round the windswept skyline while, faint in the background, there is the cry of a single bird'). After his unexpected release, Erik meets Esther and Robby, who are later coerced into collaborating with the Nazis; the Germans threaten to send the supposedly-Jewish Esther to an extermination camp. Erik finally manages to escape to England, on the same boat as Guus and Will (Peter Faber). In England, Erik is introduced to (and questioned by) Colonel Rafelli (Edward Fox) and Van der Zanden (Guus Hermus). After Erik, Guus and Will have been introduced to Queen Wilhelmina (Andrea Domburg), Erik joins the Dutch secret services. He joins Guus on an operation, back in Holland, to establish new permanent political contacts, and set up a radio post, for which he is forced to work with Robby, who has been coerced into cooperating with the Germans. Suspecting foul play, Erik goes back to the Netherlands and tries to contact Guus. Robby sets up a fake raid on his radio post to convince Guus he can be trusted (he pretends to shoot two militia men), and takes the Resistance members into a military camp near the beach, under the belief they are safer there. Here, Erik unmasks Robby, and he and Guus manage to escape, amidst chaos and explosions. Back in England, Erik joins the RAF. In the Netherlands, Guus assassinates Robby, but is caught by the Germans, who torture him. He is given a lethal injection, and when he lies in his cell, dying, we hear RAF bombers pass over his cell, intimating Erik's presence in one of the planes. Meanwhile, Alex, who has voluntarily joined the German forces, is killed by the Resistance. Soon after, Erik accepts the position of personal assistant to the Queen, and, when the war is over, he escorts her back to her home country, a hero himself. Erik sees Esther again, her hair brutally cut by townspeople, who accuse her of collaboration (a sharp reference to post-war repression). Finally, Erik revisits the pre-war past when he meets up with Jacques (Dolf de Vries), the only person left seemingly unaffected by the war. 'We are back where we were five years ago', he states, while Erik looks at a photograph of the friends, taken shortly before the war. He and Jacques are the only ones left alive.

The relationship between the individual characters, and their representation of wartime opinions, is essential to *Soldier of Orange*. Each one of them is a microcosm of Dutch society during the war. Throughout the film, Erik is the epicentre of the action and themes. The fact that the narrative follows Erik's return to England first (and shows him linking up with Guus' girlfriend Susan (Susan Penhaligon)), and only then switches back to Guus' mission, which has more narrative potential, is proof of how much the film focuses on Erik. But Erik is no traditional film hero. Although transforming into one, he has no goals or ideals. Far from nobility or heroism, Erik acknowledges that it is the adventure which attracts him to the life of the Resistance, and this candour is the trademark quality that distinguishes him as the central character and allows him to accept the different choices his friends make, even Alex, who functions as his alter ego and is technically his 'enemy'. When the two meet at a parade, rather than reproach, there is a mutual affirmation that friendship is more important than political or national allegiance. As Verhoeven puts it in Rob Van Scheers' biography, 'Erik is not a Resistance fighter. He is an adventurer. History is on his side, and he embraces it in a carefree way'. (Even when engaged in serious business, he still takes the time to make advances towards the Queen's assistant.) While Alex's decision to join the Waffen SS was made after seeing his German-born mother interned, Erik is aware that he has been relatively free to choose – and he chooses for the romanticism of Resistance life, rather than the structure and relative stability offered by the German military.

Besides Erik, the multitude of characters is a device that grants the film an extra importance. On one level, most of the characters portray Dutch stereotypes. Consider some of the less important characters: true to his maternal heritage, Alex becomes a German officer; Robby staunchly resists the Germans until forced to collaborate; Nico becomes a Resistance leader; and the unimaginative Jacques remains passive and impartial – a notably different approach to that of Robby's girlfriend Esther, who resists *and* collaborates. Guus is, in every way, the aristocrat and opportunist, and Will is just attempting to survive. At face value, they seem templates for wartime roles. On another level, however, their mutual interaction expresses the complexity of the fabric of Dutch society at the time. Neither one of them is only right or wrong, good or bad, possessing a duality which turns them into more representative characters than mere stereotypes (in fact, as Cowie remarks, the only real stereotype in the film is the German officer 'behaving like a comic-book caricature as he tries to stop Dutchmen taking ship'). Through the interaction of the characters the social issues dominating wartime Holland are not only made human by connecting them to real people, they are also brought into the open, as part of a debate on how a war changes people and their opinions – as if the film is asking us not to judge but to understand the motives of both friend and foe. This is true of even the smallest of roles. When Guus re-enters the Netherlands and meets with local political and (Dutch) military representatives to discuss the ways in which Dutch society should/could be organised after the war is over, there is a brief but telling exchange of opinions that captures an entire political discourse. The former general wants to remain neutral, while the former (socialist) member of parliament agrees to cooperate but openly distrusts the Queen's motives ('she doesn't care for democracy,' he says, 'she is into religion too much. She wants to play God').

One scene illustrating this diversity of opinions takes place as Erik, Guus and Robby pass through the German camp crowded with soldiers, militiamen and prostitutes. The atmosphere is one of baroque decadence, rather than of military structure, and at times it is hard to distinguish who is who; who is a prisoner in the camp and who is not (Erik seems to be entering and exiting at least three times), and who is involved (both in the plot and in the narrative) or not. There is no straightforward demarcation between sides here (as becomes apparent when Robby is unmasked), and this chaos elegantly reflects the complexity of Dutch society at that time, where roles were shifting and occassionally interchangeable. Both want clarity, but that is impossible. *Soldier of Orange* even questions gender stereotyping. In one scene Erik and Alex dance a tango together, applauded by bystanders, while discussing their political affiliations – a strange homoerotic moment in an otherwise almost purely macho film.

Soldier of Orange was the first of its kind – a film that openly looked at the dilemmas and the divided loyalties faced by the Dutch under Nazi occupation. While films such as *A Bridge*

Too Far (Richard Attenborough, 1977), which was shot on location in the Netherlands around the same time, focus on the enormity of the conflict and the well-known heroics of the battle-field, *Soldier of Orange* is about the ambiguities that confront 'normal' people, and the tension that arises when they choose different paths to meet the same challenge – survival. Rather than condemning collaborators and Germans alike as 'history's villains', the film acknowledges the complexity of this challenge and so invites criticism from those who prefer a more 'black and white' approach. Verhoeven reminds us of the grey areas; Robby betraying his colleagues to save his Jewish girlfriend; Germans and locals treating each other with mutual respect; Dutch people doing nothing to help the Jews in their midst. It is a reminder that of the 140,000 Jews in Holland, 100,000 were deported to the concentration camps – a higher ratio than anywhere else in Europe, and a damning reminder of the passive acceptance of the many that lay behind the outright collaboration of the few.

In such circumstances, individual responsibility becomes a difficult issue. As the story develops, the question arises as to whether intentions or results are what matters. Of the two survivors, Jacques has harmed no-one by spending his time preparing for a post-war career; Erik has to live with the knowledge that his efforts to help the Resistance have been directly responsible for the deaths of Guus and Nico. They are the only ones who have not taken up responsibility, one by not doing anything, the other by letting himself be led by events. The fact that Erik's right eye is nearsighted almost functions as a metaphor for his position – he does not see the bigger picture, only small events to which he reacts, and which he is unable of prevent-ing (it is notable that he never actually saves anyone). As it turns out, the two people who did not take responsibility for their actions – or lack of actions – are the survivors.

Verhoeven's interest in making *Soldier of Orange* was not just academic. Born in Amsterdam, and only a child during the War, Verhoeven was nevertheless deeply affected by what he experienced at first hand – from destruction to rebuilding, and collaboration to bravery against impossible odds. Conversely, Verhoeven's personal knowledge of the film's subject matter lends depth to the story, the characters and the underlying themes – while his youth during the War may have blurred some of the facts in his memory, there can be little doubt that the *issues* he encountered at this early age have affected him ever since. In various interviews, Verhoeven has described the awareness of the realities of death while still a child – it is something, he believes, that one never forgets. He spent six years at the University of Leiden, studying for his doctorate in Mathematics and Physics. At the same time he made various short films. His interest in filmmaking grew further during his time with the Dutch Navy, in which he served in the Marine Film Service, making documentaries. Most notable of his accomplishments here was his 23-minute piece to mark the tercentenary of the Marines. Known as *Het Korps Mariniers* (*The Marine Corps*, 1965), this documentary won the Silver Sun, a prestigious award given to military films in France. After his time in the military, Verhoeven embarked on a career in Dutch television. His 12-episode *Floris* (1969) won him national fame, and he moved into full-length films with *Business is Business* in 1971. After that, he rapidly became Holland's most successful director. To this day, only few Dutch films have brought in more at the box office than Verhoeven's, and his *Turkish Delight* and *Keetje Tippel* (*Cathy Tippel*, 1975) received notoriety as well as commercial success.

In the mid-1970s, Verhoeven became fascinated by the memoirs of Erik Roelfzema, a Resistance fighter who fled to England, flew as a pilot in the Royal Air Force and finally returned to the Netherlands as aide to Queen Wilhelmina. When Verhoeven set out to put these writings on the big screen, the result was a film with a difference, a film which focused on the microscopic aspects of occupied life as much as the more common stories of bravery, death and betrayal. Even when the war appears secondary to other events, there is a constant awareness that all is not well – that each individual's actions are being played out in an unnatural setting.

Working with Verhoeven, producer Rob Houwer (who had worked with the director on his previous films), and director of photography Jost Vacano, managed to preserve this feeling of an overwhelming backgroud presence by using their limited means wisely. Explosions often occur in the background, a couple of tanks are filmed in a way as to suggest the presence of a whole unit. Likewise, the placement of SS flags on Dutch housefronts conveyed the sense of an entire nation under occupation. Still, *Soldier of Orange* was at the time the most expensive Dutch film ever produced, costing somewhere between 3.5 and 5 million guilders (yet a lack of funds was responsible for a five-month delay in production). It is clear that Vacano put this to good use. He organised the action with great skill, from the full-scale parades to the air raid in Leiden. But just as the scale of the war is contrasted with the intimacy of each character's life, these impressive events are accompanied by smaller moments that are no less meaningful – such as the replacement of the silver in coins with zinc, a small but ever-present reminder of the turbulent times.

Soldier of Orange is not only proof of the impact wartime, university and military experiences had on Verhoeven. The wide acknowledgment of its place as one of the best Dutch films ever made (and Verhoeven's personal favourite among his Dutch films) appears to support its relevance for contemporary Dutch culture. While successful at the box office, *Soldier of Orange* was not received well by critics. It did meet with resounding approval in the USA, winning the Golden Globe for Best Foreign Film and causing Steven Spielberg to invite Verhoeven to the United States because, 'It's much better here.' But while *Soldier of Orange* brought a refreshing new perspective to an American audience, many viewers in the Netherlands saw it as an insult to the efficiency of the Resistance, the character of the Dutch and the impact the Dutch made as a whole on the outcome of the War. The film claims that only 50 Dutchmen fought on in exile from England; it hints that the post-war democracy in Holland would begin with communists and socialists and also suggests that the Resistance's activities were little more than diversions to keep the Germans from focusing their entire efforts on the War. The British Army in the film certainly do not hesitate to sacrifice Dutch agents when necessary. Even the six central characters are a backdrop for deeper societal issues such as the underlying 'fascist' behaviour that was more or less accepted in civilian society – such as the brutal 'hazing' undergone by shaven-headed newcomers to the fraternity, at the very start of the film. Nor does *Soldier of Orange* shy away from nudity and sexuality, starting with amicable rivalry for sexual supremacy among the friends. As with other Verhoeven films (*Basic Instinct* or *Turkish Delight*, for example) sex plays an important part in the characters' lives – but here, Verhoeven seems to acknowledge their very real need to have some sort of normality and tenderness among the surrounding chaos and violence. All these issues made *Soldier of Orange* into a *cause célèbre*, a film which was discussed widely, seen by many, but officially 'not approved of', much like the acts of the Resistance itself.

After *Soldier of Orange*, Verhoeven made several other films in the Netherlands, more or less returning to less ambitious narratives with *Voorbij, voorbij* (*All Things Must Pass*, 1979), *Spetters* (1980), and *De Vierde Man* (*The Fourth Man*, 1983). Like many of his previous films, these received both commercial and critical success, and the necessary controversy (mainly for violence and nudity). By the time Verhoeven went to Hollywood, he was the Low Countries' most successful director. *Flesh and Blood*, made in 1985, again with Rutger Hauer in the lead role, proved his transitional film. Internationally financed, with large American input, it still resembled his Dutch films, not least because of the moral ambiguity it has in common with *Soldier of Orange*. After this, Verhoeven permanently moved to Hollywood, where his films continued to stir trouble. The story of a policeman brought back from death to serve a sinister corporation as a part-human killing machine, *Robocop* was a major hit and point of discussion around the world in 1987. The central character struggles to recover his humanity and make sense of a utilitarian world in which, for some, the ends always justify the means. *Total Recall* was a major blockbuster success in 1990. This time, the central character (Arnold Schwarzenegger) is faced with perhaps the ultimate nightmare, of not knowing what is real, of who to trust. *Basic Instinct* (1992) saw a return to the level of controversy that surrounded his earlier films, but was only a foretaste of the opprobrium that was showered on *Showgirls* (1995), which attempted to look at the seedier side of Las Vegas. Verhoeven returned to military issues with *Starship Troopers* (1997) which won respect worldwide, as he poked fun at everything from military clichés to Hollywood stereotypes, and his own special brand of tongue-in-cheek patriotic bravado.

Many films and books have described the end of innocence on the battlefield, but few so effectively as *Soldier of Orange*, a two-and-a-half-hour tale of adventure, friendship and rivalries both political and personal ('an eight-course meal that leaves you hungry for more', to quote critic David Ansen). It is very different from Verhoeven's American films and focusing more on characters and story, it may still be his best. His work fits well within twenty-first-century society, with its mixed messages and blurred lines between dreams and reality. Behind the sex, violence and shock, Verhoeven's films are a rich tapestry of societal flaws and hypocrisies. They are a statement about the individual's need to distinguish himself or herself in his or her own way – in an environment, which demands acceptance, rather than questioning.

Johan Swinnen

TWEE VROUWEN TWICE A WOMAN

GEORGE SLUIZER, THE NETHERLANDS, 1979

Twee vrouwen (*Twice a Woman*) was director George Sluizer's third feature and has remained, in many ways, typical of his career. Internationalism seems to be key to the fourteen films Sluizer made up to 2002. After completing a short film in 1960 and a musical documentary in 1971, Sluizer directed his first feature film, *João en het mes* (*João and the Knife*) in 1972. It turned out to bear all the marks of his subsequent career. An international production – Dutch-Brazilian in this case – it featured a multinational cast, and was based on a novel by the author Odylo Costa-Filhos. When these features are compared with Sluizer's most recent film, *The Stonecraft* (2002), the similarities are remarkable. It is a Portuguese/Spanish/Dutch co-production, again with an international cast and is based on the source material (*La Balsa de Piedra*) of another international writer, Nobel Prize-winner José Saramago.

Twice a Woman was made in a period in which Dutch film production was steadily increasing to about 15 films a year. Public interest matched this upward trend. This success is largely due to the popularity of literary adaptations, a trend that culminated in 1976 when no fewer than 16 such adaptations were produced. To fully understand *Twice a Woman*, it is necessary to take a closer look at its internationalism, and the Dutch film adaptations of the time.

The Netherlands are a minor film nation, whose annual film production is hardly significant when compared with the output of other European countries. But adaptations of literature from the Netherlands make for some remarkable statistics. In the period between 1912 and 1999, no less than 287 novels by 179 Dutch-language authors were filmed. In the Netherlands and abroad, a total of 176 different directors are credited with the filming of a Dutch-language book or play. As far as is known, 17 titles were filmed by directors whose nationality was neither Dutch nor Belgian (many Belgian directors having some linguistic affinity with Dutch literature). Novelist Jan de Hartog (1914–2002) appears to have been particularly popular abroad. In the 1950s and 1960s, seven of his novels were filmed, the majority of which in the United States. In the Netherlands, however, not even one of his titles was filmed for the cinema. Anne Frank's (1929–45) diary, too, has frequently been filmed abroad, both for cinema and for television.

In October 1975 Harry Mulisch published his short love story *Twee vrouwen*, which was translated into English in 1980. Reception of the novel was mixed. Critic Kees Fens thought it was a gripping book in which 'a lot is left to the imagination due to the characters' taciturnity towards each other; the first-person perspective maintains that taciturnity because all that can be told is as much as the narrator knows in this uncommunicative company'. Another critic, Jaap Goedegebuure, called it an ingenious but chilly melodrama whose emotions resemble those of successful films. Immediately after the novel's publication, Sluizer attempted to buy the film rights, but producer Matthijs van Heyningen bid for them first, narrowly beating him. However, Van Heyningen failed to get the project off the ground and Sluizer was able to option the book.

The film features three principal roles, which Sluizer cast with an eclectic group of actors. Bibi Andersson played the role of Laura. Famous through her work with Ingmar Bergman, it was her performance in his *Scenes from a Marriage* (1973) that drew Sluizer to casting her. He had previously approached a number of other actresses, but they were reluctant to play the part of a lesbian. Sluizer commented upon this in an interview with Ab Van Ieperen: 'Perhaps we tend to assume rather easily in the Netherlands that such a relationship will now [1978] be accepted as a given, but when I was preparing the film, I experienced that this is by no means the case. The company that releases all films by Ingmar Berman in the US let me know they thought the screenplay was very good but they didn't want films with a "lesbian touch".' Laura's friend Sylvia played by Sandra Dumas. Finally, Sluizer cast Anthony Perkins in the smaller part of Alfred, Laura's ex-husband. According to Sluizer, 'Alfred is a man who's going through a bad patch in his life, preventing him from doing anything but nasty things. If you want such a character to go beyond the one-dimensional, you need an actor who can make his nicer sides shine through as well.' International actors also made the film easier to sell abroad.

In July 1978 Sluizer began shooting in the Netherlands and France, with the entire shoot taking seven weeks. The production cost a relatively modest 700,000 euros: 'Actually it's just a low-budget film on the scale of *Nosferatu* by Werner Herzog: two highly-paid actors, a very small crew and a fast shooting process.' He filmed on location with direct sound. Costumes were designed to allow him to work with hidden microphones. Jazz composer Willem Breuker composed the music for the film and performed it with his internationally acclaimed Willem Breuker Kollektief. *The Penguin Guide to Jazz on CD*'s description of the score could have been used to describe the images that accompanied it: 'The orchestration and arrangements are typically imaginative but there is something slightly drab and functional about the music.' The film was released in 28 cinemas on 23 May 1979.

The story of *Twice a Woman* follows a non-linear narrative structure. A woman with close-cropped hair gets into her car one evening and drives off. We switch to an old woman who chases away a young girl with her walking stick. The woman on the motorway pulls over. Forty-year-old Laura Tinhuizen is a curator in a museum. Three years earlier, she was divorced from Alfred Bloch, with whom she had been married for seven years. The main ground for their divorce was Laura's infertility. On the streets of Amsterdam, Laura meets twenty-year-old Sylvia Nithart and strikes up a relationship with her. For Laura, this is her first affair with a woman. Sylvia's parents are not supposed to be told but Laura's circle is soon informed. Laura and Sylvia visit the zoo, where Sylvia has her picture taken with an unknown passer-by. This picture comes in handy when Sylvia's mother pays an unexpected visit. Sylvia introduces Laura as the mother of Thomas, her boyfriend, with whom she was photographed in the zoo. Laura's ex-husband, Alfred, pays Laura a visit in the museum and is exasperated by her current involvement with a woman. Laura and Sylvia make a trip to Nice together, where Laura's mother lives in a nursing home. Laura's mother chases Sylvia away with her walking stick. Sylvia and Alfred meet at the performance of the play *Orpheus' Friend*. The homoerotic play causes Alfred to discuss the Greek tragedy. That night, Laura and Sylvia talk about children. The next day, Sylvia swears to Laura that she must know that she will love Laura forever, come what may. It turns out that the woman in the first scene is Laura. She is sitting on her couch at home when she receives a telegram with the news of her mother's death. She takes the car and heads for Nice. The relationship between Laura and Sylvia comes under pressure. Sylvia says she wants to stay with her parents for a few days and then drops all communications. Laura visits Sylvia's parents only to find out that Sylvia has not been there recently. On her way to Nice, Laura gets tired and books into a roadside hotel. The wife of Laura's ex-husband Alfred tells Laura that Sylvia and Alfred are having an affair. Sylvia drops by to pick up her passport and then leaves for Paris with Alfred. Laura gets her hair cut short. Sylvia then returns to Laura. She is now expecting a child by Alfred and tells him so in a short note. Laura feels that Sylvia should have it out with Alfred the next day. That next day, Alfred phones Laura to tell her that he has shot Sylvia. In her room in the roadside hotel, Laura is served breakfast.

Both the film and book were structured to avoid linear temporality, albeit to widely varying degrees. In Mulisch's story, Laura writes down her experiences in a room near Avignon. These consist of childhood memories, her relationship with Sylvia, her journey to Nice to attend her mother's funeral, and her reflections during the writing of these stories in her room. Not all of these four storylines survived the film. It shows only one childhood memory and audiences were told nothing of Laura's reflections on the events in the story and her life. The main storyline – Laura's relationship with Sylvia – is presented in chronological order in the film; the journey to Nice and the one childhood memory function as brief interruptions in the journey.

The very literary first-person narrative is unusual in film. Experiments in this field, such as *Lady in the Lake* (Robert Montgomery, 1947) or *Dark Passage* (Delmer Daves, 1947), in which the camera takes the viewpoint of the central character, who can only be glimpsed in a momentary shot of a mirror or window, were interesting, but ultimately unsuccessful. It is, however, common for films to focus on one particular character and not to show audiences information from any other narrative point of view. This is the strategy of *Twice a Woman*. In every scene we see Laura, and the viewer only receives information through her. The only times that he breaks this pattern, is when he follows Sylvia and Alfred to Paris. This change of style enabled Sluizer to film a love scene between a man and a woman, to contrast with the relationship between Laura and Sylvia.

In both the film and novel, classical references are tangible, not least because of the choice of two names – that of the protagonist and the play that is being staged. Laura is the name of the lover of the Italian Renaissance poet Petrarca, whose family moved from Italy to Avignon. To Laura is linked the classical theme of the polarity between culture and nature. Laura is unmistakably culture. She is forty years old, lives in Amsterdam, is a museum curator, and used to be married to Alfred Bloch (in Mulisch' book, his last name is Boeken, which means 'books'), a theatre critic. She is part of civilised life and is therefore quite astonished at herself for striking up a relationship with another woman, moreover a girl. In everything, this girl, Sylvia, is her opposite i.e. nature. She is young, a hairdresser, comes from a small village (Petten), and is as merciless as a natural phenomenon can be. Her surname – Nithart, an oblique reference to *niet hart*, 'no heart' – underlines her 'nature'. But culture and nature do not just form an opposition; they are also inextricably linked. This connectedness we recognise in how Laura and Sylvia are named. The beginnings of their surnames are a reversal of each other: Laura TINhuizen and Sylvia NIThart.

The second naming concerns the play attended by Laura and Sylvia: *Orpheus' Friend*. In this play, the heterosexual relationship between Orpheus and Euridyce becomes a homosexual one. Euridyce is played by a man. This relationship is mirrored in Laura and Sylvia's lesbian affair. Sylvia ('Euridyce') then descends into a symbolic underworld when entering into a relationship with Alfred (they even share a basement together). For a short time, Sylvia returns to the land of the living, but Laura ('Orpheus') insists that she confront Alfred. Instead of looking ahead into the future, Laura, like Orpheus, only looks back to the past, which is why Sylvia must die. Not only does the play refer to this second theme, it also has a narrative function. It is at this moment that Sylvia and Alfred meet and Alfred espouses his ideas on Greek Antiquity. In classical antiquity, homoerotic love was privileged. In the theatre, all female roles were played by men. In Alfred's opinion, however, men or women alone cannot produce tragedy. For that, a third party of the opposite sex is necessary. The parallel with his own role is obvious. Of course, his assertion refers to the relationship of Laura and Sylvia, a relationship between two women that can never result in a tragedy. For that, a man is required. Thus the film points to the tragic ending.

Harry Mulisch was pleased with the dogged faithfulness of Sluizer's adaptation. The Dutch press was less enthusiastic, for the same reason. There was general praise for Bibi Andersson and Sandra Dumas' acting, whilst Anthony Perkins creepiness was too reminiscent in his most famous performance, as Norman Bates in Alfred Hitchcock's *Psycho* (1960). Criticism was mainly directed at the story, which reminded critics of a pulp novel, in which the characters 'exchange empty words about events that do not affect them'. Film critic Peter van Bueren went so far as to accuse the film of being 'bland and anaemic. You watch everything passing in front of your eyes without being touched in any way.'

Besides Mulisch, the film found other champions. It attracted large audiences and was sold to various foreign markets. Jan Hein Donner praised Sluizer for emphasising the melodramatic aspect of Mulisch's novel, namely the vicissitudes between woman, girl and man, and skilfully weaving them into engrossing cinema.

Twice a Woman is a film that broke new ground. It was the first adaptation of a book by Harry Mulisch (three further novels were turned into films – *De Aanslag/The Assault* (Fons Rademakers, 1987), *Hoogste Tÿd/Last Call* (Frans Weisz, 1995) and *De Ontekking van de Hemel/The Discovery of Heaven* (Jeroen Krabbé, 2001). It has also been regarded as the ideal platform from which to debate the idea of literary adaptation. The film's subject was radical for its time. It was not until the 1980s that presenting a lesbian relationship in a popular film became even marginally accepted. The controversy caused by *Een Vrouw als Eva* (*A Woman like Eve*, Nouchka Van Brakel, 1979), another film with a lesbian theme from the same year, was a reminder of how sensitive such issues still were in Dutch society. Finally, in production terms, this international enterprise was ahead of its time. Today almost every film is an international production, but this was uncommon in the Netherlands at the time and the film's success proved the viability of taking such a route.

Hans Van Driel

DE STILTE ROND CHRISTINE M. A QUESTION OF SILENCE

MARLEEN GORRIS, THE NETHERLANDS, 1982

De Stilte Rond Christine M. (*A Question of Silence*) was described, some three years after its eventually successful initial distribution by Cinema of Women in 1982, as a '*cause célèbre*, referred to in some reviews to lure audiences and mentioned disparagingly in others as an example of shockingly uncontrolled feminism'. Twenty years on, while the restaurant or bar next door to the cinema may no longer resound to the sound of what Jane Root described as 'couples engaged in deep and sometimes angry arguments about the film', Marleen Gorris' first feature film still generates animated debate in undergraduate film classes, particularly among adults. A close reading of *A Question of Silence*, and especially of the central 'dream' sequence, highlights the sexual politics of the film. As has been documented, *A Question of Silence* was produced, marketed and distributed not, as may casually be expected, as a European 'art' film, but as a kind of psychological thriller with particular appeal to female audiences – as a brief account of the plot should make clear.

Before and during the credits, we are introduced to criminal psychiatrist Janine van den Bos (Cox Habbema) and to Christine (a housewife, Edda Barends), An (a bar worker, Henriette Tol) and Andrea (a secretary, Nelly Frijda). The latter three have been arrested and charged with the murder of a male boutique owner. It is immediately made clear that the women have no connection with one another. Janine's job is to investigate the mental state of the three women (incidentally not, as she points out during the trial at the end of the film, to establish motive). Sequences showing Janine's interviews with the women and her life at home with her husband are intercut with three flashback scenes which show the events leading up to and culminating in the killing of the shop owner. While the editing is clearly not rigorously pre-programmed, events relating to the other three women are generally presented in the sequence Christine-An-Andrea.

Janine's investigations are also intercut with flashbacks which sketch the three women's life experiences, and with another series of flashbacks which detail what each of them does after leaving the boutique: Christine visits a funfair with her son, An cooks and enjoys a meal alone, and Andrea, while crossing a street eating an ice-cream, is mistaken by a man in a car for a prostitute: she 'accepts' the man's 700 guilders and pointedly goes through the motions of having sex with him before climbing off and laughing dismissively as she leaves the surprised punter on the bed.

The key 'dream' sequence, following a meal with friends at which Janine becomes increasingly aware of her husband's overbearing overconfidence, will be discussed in some detail below. The result of the epiphanous 'dream' is a growing awareness on Janine's part of the fundamental sanity of the three women and the oppression she shares with them. At the trial which follows, Janine declares the women sane and quarrels with her husband (whose principal concern is clearly his own reputation); the patriarchal bias of the court is made especially clear by the Public Prosecutor, whose crass remark, that he sees no difference between this case and one in which a female shop-owner has been killed by three men, is greeted by prolonged laughter first from Christine, then from all the accused, the four female witnesses who had been in the shop, and, eventually, Janine. When the court is cleared, Janine finds herself on the steps of the courthouse, making a choice between her husband – aggressively blowing the horn of his car to gain her attention – and the four silent witnesses, who stand just behind her. As the music prepares for the end credits, a freeze-frame makes it clear whom she has chosen.

The 'accessibility' of the film – as opposed to the narrative and character complexity associated with much 'art' cinema – is exemplified by the narrative motivation of the flashback structure within the crime/psychological thriller and, with the exception of the boutique sequences, by the unstylised 'realist' camerawork, sound, editing and *mise-en-scène* associated with such a genre: the green-blue tint of the prison corridors, the suspense element in the gradual revelation of events in the boutique, the combination of electronic music and the 'realist' sound of prison protocols, and the (overly simplistic) signaling of suspense on the soundtrack when Janine asks Christine and then An whether there was anyone else present in the shop.

In keeping with the generic aspect of the film, the title itself is enigmatic. Does it refer to Christine's refusal to speak or to the silence – both literal and symbolic – of the four witnesses to the killing? Or is it both? The enigma of the English language title is different from that of the original Dutch, *De Stilte Rond Christine M.*, as the latter already installs Christine as the centre of a silence, and, as Jane Root describes, also implicitly makes her a (or the?) central character. Indeed doublings, repetitions and echoes pervade *A Question of Silence* – a banal observation which may nevertheless lead us somewhere interesting.

Over and above the 'obvious' male/female polarity, one key contrast in the film is that between individual consciousness as embodied by Janine and the collective feminist consciousness which she comes to embrace at the end of the film. Janine's journey starts out from her own perception of her role as a clinical psychiatrist and as her husband's partner. At the start of the film the couple appear to enjoy an egalitarian relationship: sexual horseplay is enjoyed by both, an afternoon spent entertaining another couple is sweetness and light, there is an affectionate kiss as she takes the telephone from her husband after he has affirmed their shared social standing – both are 'doctors' – by casually responding, 'I'm the lawyer, my wife's the psychiatrist.' Judging from conversation at this social occasion, he has libertarian anti-censorship views and is aware of the oppressive nature of the legal system. It seems that he cooks regularly. Indeed the Dutch social context and its relatively realist filmic representation, particularly for 1980s audiences, would surely initially have been perceived as permissive, hence unrepressive; there are policemen with long hair tolerating anti-police jokes, Janine's husband is shown full-frontal nude (Janine is not), and later in the film we have the scruffy courthouse, covered in graffiti, with its apparently matter-of-fact and unpompous procedures presided over by a very cool judge. In a British context in particular, these initial signals do not signpost male dominance and oppression of women.

Janine functions as a central identification figure in a number of ways. She – together with her husband – appears in the opening shot and the film ends with her in freeze-frame close-up. The opening credits are accompanied by scenes of the other three women at home, work, being arrested and then together at the police station. Though at this stage any of the other women, or indeed the husband, could be putative identification figures – as has previously been noted, the original Dutch title includes Christine's name – it is with the subsequent focus on Janine's home life and on her quest to understand the other three women that she emerges as the investigator, as prime identification figure. On first viewing the film, a male viewer may indeed be confused and perhaps frustrated by the absence of an appropriate male identification figure. The problem for male viewers is the extent to which one accepts the subsequent relegation of almost all male characters to the status of villains, dupes, fools or, at best, walk-on parts.

Yet if Janine's investigative function conforms readily to the generic characteristics already evoked above, it becomes evident before long that this particular investigation is not going to conform to an archetypically male 'sadistic' scrutiny of woman: we are indeed forewarned by a colleague of Janine's who immediately summarises the case: 'women that you can recognise from a mile away'.

Janine soon encounters difficulties with her work with the women. Christine refuses to speak; An talks (and laughs) so much that despite her professional training Janine is troubled by the flood of words, her middle-class sensibility unable to understand An's cackling laughter at the suggestion that she may have wanted to re-marry. Andrea is initially hostile and explicitly casts doubt on the relevance of Janine's work. Gradually, Janine is forced to recognise the 'ordinariness' of the women (chosen in the scenario, of course, to typify a cross-section of female experience), despite the fact that she is still not really getting through to them. During one extended conversation with her husband, still confident of her professional objectivity, she declares the women's sanity. There is an interesting use of diegetic sound here: after her husband fails to hear the assertion, first uttered rather diffidently, Janine turns on some loud and appropriately dramatic music, then repeats: 'I don't think those women are insane.' We do not see the husband's response, but he is unlikely to have heard. In any case he is clearly deaf to such a view.

Paralleled with Janine's growing concerns about the murder case is an increasing tension in her domestic life, evident not only in his refusal/inability to listen to Janine's prognosis, but on a second social occasion in the company of the couple already seen earlier in the film. In one of the characteristic doublings/repetitions highlighted below, what had previously been a harmonious occasion has now become a source of tension, at least for Janine; she is driven to abruptly interrupt a particularly self-absorbed speech from her husband, after he has effectively ignored her correction of his sexist male-centred use of 'he' (she intercedes 'or she') and continued to rely on the male pronoun. This is also a doubling/repetition of a previous occasion on which he had ignored her correction and continued to refer to her 'clients' as 'patients', implicitly diminishing the status of her work.

It is during the night after this last conflict that the central 'dream' sequence takes place and signals a radical shift in the object of Janine's investigation, from the three women's sanity to her own position, both professional and personal, in relation to the abuses of patriarchy. It begins with a static rear shot of Janine, pensive before the mirror, smoking a cigarette (the first time she has been seen smoking; she is known to have given up the habit) and combing her hair. Her husband enters from left, naked, remarks on her good cooking and the quality of the brandy, then leaves frame right. 'Coming to bed darling?' The next shot is a 12-frame still of Christine, An and Andrea standing over the body of the man in the boutique. Janine, troubled, sits before the mirror, then moves left to turn off the lights; the camera pans round to follow her as she gets into bed, still smoking. Her husband makes amorous advances. The 12-frame insert is repeated, then the husband continues his advances despite Janine's lack of interest ('not now') and obvious preoccupation. As he insists, we see a further shot of the boutique, but this time one or two shadowy figures can be discerned through the boutique window. The husband continues to insist, eventually taking the cigarette from Janine's hand and stubbing it out.

The shot of the shop appears for a fourth time (for some 22 frames), this time with two or three figures more clearly visible in the background, which inaugurates the 'dream' sequence. First, a medium-shot of Janine, facing right of frame; she turns left. Then a medium-shot of Andrea, same movement: she is turning away from Janine. Another shot of Janine, then Christine turns from right of frame to left, again turning away. A medium-shot of Janine looking confidently is followed by An turning from right of frame to left, again turning away. A medium-shot of Janine at her desk, looking lost/confused, making a similar head movement, is followed by a medium-shot of An, knitting and laughing. After a medium-shot of Janine, confused, this time looking from left to right of frame, and a medium-shot of Andrea, smiling and confident, we see another medium-shot of Janine in her office; she turns from right frame to face the camera, looking down. The next shot is a medium-close-up from a similar angle. Janine looks up at the camera. A fifth shot of the boutique is similar to the others, but this time Christine, An and Andrea are looking up and smiling, and the three background figures are clearly visible, as are the backs of two other figures in the foreground. All the figures are clearly female.

Next we see Janine crouching by the music centre in the living room, turning right frame to left; her husband is in long-shot with his back to the camera. A medium-shot of Andrea turning from left frame to look right of frame is followed by a medium-shot of Janine turning from left frame to look right of frame, turning away from Andrea. A medium-shot of An turning from left frame to look right of frame is followed by another shot of Janine turning away; there follows a similar pairing for Christine. Andrea stands by some shelves, turns to look frame right; Janine turns away. Christine looks up and frame right; this time a longer medium-shot has Janine turn frame right and towards the cell door, head and hair turning more quickly. A close-up of Janine in her study shows her looking more distressed; the left–right movement is continued, and is followed by an extreme close-up of Janine, with rapid head & hair movement frame right to frame left. This is followed by three very brief very similar shots, then by a shot from the set-up used earlier for the couple in bed. Janine awakes from her dream, sits up sweating and alarmed. 'Jesus!' She turns on the light, calls her husband's name (indistinctly); there is no response. She gets out of bed and leaves frame left with a little display of nudity. The static camera remains on the sleeping husband for some five seconds.

There is no synchronised speech during the 'dream' sequence itself. Amid a jumble of sound signifying Janine's confused state, An's laughter and disorienting electronic music combine and build rapidly to a crescendo when Janine wakes up. In the fragments of super-imposed remembered remarks, four are subtitled. During the first part of the dream, the most distinct snatches are 'those women are completely deranged', 'they're utterly mad' and 'she had nothing else to do all day'. The only audible statement following the final flash of the shop interior is 'your report will be of no consequence whatsoever'.

A number of things need to be noted about this sequence. First, the speed of the editing rhythm for the 'dream' sequence itself: most shots have a duration of approximately one second, reduced to under a second for the last four shots. The pace here is underlined by an overlapping confusion of sounds, mostly fragments of the interviews Janine has conducted, merging into a vertiginous crescendo of repetitive music as Janine's head spins just before she awakens. Secondly – and this has been remarked on relatively little – there is the crucial punctuation of the sequence by the five interposed shots of the women in the boutique, most lasting for only 12 frames and hence verging on the subliminal. Even the shots that are almost one second long (the last two) have not been subject to much analysis; in 1982, when the film first appeared, private ownership of video recorders was spreading rapidly in Western Europe, but VCRs were not yet as ubiquitous as they are today.

A close analysis of this sequence clarifies its central revelatory status. The take in which Janine sits before the mirror and then gets into bed is interrupted by three 12-frame 'flashes' of the women in the boutique: the first just after her husband has said 'Coming to bed darling?', the second as he has begun his advances towards her, the third after Janine has said 'not now'. The fourth 'flash', lasting some 22 frames, inaugurates the 'dream' sequence proper, and immediately follows the husband's removing the cigarette from Janine's hand and putting it out: a clear doubling of the unthinking male violation of Andrea's physical autonomy which we have observed in an earlier flashback, when a male colleague, following an encouraging glance from his (male) superior, puts his hand on hers to forcibly stop the clinking noise she is making while absent-mindedly stirring her coffee. As these instances of male incursion lead to the 'dream' sequence, there are crucial changes in the brief 'flashes' of the boutique: in the second, third and fourth of these shots, two or three indistinct figures become gradually more visible in the background, outside the boutique window: an emergent answer to the question of silence which has been gnawing at Janine: were there other women present at the killing? If so, where and who are they?

After that last shot, the fourth 'flash', in which for just under a second three figures are now visible in the background, the 'dream' itself can be divided into five segments. The first segment consists of three pairs of shots; in the first of each pair Janine is shown in confident 'professional psychiatrist' mode, generally looking/glancing to the left of the frame, and each of these shots is followed by one of the other three women turning or looking away to the same side. The three women are thus averting the gaze, rejecting Janine's approach.

In a second segment, the pairing continues, but now Janine appears lost, and the intervening shots are of An and Andrea looking happy and confident – as Janine has already described them, 'normal'. The second shot of each pair shows Janine turn from frame left to frame right.

A third segment consists of four shots which contain the climax of Janine's revelatory experience. The first two shots show Janine in her study as if interpellated by the camera; she then looks up, only to clearly see, in the next shot (for about 18 frames), the final 'flash' of the boutique. This time all becomes clear. Three figures are visible in the background, while another two figures block out part of the frame in the foreground. All the observing figures are recognisably female, and neatly add up to five: the four witnesses to the killing plus Janine herself. The following shot takes us back to a key scene, already remarked upon, in which Janine asserted to her husband that she considered the women sane of comitting the crime.

The fourth segment contains ten shots, arranged as five pairs – and it seems that virtually all the shots in the 'dream' sequence are fragments from shots earlier in the film – in which one of the other three women turns and/or looks frame right, and the following shot each time shows Janine turning or looking away frame right, thus echoing the first segment, but this time it is Janine who averts the gaze of the other women.

Finally, a fifth segment, including a series of five shots of ever-shorter duration continue Janine's head movement of the last shot of the previous segment (though now repeatedly from right to left of screen), this time in extreme close-up. The dizzying, spinning effect is augmented by the crescendo of music until, abruptly, Janine awakes in a cold sweat.

After the last shot, having failed to awaken her husband, Janine goes downstairs to her study and, clearly dazed, sits and thinks, and replays on her tape recorder a lucid analysis of Christine's muteness provided by Andrea. Then she (perhaps overly dramatically) sets a Newton's cradle in motion on her desk, a diegetic rhythm taken up by extradiegetic music which then bridges into the next sequence.

On the theme of doubling, it may indeed be no accident that Janine begins the extended 'dream' sitting in front of a mirror, in which we see her reflection (and that of her husband). We can perhaps press into service here the notion of *catoptromancy*: the mythologically resonant practice of the use of mirrors for finding lost objects, evoked in films from *Snow*

White and the Seven Dwarfs (Walt Disney, 1937) to *Harry Potter and the Philosopher's Stone* (Christopher Columbus, 2001) via the fascinating *Combat d'amour en songe* (*Love Torn in Dream*, Raul Ruiz, 2000).

It is widely accepted that mirrors play an important role (metaphorically or, according to psychoanalytic theory, in some kind of reality) in how people are socialised and framed within existing positions of power and ideology. Janine's social position at the beginning of *A Question of Silence* is clearly that of the successful career woman: a dinky (double income no kids yet) household. In accordance with the material progress and perceived increased egalitarianism overseen by feminism since the 1960s (perhaps especially in countries such as the Netherlands and Sweden), the submission to patriarchy seems to be a thing of the past. Yet as she investigates the three women, Janine comes to see that this is not the case: that she has instead been co-opted as a surrogate man.

The mirror shots are highly significant, coming as they do immediately before the 'dream' sequence. The effect of the rapidly-edited shots of Janine interspersed with those of the other three women is to destabilise and eventually to shatter the individual male-modeled image of herself which Janine initially contemplates: remember that the naked husband also appears in the mirror; Janine has 'misrecognised' herself and is now learning that the subject she thought she was is but a phallocentric fiction. As Sabine Melchior-Bonnet has commented, 'the kaleidoscopic fragments of the broken mirror reveal a protean self, with infinite virtualities ... The mirror, instead of anticipating unity, breaks into pieces'. Writing of 'the young female psychoanalytic patient', Melchior-Bonnet also writes that 'the broken pieces caused an appropriate representation of herself to appear'. We should note in passing that Marleen Gorris' next film was entitled *Gebroken Spiegels* (*Broken Mirrors*, 1984).

The tropes of deconstruction and fragmentation, though now largely colonised by postmodern discourse, also continue to have other functions. Janine's shattered sense of self does not remain unreconstructed; it is precisely through the dual function of the interposed flashes of the boutique that her understanding of herself as a professional is fragmented and a new conception of her position in a collectivity of women – literally, as the 'fifth woman' in the last of the flashes – can emerge.

The broader positioning of the 'dream' in the film text also supports such a reading. This is especially connected to the shift in representations of the husband from 'liberal' to male-chauvinist; it is no accident that the 'dream' happens when he forces his sexual attentions on his unwilling partner; as we have seen, the 'flashes' of the boutique keep time with his insistence.

The entire sequence is moreover further bracketed by the flashbacks of Andrea's post-homicidal sexual act, of which she remains entirely in control; this begins before the night of the 'dream' and is completed after it. Andrea's position on top of her 'client' is pre-echoed in the very first moments of the film when it is Janine who takes the upper hand and lies on top of her husband. And Janine's playful teasing gesture in the opening scene of running a pen down her husband's chest towards his genitals cannot but deliberately prefigure the later mutilation of the boutique proprietor.

In the aftermath to the central sequence, there are scenes which explicitly reverse the themes of non-communication and evasion so evident in the 'dream'. Thus when Janine expresses her desire to communicate with Christine in personal terms, the latter speaks for the first and only time in the film, and this evinces a physical response from Janine as she touches Christine's hand. Immediately after this comes the cryptic scene in which Andrea passes her hands over the length of Janine's body, which, as Jeanette Murphy and others have pointed out, is a barely coded lesbian encounter. The interruption at the end of this scene ('sorry, wrong door') serves as a reminder of the predominance of male control and surveillance over female sexuality.

Through her investigative journey Janine thus arrives at a realisation of her place in a (separatist) feminist collectivity and rejects her previous complicity in upholding repressive patriarchy. Signs of the latter in the film are manifest, from the economic exploitation suffered by all three women to the physical restriction of Andrea's hand, from the 'joking' sexist banter to which An is subjected to Christine's virtual imprisonment in her home.

When Janine first arrives at the prison at the start of the film, a colleague politely holds the door open: 'after you.' As she leaves the courthouse at the end of the film, Janine is rudely jostled by a passing man. The theatrical distribution subtitle reads: 'Look where you're going, you cunt.' Though the abuse remains untranslated in televised versions, it is a ready index of the change in Janine's status, and of how much she has had to learn. Indeed, though Gorris' choice of subjects for her films of the 1990s (*Antonia's Line*, 1995 and *Mrs. Dalloway*, 1997) may have signaled a turn to more literary concerns, her investigation into a woman's place in society continues.

Jan Udris

CRAZY LOVE

DOMINIQUE DERUDDERE, BELGIUM, 1987

Dominique Deruddere's 1987 film *Crazy Love* is one of the very few Belgian films ever to be distributed in America. In fact, it is one of the very few films from that country to make any kind of impression on the world's screens.

Belgian films that get seen abroad tend to be the ones that have sex in them or that deal with controversial subject matter. And *Crazy Love* has exploitable elements aplenty. Male masturbation, voyeurism, necrophilia and suicide all feature in its relatively brief running time. Yet, for all that, the impression left when the film ends is a rather surprising one. The controversial aspects recede into the background and what remains is an overriding feeling of melancholia and an immanent, hovering sense of mystery; the kind of mood that comes from looking at a painting like René Magritte's *The Empire of Lights*. It is a dreamlike glimpse of a place you can never really enter. A feeling that a better world exists somewhere else; but maybe only in our dreams.

This melancholic mood is a feature of certain forms of Low Countries art. It saturates the paintings of Xavier Mellery, is woven through the writings of Jean Ray, and filters into cinema via the likes of André Delvaux's *Un soir, a train* (*One Night … a Train*, 1968) and Harry Kümel's *Les lèvres rouges* (*Daughters of Darkness*, 1971). Both of these could be loosely defined as 'film fantastique' and while *Crazy Love* is definitely not that, it draws many of its images and much of its power from the same tradition. It is a tradition in which the everyday becomes imbued with the unreal. The human element is removed from streets and landscapes; shadow, mood and mystery come to dominate.

This Low Countries genre of 'film fantastique' encompasses only a very small and select group of titles, which at least gives them the advantage of being easily identified. They stand out from the mass of Low Countries cinema, as Raymond Chandler would say, 'like a tarantula on a slice of angel cake'. Their main attributes are a certain literary pretension; a sense of being between two worlds; a conservative and consequently rather uneasy sense of rebellion and finally – and most importantly – a definite touch of *l'amour pour la mort*. So marked are these traits in Low Countries fantastic that even a foreign production set there (for example Giorgio

Ferroni's 1960 Italian production *The Mill of the Stone Women*) seems bathed in these same melancholy moods.

It is this dark and yet elegiac atmosphere that lifts *Crazy Love* out of the ordinary and makes it a very different kind of film from the one it could so easily have been. On paper, it reads as a combination of two well-worn genres: the male coming-of-age movie and the European tradition of literary art cinema. That the final product is a long way from either is a tribute to the skill of first-time director Derrudere and his fresh and inspired approach to the material. Anyone reading the film's synopsis and expecting a *Porky's* (Bob Clark, 1981) or *Road Trip* (Todd Phillips, 2000) experience would soon find the smile fading from their face when confronted by – for instance – the uncomfortably intense scenes of male masturbation.

Literary purists too might find themselves confused by the way the film uses its sources. Ostensibly based on stories by Charles Bukowski, *Crazy Love* takes a far from traditional approach to this material. Bukowski was a poet of the tenement and the welfare line, a chronicler of the dead-end job and the down-beat drunk. His work is strongly autobiographical, with the recurring figure of Henry Chinaski acting as a compendium of some of the things Bukowski had been and some of the things he saw in those around him. This figure, Belgianised into Harry Voss, is the main protagonist of Deruddere's film which tells his story in three short episodes that take place over a period of 21 years.

Other films based on Bukowski's work, of which *Barfly* (Barbet Schroeder, 1987) and *Tales of Ordinary Madness* (Marco Ferreri, 1981) are the most famous, tend to concentrate on the drinking and the despair. However, *Crazy Love* reminds us that Bukowski was a poet as well as a kind of bleak humorist. And in that way it certainly comes closer to the spirit, if not the letter, of his work than most of the other films derived from it. Bukowski, on seeing the film, told Deruddere that he had vastly improved on his source material. 'You put wheels on my tires, baby!' he announced joyously as the film ended.

A wolf howls. Clouds pass across the face of the full moon. We are in the sepia wonderland of 'black-and-white' film. On-screen titles tell us it is 1955. A beautiful princess waits for her handsome knight. A shaft of mystical light from above pierces her gloomy thoughts and there he is, riding through the castle gate. Prince Charming on a charger comes to wed his lady in waiting. As the titles announce *The End*, we cut to colour and see a young boy in the darkness of a deserted cinema still dreaming in his seat, not wanting the fantasy to end.

This is young Harry Voss, twelve years old. The hero of our story. As he leaves the cinema he filches a black-and-white still of the beautiful princess from the front of house display. That is his first attempt to bridge the gap between dreams born in the darkened cinema and the reality of a mundane life outside it. The photograph becomes Harry's first fetish. It is also the first step on the road to his destruction. Harry's second attempt to force reality into the shape of dreams comes when he asks his mother how she got married. Listening to her fantastic story about being kidnapped by his father and held captive in a cabin in the woods, Harry says wonderingly: 'That's as beautiful as a film…' 'Much more beautiful', his mother replies as she looks across at her husband in his dirty vest, sleeping off a Sunday lunch on the sofa.

In Bukowski's stories and in Deruddere's film, the father is a shadowy figure at best. Women are the subjects of fantasy and also its wellspring. It is Harry's mother who tells him the fairy story about her marriage and it is to women that Harry later dedicates his poems of unrequitable love. But there are other aspects to the relationship between men and woman as Harry is about to find out.

An older male friend tells him about sex, showing him a photograph of a naked girl. In an attempt to feed their twitching libidos, the two boys visit a fairground. There they come across one of Harry's classmates and his Italian mother. The sight of this exotic older woman spins Harry's friend off into a reverie. He insists that they visit her house. Like a fairytale cottage, it is set deep in the dark woods. As the two boys enter the house they find the woman lying on her bed, barely covered by a diaphanous night-dress, like some sluttish sleeping beauty. 'Dead drunk', Harry's friend informs him, instructing the younger boy to climb on top of her. The woman awakes and her screams send them running. Later, all fired up and with nowhere to go, the older boy teaches Harry the delights of masturbation as they sit in the wreck of an abandoned car. Harry returns home and hears his mother admit that her kidnap story was just a fantasy. 'Everything is ugly', Harry concludes. But that night, clutching the stolen photograph of the princess, he masturbates himself to climax.

The next section of the film is set in 1962. The camera pans round a room, past a photo of Harry's mother marked with the black band of death. The Everly Brothers' *Love Hurts* is playing. The pan comes to a jarring halt on a close-up of the teenage Harry. His skin, now hideously scarred by *acne vulgaris*, resembles the cratered surface of the moon, but scraped red and raw. We learn that it is the last day of school. But Harry – known to his classmates as Harry Frankenstein – will not be attending.

A friend visits him that night to persuade him to come to the school prom, but instead they visit the local freight yard and break into a wagon full of whiskey. They get wrecked as Harry reads out his painfully tender love poetry – dedicated to the beautiful Lisa, belle of the school ball. Fired up by drink, Harry decides to visit the school. There he dares to approach Lisa to ask for a dance, but before he can reach her he is brushed aside by a handsome jock. As consolation, Harry's friend sets him up with a supposedly willing girl in the back seat of a car, but even she rejects him. As the dance draws to an end, the teen pop band begin a smoochy rendition of *Love Hurts*. A strange apparition then enters the hall. It is Harry, but looking like a mummy from a horror film. His pock-marked face is wrapped not in strips of cloth but in toilet paper. He holds out his hand to the lovely Lisa, who is amused enough by his originality to accept an invitation to dance. 'You made it!' his friend whispers to him excitedly. 'Yes – with shit paper', sneers Harry as he storms off to finish the whiskey.

In a final irony as Harry rolls dead drunk on his doorstep that night, the police turn up. They found the discarded poem with his name on it in the bottom of the freight car and have come to arrest him for robbery. (All poetry really does is let the world know about our crimes.) In the back of the wagon on his way to the lock up, Harry begins to laugh; furiously and bitterly, as funereal strings flood the soundtrack.

The third part of the story is set in 1976. It is fourteen years later and 33-year-old Harry still has not stopped laughing. A mask-like grin permanently plastered over his blank face, he listens to a sleazy rock band in a waterside dive filled with drunken sailors and cheap whores. The loud music, the wooden walls and gaudy flashing lights make the place a kind of grown-up version of the fun fair Harry visited as a child.

As in the first two sections, there is a best friend. Here it is Bill, another hopeless drunk, who is just out of prison. He and Harry go on a bender. On their way home in the misty early morning, they see a hearse parked outside a block of flats. With nothing better to do, they steal the body. Back in Bill's cavernous squat, Harry unzips the body bag. To his astonishment the girl lying there is the Princess of his dreams – the girl from the film all those years ago; but perfectly preserved. 'She's dead', says Bill. 'But she lives…' Ignoring his friend's protests, Harry fucks the still-warm corpse, as though pumping new life into the dead dreams of his childhood.

In a final act of closing the circle, they drive to the sea and there on the pebbly beach, in the glaring headlights, Harry re-enacts the marriage scene from the old black-and-white film. Then, taking the Princess in his arms, he walks off into the sea. As at the film's beginning, clouds pass across the face of the moon. A moon now sickly yellow with the pallor of death.

Deruddere began making 8mm shorts as a teenager. He progressed to 16mm and eventually attended film school in Brussels, where he made short films like *Killing Joke* (1980) and *Wodka Orange* (1982), which are still regarded as excellent. After a number of false starts and odd jobs in the industry, he began work in 1984 on a 35mm short based on a Bukowski story called *The Copulating Mermaid of Venice, California* (eventually released as *Foggy Night*, 1985). The success of this 20-minute piece convinced the producers that Deruddere was ready to make a full-length feature. He decided to dramatise two more stories of Bukowski's and weave all three of them into a continuous narrative.

It is a technique that has been tried before, but rarely with such success. In fact, *Crazy Love* is a rare example (Walerian Borowczyk's *La Bête*, 1975, is another one) of a feature based around a short film that seems originally to have been conceived within the detailed framework of a full-length narrative, as opposed to a compressed version of that narrative. In both cases, the material added to the short expands its meaning, rather than simply stretching out the dénouement. The identity of the dead female, for instance, is so important to the emotional meaning of *Crazy Love*, that without knowledge of the film's first part, the whole impact of the necrophilia scene would have been radically different; little more than a shock effect, in fact, rather than the emotional punch that it becomes in the full-length feature.

Again, the look of the film is the kind of lucky choice that in retrospect seems obvious, but was one of a number of possible options. When planning the original short film, with cinematographer Willy Stassen, Deruddere knew only that he wanted a dark, 'poetic' look; one with some texture and mystery to it. In fact, they began by studying the paintings of Van Gogh to find the sort of muted pallette that they were after. In the full-length feature, this mood of autumnal melancholy is the perfect conclusion to the development of a trilogy that begins as a lyrical summer fairytale in black-and-white. From the exact sepia tone and lighting of this black-and-white beginning, through the perfect kitsch of the teen band at the school prom, the film is a triumph of tiny details and perfect nuance.

But it is in his accurate staking of much more ambitious targets that Deruddere really impresses. Using his source material as a framework, he laid over it a rich cloak of fantastic imagery. This appropriation of the mood and manners of fantasy allowed him to make, out of the otherwise realistic material, a kind of horrifying fairy tale. From the gritty details of Bukowski's autobiographical fragments, he fashioned a universal fable about the power and penalty that come from fuelling your life with the stuff of dreams.

The germ of this approach was there in Bukowski, but it was Deruddere's use of the tropes of the 'film fantastique' that set this notion free and is most obvious in the last third of the film. The scene where the two drunken men discover the body is pure horror movie – but in the European tradition; it is Mario Bava – or better still Jean Rollin – rather than George

Romero. The lighting and tone palette capture the stillness of early morning when the fragile darkness has yet to be broken by the light of dawn: *the hour between dog and wolf*. Then there is the hearse. Like Dracula's carriage, it waits for lost travellers on the road. These are almost archetypal images; the deserted city, the fog, the haloed street lamp, the wet cobblestones – the essential elements of Belgian surrealism.

The Bukowskian mood is re-established when the two men steal the body. There is a sense of inevitability but also of transgressive joy about the act. They have shattered nearly all the codes of accepted behaviour in the course of their rundown lives: now they are going to break the final taboo. They take the body to Bill's squat. But rather than an empty warehouse or derelict tenement, we find ourselves entering a contemporary take on the gothic castle, wreathed in pale green mists and surrounded by wild woods. This might not make the necrophilia that follows any less 'shocking', but it places it in a context where the sad poetry of the situation confronts us first, rather than the transgressiveness of the act.

The ambience that Deruddere creates so skillfully in the film allows him to get away with things that might have been howlingly pretentious if they were not bathed in the light of the fantastic. The creative tension between Bukowski's raw portrayal of life's losers and the fantasy treatment allows Deruddere to deal in archetypes and symbols without once ever seeming precious or falling prey to the kind of tweeness that sometimes affects the European literary art movie (Jeroen Krabbé's *De Ontdekking van de Hemel* (*The Discovery of Heaven*, 2001) is a good example).

In Deruddere's film, the figure of Harry Voss comes to assume the epic aspects of the heroes of classical tragedy. There is a kind of cosmic inevitability about his fate. In a sense he is born in that moment when the bright shaft of mystical sunlight pierces the womblike chamber of the Princess's thoughts. Freud said that all men are trying to get back inside their mother, and that is certainly Harry's trajectory in the film. It is no accident that it takes 21 years – traditionally the age of maturity – for him to find his princess/mother again and possess her in the flesh, just as his purloining of the black-and-white still had dictated he would. The film he watched as a child planted a seed in Harry's head that took 21 years to flower.

If the film's opening sets in motion the rolling stone of inevitability, the ending is a perfect closure. For where else could Harry's journey conclude but in the sea – the eternally cleansing and nurturing womb of the world? The sea has an important place in the Low Countries tradition of the fantastic. Jean Ray's *Malpertuis* reeks of the salty air of Antwerp's docks. Many of his stories are related by sailors returning from long voyages. Most of Kümel's *Daughters of Darkness* takes place in a huge, deserted hotel in Ostend. It is a kind of end of the line for everyone in it. And before these, there was the masterpiece of late Belgian surrealism, *Monsieur Fantomas* (Ernst Moerman, 1937) with its delirious beach scenes. The sea perfectly illustrates the seemingly opposed aspects of the Low Countries' fantastic tradition: the real that reveals the unreal. The unavoidable physicality of the sea, its wetness, its distinctive smell and taste, is somehow combined with the dark and deep mystery of the endless oceans where, lost in its vastness, sailors fall prey to irresolvable fantasies about sea creatures and mysterious, uncharted lands.

Deruddere was well aware of the tradition into which he was pitching his film. In interviews he defended himself from charges of gloominess with the remark that: 'Well, I'm Belgian. We have a taste for that kind of surrealist symbolism.' This may have been interpreted as a form of jokey defence. But Deruddere was quite serious when later acknowledging that the film was a fairytale and consciously used the traditional structure of such narratives. Fairytales are often journeys. We venture into the dark wood without really knowing what we are doing. On the way we learn about ourselves and pick up, by accident, things that help us to make sense of the journey and to triumph when we reach the end. In Harry's case, we are in a kind of 'anti-fairytale': his journey is a circular one. Everything he experiences seems to force him further towards the abyss of his doomed desires. Even his higher thoughts – his poetry – only serve to make him seem ridiculous and, finally, to identify him as a thief. Life seems to hold out promise for him – like the hot-blooded Italian mother in Part One. But when it comes down to it, she is just a drunk, asleep in a state of undress – not Sleeping Beauty in her enchanted cottage in the woods.

Women are the source of Harry's dreams. They inspire and nurture fantasy – like his mother's tales of her romantic courtship. But they are also perfidious. 'Why did you lie to me?' Harry asks his mother. 'Because you're so young', she tells him. The girl that Harry's friend sets him up with is happy enough to accommodate him in the back of a car, but is repulsed by his physical appearance. This last episode is filmed like a horror movie, with Harry advancing on the girl like a stalking monster. It is the kind of scene that makes explicit the film's particular debt to fantastic cinema. It acknowledges that it draws on the same source as all good horror films: sex; the fascination of it, the fear of it; a boy's adolescent anxiety that his need for sex makes him somehow monstrous and that women will never accept this.

But of course, there's always another view. In the film this is represented by the 'best friend'. In Part One, the older boy's straightforward approach to sex seems healthy and matter of fact. However, his gift to Harry of the secret of masturbation serves as yet another curse, pushing the younger boy ever more profoundly into the world of the watcher rather than the doer. In Part Two, Harry's friend, whom we know to be more experienced with women, assures him that girls do not care about physical appearance. In a scene as subtle as any in the film, Deruddere undercuts this sensible advice when Harry first approaches the lovely Lisa. Although she is momentarily repulsed by his pock-marked face, the brief smile she gives is genuine enough. But Harry cannot see that. All he sees is the handsome jock who gets to the girl first.

In Harry's world, real girls do not see through his hideous mask. But why should he care? He does not need real girls. For him there is only one woman; the woman who never existed; the woman of his dreams – the woman of his film. Finally, when there is nowhere else to go, he steps over the line that divides dream from reality and there she is, waiting for him. Perfectly preserved in death – because, of course, she never existed in life in the first place. After that realisation, there is only one course of action left for Harry. His life is at an end. In fact, it was already over when he first fell in love with the beautiful, but lifeless, Princess all those years ago. As he enters the sea, Harry finally enters the world of dreams through the door opened up by the childhood film. The titles that announced *The End* right at the beginning of the film were not just a fancy cinematic trick. They were a premonition and an on-screen warning.

As already noted, *Crazy Love* was picked up for distribution in the US and the resulting good notices brought Deruddere a number of offers to work in Hollywood. Aware that the strength of his first film came from its careful appropriation of familiar cultural flavours, he was wary of invitations to work overseas, where he would be on much less recognisable territory. The only offer he accepted was from Francis Ford Coppola, who was keen to film a story by the writer John Fante, *Wait Until Spring, Bandini*. Deruddere had the same idea. And he had already acquired the rights to the book and completed an adaptation of it. By chance, an acquaintance of Deruddere's sent the script to Coppola. He took a look at *Crazy Love*, liked it and suggested a collaboration on the new film. With Coppola's influence things began to change. Names became attached to the project and it transformed into the kind of big-budget Hollywood project that Deruddere had been avoiding.

The film was released in 1989 and proved to be a commercial failure. It was another five years before Deruddere began work on another feature film. This time it was very much as a hired hand on a project set up by British novelist and comedy writer Charlie Higson. The film, *Suite 16* (1994), was a Belgian/Dutch/UK co-production starring Peter Postlethwaite. Controversial for its use of sex and violence, it received a number of negative and vitriolic reviews before vanishing from sight. Aware of the fact that his first film had succeeded *because* of its Belgian background rather than in spite of it, Deruddere decided to revisit his home territory. He fashioned a script that could be made very quickly and cheaply in real locations. The result, *Hombres Complicados*, was shot over thirteen days in 1997. It was very much a personal project – a recharging of the batteries – that united some of the same team as *Crazy Love*. A couple of years later several of them returned to the fold one more time for Deruddere's fifth feature film. A satire on the world of showbiz, *Iedereen Beroemd!* (*Everybody Famous!*) was released in 2000 and was nominated for an Academy Award as Best Foreign Feature.

Like *Crazy Love*, the film deals with the spaces that exist between dreams and reality. However, here the world it depicts is that of a camp, kitschy television show and the mood is one of gently ironic parody rather than horror movie fatalism. The background to the story is once more the lower-middle-class Belgium that Deruddere grew up in and he seems very much at home with the material. He claimed that, like *Crazy Love*, the film deals with the impossibility of having our dreams come true. And that this 'longing for something you can't have', while a universal human trait, is perhaps most keenly felt in Belgium with its fractured sense of identity.

Can an artist whose best work so obviously draws on a nuanced sense of cultural tradition find a subject that can do that and still have the universal appeal that is needed for a commercial hit? That is the dilemma for Dominique Deruddere and in a way it is the dilemma for all Belgian filmmakers. In a market that is not large enough to support an indigenous film industry, is the only way forward to make films that ignore that cultural background and try to compete with the mass appeal of Hollywood? That is one approach, but it is pretty much a doomed one given the greater firepower of the US product.

The last few years have seen a number of films gain wide distribution from countries that had formerly been considered outside the loop of commercial productions: Argentina, Mexico and Thailand. All of them shared a common thread in that they used genre conventions (the road movie, thriller, western) which they reinvigorated by injecting them with local colour. In a sense this is what Dominique Deruddere did with the fantasy imagery of *Crazy Love*. And in doing so he revived a tradition (the Low Countries fantasy genre) that was in danger of disappearing. Given that tradition's unique ability to invoke a very specific Low Countries cultural identity, it seems strange that it is been allowed once more to languish on the sidelines. Let us hope it is only a matter of time before another adventurous Belgian filmmaker picks up this particular gauntlet and runs with it.

Pete Tombs

SPOORLOOS THE VANISHING

GEORGE SLUIZER, THE NETHERLANDS, 1988

Het Gouden Ei (*The Golden Egg*), a best-selling novel published in 1984 by Dutch journalist and author Tim Krabbé, serves as the source material for director George Sluizer's highly acclaimed 1988 thriller, *Spoorloos* (*The Vanishing*). Both book and film tell the story of Rex Hofman (played by Gene Bervoets in the latter text), a young Dutchman whose girlfriend Saskia (Johanna ter Steege) mysteriously disappears at a gas station in central France, while the couple are on vacation. Obsessed with finding out what happened to her, and tormented by the memory of her loss, Rex single-handedly launches an international missing-persons campaign that completely takes over his life.

Years later, long after the trail has gone cold and the police have closed the case, Rex still scours the countryside out of guilt and as a tribute to Saskia, alienating and eventually losing his new girlfriend in the process. When Saskia's unlikely abductor, a French chemistry teacher named Raymond Lemorne (Bernard-Pierre Donnadieu) who just happens to be a sociopath, turns up with an offer to tell Rex everything if only he will agree in advance to undergo the exact same experience as his girlfriend, Rex hesitantly agrees. This is because, for Rex, the worst thing of all is 'not knowing'. Raymond explains that he did indeed kill Saskia, not for sexual or personal reasons, but merely because he wanted to find out if he was capable of committing such an evil act. Rex willingly takes a sedative, and in the film's (and the book's) penultimate scene, awakens to find himself buried alive inside a narrow coffin. 'Now he knew. It was too awful to know.' *Spoorloos* ends with a slow zoom-in on a newspaper headline concerning the mysterious 'double vanishing' of Rex and Saskia, while Raymond sits contemplatively at his cottage, his unsuspecting wife watering the plants which mark the couple's otherwise anonymous graves.

Sluizer's filmmaking career began in the late 1950s, when he served as assistant director on Bert Haanstra's popular Dutch comedy entitled *Fanfare* (1958). From the 1960s up through the 1980s he produced and directed a number of documentaries and television specials. He also worked as a producer on such highly-regarded films as Werner Herzog's *Fitzcarraldo* (1982) and Rudolf van den Berg's *Bastille* (1984). In 1961 he directed a short documentary, *Hold Back the Sea*, which won a Silver Bear award at the Berlin Film Festival. Ten years later he wrote and directed his first feature, a Dutch/Brazilian co-production entitled *João en het mes* (*Joao and the Knife*, 1971), which was followed in 1979 by *Twee vrouwen* (*Twice a Woman*). Though highly regarded in Holland, no one could have predicted either the amount or the degree of praise that would be lavished upon Sluizer after the release of *The Vanishing*. At the 1988 Nederlands Filmfestival, the director picked up the prestigious Dutch Film Critics Award. Later that evening, his entry won the Golden Calf Award for Best Feature. The Americans too were impressed with Sluizer, 'whose direction', *New York Times* reviewer Janet Maslin wrote at the time, 'has the spooky precision of non-fiction crime writing.'

Sluizer was not the only one to earn kudos for *The Vanishing*. At the 1988 European Film Awards, ter Steege won Best Supporting Actress for her role as Saskia. Donnadieu was lauded for his 'sterling performance' as Raymond, one in which he was held to 'create a credible, chilly fusion of humanistic and sociopathic impulses'. And Bervoets was praised by numerous critics for making Rex strong 'even in the face of unbearable strain'. Such unanimously positive response led to the film's being optioned to Twentieth Century Fox. Five years later, in 1993, Sluizer himself directed a big-budget remake (released as *The Vanishing*) which was severely dumbed-down as a result of studio interference and a misguided desire on the parts of the studio heads to make the original more accessible and appealing to American audiences.

Unlike the remake, the screenplay of which was significantly altered by a Hollywood script doctor, *The Vanishing* is faithful to Krabbé's novel, with Sluizer adapting the story with assistance from the author himself (the two share writing credits). The main differences between the book and the film can be summarised as follows: first of all, *The Vanishing* has a more complicated plotline than *The Golden Egg*, one that is filled with flashbacks and temporal ellipses as well as dramatic shifts in character focus. As *Washington Post* critic Hal Hinson noted shortly after *The Vanishing*'s US release in January 1991, 'the film's narrative structure, which tells the film's story from two points of view – the perpetrator's and the victim's – is complex, but the facts are straightforward.' (*The Golden Egg* also 'tells the same story from two points of view', but the narrative structure is definitely less complex than that of *The Vanishing*, perhaps because the book is so short – just 103 pages.) Second, in *The Vanishing*, Rex and Raymond spend more time together than in *The Golden Egg*, and as a result of this interaction both men discover that they share a certain sensibility; there is more than a hint of mutual, albeit unacknowledged, homosexual desire in their verbal exchanges. Although it is true that in Krabbé's novel a subtle 'doubling' is effected between Rex and Raymond – for example, we learn that both men get spontaneous, non-sexual erections when they are excited, and both men have advanced knowledge of the sciences – this doubling does not carry the erotic charge provided by their interactions in the film. Finally, in *The Golden Egg*, we learn that Raymond shot and killed two hitchhikers as a prelude to his kidnapping and murder of Saskia, a fact which serves to render him more conventional – and therefore less compelling – than he is in *The Vanishing*.

By revealing the killer's identity less than a third of the way through the film, *The Vanishing* forces viewers to ask questions about the how, what and why of Saskia's disappearance, rather than about the typically all-important *who*. As Roger Ebert puts it, 'the film's unusual structure … builds suspense even while it seems to be telling us almost everything we want to know'. This is the case because the one thing *The Vanishing* does *not* tell us, at least not until it is too late, is exactly what happened to Saskia after her abduction. It is precisely this dramatic shift in hermeneutic code effected by Sluizer and Krabbé that led many reviewers – especially those in the United States and Britain – to characterise the film as manifestly 'Hitchcockian' in nature. As Steve Murray writes, 'remember [Hitchcock's] decision to reveal Kim Novak's true identity midway through *Vertigo*? *The Vanishing* is less interested in giving you a quick jolt than in planting seeds of unease that continue to sprout long after you leave the theatre.' Another critic at the time offered the following comparison: 'there's a clinicism … in Sluizer's methods; he lays out the story … dispassionately, as if he were dissecting a frog. And yet his style seems supple, and not the least bit mechanical. His work is like that of a slightly more laconic, slightly more intellectualised Hitchcock – Hitchcock in a beret.' For the most part, though, such references to the Master of Suspense indicated not so much an interest in reading *The Vanishing* as an auteurist text than an effort at sidestepping difficult questions about the film's generic status by making 'Hitchcock' a genre in its own right. In fact, British and American reviewers (as well as scholars) have consistently, even insistently, analysed *The Vanishing* in generic terms, if only to highlight Sluizer's innovative 'take' on mainstream/Hollywood horror, thriller and suspense conventions.

So, for example, Marion Pilowsky offered that *The Vanishing* 'represents one of the most extraordinary realisations of the psychological thriller captured on film', the superlative 'extraordinary realisation' a near-oxymoron which serves to simultaneously mark the film's distinctiveness from *and* conformity with an established tradition of thriller cinema. Similarly, Ebert states that Sluizer's film 'is a thriller, but in a different way than most thrillers. It is a thriller about knowledge – about what the characters know about the disappearance, and what they know about themselves. [Its] plot … makes you realise how simplistic many suspense films really are.' In a recent essay, meanwhile, Kevin Sweeney proposes to 'discuss the film's nature as a horror film, paying attention to why it should be considered as such even though several respected theories of cinematic horror would exclude it from such a classification'. Sweeney's sensitivity to the question of *The Vanishing*'s generic status is signaled by his awareness of the problems involved in labeling it a horror film. But even while acknowledging the virtues of his subsequent argument, one can identify a symptomatic flaw in his stated aim: if the only or best way to prove that *The Vanishing* is indeed a horror film is to discuss its underlying 'nature' in contrast to those surface (presumably generic) features that have led 'several respected theories of cinematic horror [to] exclude it from such a classification', then the most it seems Sweeney could even hope to show is that *The Vanishing* is *horrifying*, not that it is a *horror film* as the term is conventionally understood.

At the other extreme, and none too surprisingly, the Dutch film community elected not to read *The Vanishing* as a genre picture at all, stressing instead its unique 'artistic' and 'intellectual' merits. In The Hague's own annual survey of Dutch releases, for example, Sluizer's film is held to 'succeed without star actors, sex, horror or sensational speedboat stunts in the canals of Amsterdam. Instead it offers a chilling plot … well-timed doses of humour and some memorable observations on an age in which romanticism has given way to cold cynicism. The film does not provide mindless entertainment and Sluizer demands some intellectual effort from his audiences.' (The reference to 'sensational speedboat stunts in the canals of Amsterdam' is a sly dig at Dick Maas' serial-killer film, *Amsterdamned*, 1987.) As Krabbé himself has stated, 'I've never thought of … *Spoorloos* as belonging to any genre, and I certainly didn't mean it to belong to any. I know nothing about the horror genre.'

The reason why such a domestic response is none too surprising is explained in part by Joke Hermes. In a discussion of recent Dutch television crime series prior to the late 1980s, she notes that 'virtually all television fiction and feature film production [in the Netherlands] … resisted the idea that to follow a generic formula could lead to a quality product'. Hermes explains this resistance primarily in terms of 'the enduring sensitivity of the Dutch to the high–low culture divide. … Genre is associated with cheap American mass-produced fiction. Not something that one would want to make or could make for that matter with money funded by the Dutch government.' If generic convention was largely eschewed in Dutch cinema for its low-culture connotations, however, it is also the case that Dutch filmmakers of the time were ill-equipped to make successful genre pictures at home, much less abroad, and not just because of a relative lack of financial backing. One consequence of the Dutch film academy's preference for European art and auteurist product – its emphasis on traditional, romantic notions of artistic originality and innovation – was that it did not focus on the instruction of genre codes and conventions.

Things have changed following the blockbuster successes of Dutch directors such as Paul Verhoeven (*Total Recall* (1990), *Basic Instinct* (1992), *Starship Troopers* (1997)) and Jan de Bont (*Speed* (1994), *Twister* (1996)) in America, and the realisation by Dutch producers that 'genre rules are not to be looked down on but to be used inventively' in order to ensure larger and more reliable audiences. But even after a recent tax-incentive scheme introduced by the Dutch Ministry of Finance to encourage private investors – foreign as well as local – to invest in Dutch film production, judging from the major international releases of the past several years (*Antonia* (*Antonia's Line*, 1995), *Karakter* (*Character*, 1997) and *Twee koffers vol* (*Left Luggage*, 1998)), it would seem that Dutch filmmakers still have far less interest in utilising generic conventions than their Hollywood counterparts.

Despite its surface adherence to the mystery/horror/suspense form, and its international promotion and reception as a paradigmatic example of Hitchcockian moviemaking, *The Vanishing*'s plaintive score, melodramatic tone and focus on subjectivity rather than detection all serve to make the film extremely difficult to analyse in traditional generic terms. Instead of forcing it into a preexisting and loosely defined category, or alternatively, interpreting it as an idiosyncratic and wholly unique auteurist text, Sluizer's picture shows much similarity to a tradition or cycle of distinctively Dutch 'thrillers', all of which possess an essentially national, culturally specific dimension. Other entries in this cycle include Paul Verhoeven's *De Vierde man* (*The Fourth Man*, 1983), Dick Maas' *De Lift* (*The Lift*, 1983) and *Amsterdamned* (1987) and, to some extent, Marleen Gorris' *Gebroken spiegels* (*Broken Mirrors*, 1984). Despite their specific incorporation of conventions from otherwise disparate genres, and the undeniable presence of auteurist elements in each of them, it is possible to identify an underlying thematic preoccupation across all of these films: namely, the male protagonist's severe anxiety about being bound to a female partner in a normatively-constituted/determined relationship, with the expectation or reality of marriage and all that this legal and social institution entails – monogamy, heterosexuality and life-long commitment. As with other European genre-like films we might hold that Dutch thriller cinema, of which *The Vanishing* is a key example, is not so much a genre as a body of films that resists definition as a genre. Yet at the same time, the Dutch thriller can be understood as a coherent set of texts open for theorisation, study and criticism.

In *The Vanishing*, Rex's apprehension about committing to a lifelong partnership with his girlfriend, as well as his own repressed/unconscious homosexual inclinations, are only revealed by the text *indirectly*. These aspects of Rex's personality thus form part of *The Vanishing*'s implicit meaning. On the surface, the film tells the story of Rex's obsessive, life-consuming quest to unravel the mystery behind his girlfriend's disappearance, his psychological refusal to break the vow he made to Saskia – to never abandon her, no matter what. A closer look at some of the film's dialogue, characterisation and *mise-en-scène*, however, indicates that, at a deeper level, this is actually a story about Rex's *inability* to obtain release from his commitment to Saskia, and to normative heterosexuality more generally.

The underlying tension in Rex and Saskia's relationship is evident from the very beginning of the film, as the couple bicker about seemingly trivial matters while driving towards their holiday destination. Throughout the opening scenes, Rex's insecurity with his masculinity is revealed through the harsh, clumsy manner in which he seeks to impose his will upon Saskia, while simultaneously (and for the same reason) attempting to force her into the role of member of the 'weaker' sex. So, for example, when Saskia states that 'I'm just looking at the gas meter', Rex snaps 'You just look in your mirror', implying that Saskia should be more like 'normal' women: vain, unconcerned with practical matters, and focused on their own image rather than the world around them. After teaching her some words in French – the master/pupil dynamic clearly feeding his ego and sense of control over the relationship – he orders Saskia to 'peel me an orange'. And when they run out of gas in the middle of a dark tunnel, Rex yells at Saskia not to be hysterical, assuming a stereotypically feminine irrational response on her part even though she makes the perfectly reasonable point that 'I'm not hysterical – I'm scared.' Knowing very well how frightened she is, Rex proceeds to leave her all alone in the tunnel in order to locate the nearest gas station. It is here that the first real cracks in Rex's psyche begin to show, as his temporary abandonment of Saskia can be interpreted as much as an unacknowledged (and ultimately unsatisfiable) desire to run away from his relationship as an effort to do the 'manly' thing and solve the problem at hand.

A little while later, after the couple take a break from driving and make up with each other at a rest stop, Saskia pressures Rex into swearing that he will never abandon her again. It is crucial to note that Saskia has to effectively put the words in Rex's mouth, straddling him on the ground and commanding him to 'repeat after me'. She then proceeds to force-feed him the lines as he squirms beneath her. One might compare Saskia with Verhoeven's femme fatale Christine Halsslag (Renée Soutendijk) in *The Fourth Man* insofar as both women are depicted as capable of binding the men in their life under virtual spells from which there is no means of (healthy) escape. *The Vanishing* is a more 'realistic' text than *The Fourth Man*, however, and so the vow of 'till death do us part' is rendered by Sluizer in psychological and emotional rather than paranormal or supernatural terms: instead of dying under mysterious circumstances or suffering from threatening hallucinatory visions (like Gerard in Verhoeven's film), Rex lets his new girlfriend Lieneke (Gwen Eckhaus) walk out on him because he is constitutionally incapable of breaking his prior commitment to Saskia. Here it is worth pointing out that the 'Golden Egg' of the book's title is a reference to a nightmare of Saskia's about being trapped in a golden egg, all alone, floating through space forever.

If we take Rex's various separations from the women in his life (Saskia physically, Lieneke emotionally) as forming a pattern, one that indicates a desire on his part to break free from long-term heterosexual relationships, then Rex's meetings with Raymond later in the film begin to take on the aspect of a homosocial, perhaps even homosexual, courtship. While waiting for Raymond to show up for their prearranged rendezvous at a Nîmes café, Rex confides to Lieneke, 'Do you know what I'm afraid of? That he stops sending postcards.' Abstracted from the literal narrative context, in which Rex pursues Raymond solely in order to find out what happened to Saskia, the above confession makes Rex sound very much like a man in love and frightened of being abandoned by his beloved; he thus adopts a traditional 'feminine' position relative to Raymond, one that is analogous to Saskia's position relative to Rex earlier in the film.

Raymond, meanwhile, seems to relish playing the role of masculine initiator in his interactions with Rex. Despite being even more firmly entrenched in a committed, long-term heterosexual relationship than his pursuer (he is married with two daughters, and is every bit the faithful family man), there is an important sense in which Raymond is more 'out' than Rex, insofar as he carefully orchestrates the entire sequence of events which will result in the development of a powerful homosocial bond between the two men. During their first face-to-face encounter approximately two-thirds of the way through the film, Raymond tells Rex that 'I thought a lot about our meeting. … Right from the start I felt the need to see you. When you left the café at Nîmes, I realised I couldn't wait any longer.' And when revealing the means by which he came to abduct Saskia at the rest stop three years earlier, Raymond interprets his seemingly random choice of victims as a clear indication that he and Rex were fated to meet: 'Destiny, Mr. Hofman.' Raymond thereby reduces Saskia's significance in the narrative to her function as a bridge between him and Rex; this is in line with observations concerning the gender asymmetry of erotic love triangles in European fiction by René Girard and, more recently, Eve Kosofsky Sedgwick. Discussing Girard's early book, *Deceit, Desire, and the Novel*, Sedgwick writes that, 'What is most interesting … [is] that, in any erotic rivalry, the bond that links the two rivals is as intense and potent as the bond that links either of the rivals to the beloved; that the bonds of "rivalry" and "love", differently as they are experienced, are equally powerful and in many ways equivalent.'

By far the most loaded conversation between Raymond and Rex takes place during their lengthy ride together to Raymond's cottage, where he has admitted to taking Saskia after kidnapping her. At one point, the pair stop by a park to stretch their legs – a seemingly innocuous activity that is strange in and of itself, considering how long Rex has been waiting to find Raymond and how desperate he is to find out what happened to Saskia. Their awkward exchange in the park, filled as it is with coded references, bilingual word play and flirtatious banter, actually sounds more like a first date between potential lovers than a civil conversation between long-time adversaries. Aware that Rex was once an amateur cyclist, Raymond – a Frenchman – attempts to show off his knowledge of the sport by mentioning a popular Dutch biker named 'Zoltemeque', saying that 'it sounds like a Mexican god, not Dutch.' Rex, however, is unmoved, noting that Raymond pronounced the name wrong: 'Zoltemeque' is really 'Zoetemelk,' a word which, as Rex explains, means 'sweet milk'. Raymond replies, 'Mr Sweetmilk. Some weird names you have there.' Though he does not elaborate, he seems to be alluding to the fact that this male Dutch name possesses distinctly feminine connotations. Instead of taking offense or reacting homophobically, Rex for his part offers up what he takes to be a similarly 'weird' Dutch name: 'Naaktgeboren. Born naked.' In a clear echo of the film's opening scene, in which Rex playfully taught Saskia some words in French, Rex now begins teaching Raymond some words in Dutch, a lesson which culminates in 'Dodeman: Mrs Deadman. Marriage produces some strange combinations.' At a level that is not merely linguistic, Rex is here calling attention to the fact that, at least where he comes from, being married can also mean being dead.

Not to be outdone, Raymond recalls that, 'In the Nîmes phonebook, there's someone called Mr Poof.' Although French marital laws do not dictate that the groom takes the bride's last name, following the logic of the conversation it would seem that the man in the Nîmes phonebook became a 'poof' (slang in English for an effeminate homosexual) upon getting married. Despite the manifest animosity Rex has been expressing towards Raymond up until now, he clearly finds this amusing, and a small smile breaks out across his face – perhaps the first time he has smiled since Saskia's disappearance. The *mise-en-scène* here is quite telling: in the background, Raymond is standing on the bars of a jungle gym, arms spread wide apart to stay balanced, his body vulnerable and receptive; while in the foreground, Rex is standing with his back to Raymond, hands in pockets. Unlike his relationship with Saskia, in which he was the dominating partner, here Rex plays a more passive role, allowing himself to be 'seduced' by the more open and aggressive Raymond. Before heading off, Rex responds to Raymond's latest comment with the words, 'Yes … Poof.'

Back in the car, Rex asks Raymond if he raped Saskia. Raymond replies, 'Come on, Mr Hofman,' as if even the mere suggestion of such a crime is an insult to his character. Although Rex drops the issue here, it is not clear why he does so. After all, Raymond is a self-described sociopath, and his answer is far from unambiguous. The possibility of rape arises again when Raymond tells Rex what will have to take place if he ever wants to find out what happened to Saskia: 'I'm going to drug you, and after that you'll experience exactly what she experienced.' When Rex rejects this plan as ridiculous, Raymond tries to tempt him by asking, 'What about the uncertainty? The eternal not knowing? That's the worst thing, Mr. Hofman.' Although on the surface level of the text, this is all in reference to Saskia's fate, at the level of implicit meaning, the 'uncertainty' and 'eternal not knowing' can be taken as referring to Rex's repressed homo-erotic impulses; in keeping with the underlying thematic of Dutch thriller cinema, it is the prospect of these impulses remaining repressed (or else being re-repressed), rather than their emergence in the form of a monster, that is held to be 'the worst thing'.

This is reinforced by the film's conclusion. After a lengthy internal debate, Rex finally musters up the nerve to put himself completely at Raymond's mercy, drinking the drugged coffee and allowing himself to be manhandled the same way Saskia was. Of course Saskia had no choice in the matter, whereas Rex consciously elects to be 'initiated' into Raymond's secret world. In the penultimate scene, Rex awakens to find himself buried alive inside a pitch-black wooden coffin. It would be too easy to attribute the power of this disturbing and memorable climax to Rex's realisation that he is doomed, left for dead with no hope of sur-vival. Metaphorically and implicitly speaking, Rex ends up trapped not so much in a coffin as in the closet, while the true nature and depth of Raymond's monstrousness is revealed: despite the freedom he initially grants Rex from normative (monogamous and life-long) heterosexual commitment, by burying the couple side-by-side in his garden he ultimately binds the young man to his girlfriend for all eternity.

The last scene of the film slowly zooms in on a newspaper headline announcing the 'mysterious double vanishing' of Rex and Saskia; the background then fades to black as the oval (egg-shaped) headshots of the couple stand alone, isolated from one another yet together forever. Thus, even while reinforcing its status as a paradigmatic Dutch thriller, *The Vanishing*'s ending brilliantly succeeds in showcasing Sluizer's talents as a filmmaker capable of inscribing a taut, gripping narrative with a lyrical, even dreamlike sensibility.

Steven Jay Schneider

A WOPBOPALOOBOP A LOPBAMBOOM

ANDY BAUSCH, LUXEMBOURG, 1989

Although the Grand Duchy of Luxembourg had its first cinematograph screenings in 1896 and shot its first moving pictures (after those by a Lumière brothers cameraman in 1899) in 1904, the Luxembourg film industry remained virtually non-existent until the beginning of the 1990s. The only professional filmmakers to establish themselves in Luxembourg were two directors, René Leclère in the 1930s and Philippe Schneider from 1946 to 1979, both of whom produced tourism and corporate-sponsored documentaries. In the 1980s, without any organised structure, a handful of amateurs started making 16mm feature films in *lëtzebuergesch* (luxembourgish, the national language). Two of these films met with resounding success. The first, called *Congé fir e Mord* (*Holiday for a Murder*) was filmed by teachers in 1983. The second was *Troublemaker* by Andy Bausch.

A young, self-taught filmmaker, Bausch began to make films in 1977, driven by a passion for cinema. He started on Super-8 before switching to 16mm, shooting short films that dealt with youth, rock, drugs and homosexuality. His work brought a breath of fresh air to the somewhat stuffy amateur Luxembourg filmmaking scene. His technique was crude and his plot structures were almost always chaotic, but among his novice actors was a certain Thierry Van Werveke whose presence was to make him Bausch's favourite actor. Werveke began by playing a small role in *Gwyncilla, Legend of Dark Ages*, Bausch's ambitious first 16mm feature film, about a troubadour in the Middle Ages in search of a mysterious young girl who is the love child of a count and a fairy. Filmed in black-and-white in German in 1985, *Gwyncilla* displayed, as the short film *One-Reel Picture Show* had in 1984, the director's unmistakable visual style. Unfortunately, the film was not a great success in the Grand Duchy, forcing Bausch to change tack and revert back to the more popular style he had employed in a number of his short films. In 1987, *Troublemaker* was released. Filming had started in August 1986, but had to be postponed for a year, due to lack of money. It was not until June 1987 that assistance from the regional German television channel Saarländischer Rundfunk enabled the production to begin again. Shot on 16mm (and later converted to 35mm for distribution) the film tells the story of two young crooks fresh out of prison who immediately hatch a new scheme. They need money to make their dream of going to America come true. Chuck Moreno (Ender Frings) and especially Johnny Chicago (Van Werveke) won over the public, as a pair of good-natured but rather dim dreamers, always willing to jump into jobs that inevitably resulted in failure. Van Werveke, in particular, made his physically- and intellectually-challenged character a destructive, but lovable rogue. A number of German technicians (including director of photography Klaus Peter Weber) lent their expertise to the film with the result that, despite its shortcomings in content and form, it looked rather more professional than anything else previously seen in Luxembourg. *Troublemaker*'s openly coarse Luxembourgish dialogue peppered with often juicy expressions stood out against the media landscape of the time, which was still dominated by a more formal televisual language and syntax, and played a major role in the success of the film, which attracted audience figures of 15,000 when it was first released locally, going on to achieve the status of a popular cult film.

In January 1989, while riding high on the success of *Troublemaker* and supported this time by a German co-producer (Frankfurter Filmproduction co-produced the film for the German channel ZDF) even though there was still no real support forthcoming from the Luxembourg government (except for an equivalent of 20,000 euros from the Cultural Fond), Bausch began filming *A Wopbopaloobop a Lopbamboom*. Once again, he worked with German technicians and because of the nature of his financial support, hired a number of German actors (Birol Uenel, Sabine Berg and Jochen Senf). He combined these with Luxembourgish actors, including Van Werveke, in addition to Serge Wolf (France) and national star Désirée Nosbusch, who two years previously had appeared in Paolo and Vittorio Taviani's *Good Morning Babylon* (1987). *A Wopbopaloobop a Lopbamboom*, shot in black-and-white on 16mm, cost a total of 14 million Luxembourg francs (approximately 347,000 euros).

Just like the heroes in *Troublemaker*, *A Wop…*'s Rocco (Birol Uenel) is fresh out of prison and dreams of leaving Luxembourg, perhaps to go to America. However, he first stops off in Dudelange, a town on the Luxembourg-French border, to pick up some money and see his girlfriend Vero (Désirée Nosbusch). The date is 31 December 1962 and that night, the paths of several characters cross, with unexpected results. Rocco's brother, Hartmut (Conny Scheel), loves Vero, but does not dare tell her. Erwinn (Nicolas Lansky), Anke (Sabine Berg) and Bruno (Jochen Senf) are planning the job of a lifetime. Petz (Van Werveke), Vero's brother, and his friends get drunk to forget their impending national service and in the course of the night are confronted by a group of French men, who came over to pick up Luxembourg girls. When Vero falls for the charms of shy French Daniel (Serge Wolf), Petz intervenes and the evening takes a tragic turn. Petz stabs Daniel to death and Rocco's hopes and dreams quickly disappear. He leaves in the early hours of the morning, this time for good.

The 1960s are Bausch's favourite period. In *Troublemaker*, a character criticises the two heroes for hankering after a time they did not even know. The same thing could be said of the director who, born in 1959, could hardly remember the period he constantly returns to. He paints a romantic picture of the age, much of it informed by the freewheeling cinema of that time.

The archive shots seen during the opening titles of *A Wop...* show farmers working in their fields, with an iron and steel works in the background. Fanfares play, athletes race each other, football players pose before the match, swimsuit-clad women laugh at a poolside, people jostle each other in an open-air clearance sale, and a bouquet is placed at the foot of a monument. The older Luxembourg audience, in particular the inhabitants of Dudelange, would recognise the people and places. For everyone else, these images simply imply the peaceful contentment of bygone days when everyone seemed to know their place. Placed as they are at the beginning of the film, they serve as an ironic counterpoint to the story that follows.

From the opening lines of dialogue, the apparent idealism of the period is swept away by the red dust so characteristic of the Minett region of Luxembourg. This region, of which Dudelange (Andy Bausch's birthplace) is one of the main towns, owes its name to the iron ore that used to be mined there and gave the Grand Duchy its wealth, well before international banking dominated its economy. At the beginning of the film, a grain of red dust flies into Daniel's eye and momentarily blinds him, a bad omen of things to come. Later, the factory dust makes Vero's father cough and we are told of a worker who lost a limb in a factory accident. After the 'red eye' sequence, the film shifts to a reminder of what used to be an everyday ritual in industrial towns and a subtle reference to the Lumière brothers' short: workers leaving the factory. It was Bausch's way of paying tribute to the glorious history of the Luxembourgish (and immigrant) working class who worked in the iron and steel industry sacrificing their health for the good of the country. If Luxembourg has a national legend, this is it. And Bausch, who prides himself of shooting 'typically Luxembourgish' films, has made it one of his favourite themes. It was a central theme he returned to in *Le club des chômeurs* (2001), be it with much less impressive effect.

In *A Wop...*, Bausch manages to combine this virtually mythical representation of the Minett with imagery and themes taken straight from American cinema. Rocco is a mysterious character (neither the audience nor the other characters ever know exactly where he has spent the last few months) who is both familiar and foreign to Dudelange and always slightly distanced from the other protagonists. He resembles a lone cowboy from a western, carrying with him the portent of tragedy. Bausch even employed one of the dominant themes of Wild West legend: the frontier. The first and last times we see Rocco, he is passing through customs between France and Luxembourg. Birol Uenel, who played Rocco, resembled James Dean, and a quality not too dis-similar to the leather-clad rebel look of Marlon Brando.

Bausch is at his best when inspired by a specific genre. His first short, *One-Reel Picture Show*, was influenced directly by the German expressionist cinema. In *A Wop...*, Anke, a beautiful woman yearning for the good life, is willing to steal from her boss to flee the town with her lover. The character is straight out of *film noir* and is complemented by the contrast in lighting, the ever-present fog and the many plays with shadows and reflections. The lighting effects, borrowed by Hollywood from the German expressionist cinema of the 1930s and 1940s, reappeared in Germany after the war, in particular, in a long series of Edgar Wallace adaptations, which quite visibly inspired Bausch. By contrast, the sequence of the training of Luxembourgish soldiers, however provincial it may seem, is reminiscent of Stanley Kubrick's *Full Metal Jacket* (which came out two years before *A Wop...*). The rivalry between the Luxembourg people and the French border inhabitants also owes a debt to the conflict in *West Side Story* (Jerome Robbins and Robert Wise, 1961). The characters of Vero, Daniel and Petz, as well as the music, are inspired by American 1950s and 1960s teenager films.

Just like today, one of the things at stake in those teenager films was whether the boy was going to get the girl and incidentally (although for a long time filmmakers would not be explicit about this), sleep with her. This is clear in *A Wop...*, and accordingly the New Year's Eve ball in Dudelange is also the equivalent of prom night in the American films. In the best tradition of the genre, Daniel's friends bet on whether or not he will sleep with a girl, any girl, before midnight.

Bausch pulls off this mix of genres remarkably well and manages to root them quite convincingly in the Luxembourg world in the early 1960s. National service was still compulsory at the time (it was withdrawn in 1967). The rivalry between the Luxembourg people and the French border inhabitants, scornfully nicknamed *Heckefranzousen* ('French from the other side of the hedge'), has always existed in the Minett border towns. In the period in which the film is set, the large influx of Italian immigrants had already been succesfully integrated. Virtually all that remained of the Italian roots of Vero and Petz (a typically Luxembourg nickname) is their family name, Zamponi. However, the German actors were present only because of the dictates of the co-production and they appear out of place in the setting of the Minett, which has never seen any sizeable influx of Germans. The mix of Luxembourgish, German and French languages spoken during the film is nonetheless not as disconcerting as one might think, since these are the three official languages of the Grand Duchy and are understood by everyone in the country.

A youth culture was gradually emerging in Luxembourg in the 1960s. In his 1993 documentary *Thé dansant*, Andy Bausch reports on the careers of the handful of groups that performed at the country's sober Sunday afternoon tea dances at the time. Some of them probably bore a resemblance to the group of amateur musicians headed by Petz in *A Wop...* or the madrigal choir (with scriptwriter, co-producer and art director Armand Strainchamps as one of the singers) that perform after them, and it is easy to imagine that young girls went to these tea dances in their best dresses, with huge ribbons in their hair, like Vero.

Music always plays a dominant role in Bausch's films. The title, *A Wopbopaloobop a Lopbamboom*, is taken from Little Richard's song *Tutti Frutti*. The Luxembourg musician, Gast Waltzing and his wife Maggie Parke, were nominated for a European Film Award for their compositions. In a further reference to *film noir*, jazz tunes punctuated the film's most dramatic moments, while twists lightened the atmosphere and even produce one of its best scenes: the rendition of the corny *Twist à Luxembourg* sung by Petz/Thierry Van Werveke with a strong Luxembourg accent and written by Bausch, in partnership with the Waltzing-Parke team.

Armand Strainchamps' sets and Klaus Peter Weber's lighting greatly heightened the tragic, as well as the dreamlike elements that pervaded *A Wop...* and remain mostly absent from Bausch's later work. The workers leaving the factory at the beginning of the film are shot against the seemingly unreal backdrop of buildings under a dark sky, lit here and there by a few lone streetlights (some of the sets were painted in *trompe l'oeil*). The strongly contrasting lighting effects, including the fog and a luminescent full moon, all added to the impression of otherworldliness. Such choices created the necessary distance from reality that enabled the director to place his dramatic and coded story in a familiar setting. Additionally, if the film worked better than later Bausch films, it may also have been because of the supervision of the German television producers who co-produced *A Wop...* and probably imposed a certain discipline on the young director; a discipline often lacking in his later films.

Nevertheless, *A Wop...* suffers from certain defects, particularly in its rhythm and narrative. Characters seem to turn up out of the blue and some scenes fail to work within the narrative, such as a boxing training sequence which has nothing to do with the rest of the story and only serves as a 'typical' backdrop for what is an unconvincing conversation between two workers about Rocco's father. The action scenes are also badly choreographed. The final scene with Daniel's death, filmed in a swimming pool where the water is reflected on the walls under the full moon, albeit visually stunning, is a good example of this lack of coherence. The film also suffers from mediocre acting by most of the minor roles played by Luxembourgish actors. However, most of the leading actors were convincing.

In addition to its two European Award nominations in 1990, *A Wop...* also won the Open Zone/New Directors award at the 1989 San Sebastian Film Festival. Bausch's future looked bright. Having attracted the attention of German television, he then made several television films and episodes for series, without ever breaking ties with the Grand Duchy of Luxembourg. In addition to a number of short films, he returned in 1993, 1997 and 2001 to film the musical *Three Shake-a-Leg Steps to Heaven* (with Thierry Van Werveke, Désirée Nosbusch, Richy Muller, Udo Kier and Eddie Constantine), the *Troublemaker* sequel, *Back to Trouble*, and *Le club des chômeurs*. This last film, again with Van Werveke and Luxembourgish actors André Jung, Luc Feit and Fernand Fox, was a resounding commercial success in Luxembourg. However, the director has yet to gain the international recognition he achieved with *A Wop...* which remains his most artistically accomplished film even though it was only moderately successful at the box office.

The Grand Duchy filmmaking landscape has changed considerably since the release of *A Wop....* Many young directors like Pol Cruchten, Geneviève Mersch, Bady Minck or Dan Wiroth have graduated from film schools and made short films, documentaries and a few feature films. The national cinema has finally become more professional with extensive support from the government. The flaws in Andy Bausch's films have hence become more obvious, especially since the director has never really managed to develop his style. All of his feature films since *A Wop...* have been in the popular comedy vein and have often veered towards the overly kitsch. This type of production is aimed mainly at the local market and, although he sometimes makes a clumsy attempt at incorporating tragic elements into the narratives, his iconic on-screen image remains the 'troublemaker' played by Van Werveke. As long as he continues to film in a rush, without taking the time to polish his scripts and work on his direction, Andy Bausch will be hard pressed to recreate the promise he displayed with *A Wopbopaloobop A Lopbamboom*.

Viviane Thill

TOTO LE HÉROS TOTO THE HERO

JACO VAN DORMAEL, BELGIUM, 1991

When, in 1991, Jaco Van Dormael's *Toto le héros* (*Toto the Hero*) was released, it took the film world by surprise. Not only was it universally acclaimed, it received four major awards at Cannes: best young filmmaker and best screenwriter for Van Dormael, best actor for Michel Bouquet (Toto) and best cinematographer for Walther van den Ende. However, a brief look at the film's history shows a film that appears lucky to have been made, especially in a country that has never been seen to have a defineable national cinematic identity or structured film culture.

It may well be that with the creation of a federal Belgian state in 1993, it is hard to specify what a 'Belgian' cinema is. How can one refer to a 'national' cinema for a country divided between French-speaking Wallonia, Dutch/Flemish-speaking Flanders and a further small German-speaking community in the Eastern Eupen-Malmédy area. In the mid-1960s, well before the official proclamation of a federal state, the country had already put in place a system for allocating subsidies that distinguished between Flemish and French-speaking filmmakers.

In his work *La Kermesse Héroïque du cinéma belge*, Fréderic Sojcher explores the possible negative effects of a division based on language. There was a temptation, he writes, for the Flemish side to promote 'Flemish' films and a 'Flemish' identity, while on the French-speaking side there seemed to be a desire, within the commission, to follow the 'French' style of auteur cinema. Neither strategy proved successful, with the notable exception of *Toto the Hero*. But even for Van Dormael, whose earlier short films had been well received, the funding was by no means straightforward. French co-producers had twice refused an advance against receipts for the script because they failed to locate financing for the film. But, having made short films in both languages, Van Dormael succeeded in obtaining financial support from both communities. Like André Delvaux before him, Van Dormael bridged the linguistic divide.

A further difficulty resulted from the recessionary climate of the early 1980s, which necessitated cutbacks in the linguistic community budgets. These cutbacks might have proved fatal for Belgian cinema, as a state-supported venture, had it not been for the promotion of cinema and television on a European level in 1988. Indeed, in the late 1980s the European Union and the Council of Europe created schemes such as *Media* (EU) and *Eurimages* (Council of Europe) that aimed at encouraging production partnerships by means of loans and advances against receipts. These new European programmes arrived just in time for Van Dormael.

Had it not been for the receipt of 26 million francs from the French community and 13 million from the Flemish community, *Toto the Hero* would not have drawn the substantial support from the newly-created European subsidies. The smaller European states and the minority languages were well-placed to obtain the assistance of these schemes. *Toto the Hero* benefited from a fortunate coincidence of circumstances: it was the first film to profit from a diversity of funding and thus from a multicultural financing. It was also to become the best-known, internationally acclaimed Belgian film for two decades. Besides the prizes awarded at Cannes, *Toto the Hero* also received accolades at Berlin, Locarno and Edinburgh, and came to be seen as representative of both Belgian and European cinema. The European fund-granting body, *Media*, revelled in the film's success because it proved the potential for a 'European' cinema especially in the strengthening of its position in relation to Hollywood.

It may have been expected that a film, heralded as being 'European', would play down a Belgian-specific tone, in favour of an emphasis on the creation of a European identity. But what would a 'European' identity be? French critic Jean-Michel Frodon observed that there was a solidarity between the history of nations and that of cinema which is not only historical but also ontological. It concerns a process of identification between the spectators and the film's narrative, between citizens and their imagined community. The idea of 'nation' might well disintegrate since it no longer reflects the evolution of the world and the collective imaginary that globalisation has brought about. If a 'European' cinema is to resist the Hollywood hegemony, Frodon suggests, it would be imperative for Europe to create a 'European' identity.

However, it remains difficult to speak of a European identity or a European cinema. European cinema is the sum of the achievements of all the cinemas in Europe. As the *Encyclopedia of European Cinema* states, 'while the European Union has come up with legislation to help script development, and the production and distribution of films in Europe, there is no pan-European distribution system able to release a European film simultaneously across Europe, and take advantage of its large collective audience with the same "muscle" as Hollywood.' American films continue to dominate European screens. The funding strategies, set up in 1988, were intended to develop a European cinema but they were also an assertive way to resist American cultural imperialism. Van Dormael's film was interesting for the way in which, without following the American model, it succeeded in blending a measure of

Hollywood verve with what Philip Mosley has refered to as 'post-modern European art film elements'. But the film did more than this. It addressed the very question of Hollywood's threat to European identity and doing so in a playful way, through the character of Thomas, who is haunted, on the one hand, by the uncertainty regarding his own identity and, on the other, by the powerful projective identification of American cinema upon his life.

Toto is a French-speaking Belgian boy whose real name is Thomas Van Haesebroek but who calls himself 'Toto' after the name of a detective who appears on television. It is here that the Hollywood influence enters the film. The boy, from an early age, is fascinated by the heroism of the television detective. His secret dream is to become a secret agent, 'Toto le héros'. But since Thomas is an unadventurous and fearful boy – the children call him 'Van chicken soup' – there is little hope for any heroic exploits.

Not only does Thomas want to become Toto the secret agent, he is also convinced that he is not Thomas, because when he was born a fire erupted in the maternity hospital and, in the panic of that moment, the wrong mother grabbed him. He is, in fact, Alfred, the only child of the rich neighbours across the street. The two boys have identical birthdays but only Thomas 'knows' that Alfred has usurped his identity. The worst consequence of this theft, according to Thomas, is that his life has been empty, and the story he tells is, therefore, that of someone to whom nothing has happened.

Van Dormael constructed the story in such a way as to leave the viewer puzzled as to what this question of identity was about. The film shows Thomas' life at three different stages: childhood, adulthood and old age. These stages intertwine as the film moves from flash forward to flashback, from old age to birth, from adulthood to death and cremation, leaving the viewer in doubt as to which events are real and which are imagined.

The film opens with a succession of three sequences, which precede the film's title and which encapsulate the narrative. The first sequence reveals a murder: a window broken by a pistol shot, then a body lying in a fountain. It then cuts to an old man who, when ready to go to bed, declares through a voice-over that he wants to kill 'Alfred'. But, 'it will not even be a murder,' he continues, 'since I will be taking back what belongs to me … the life you stole from me the very day I was born. My life.' The second sequence is located in the maternity ward of a hospital on fire. Two mothers run towards the two occupied cots, hesitate as to which baby is theirs, before grabbing one each and fleeing from the burning nursery. At the back of the room, a television set shows a detective film that announces the appearance of private detective 'Toto le héros'. The third sequence returns to the old man who, about to have his breakfast, reiterates that he has been robbed of his life and that, therefore, he has had no life. The sequence is interspersed with scenes from the past (a quarrel between him and Alfred) and the future (the murder of Alfred). These enigmatic opening images, mingling past and future, are followed by the film's title, *Toto the Hero*.

These introductory sequences set the mood for the film. American cinema intrudes in several ways: it is literally present from the moment the child is born (via a television set in the nursery) and is accompanied by the sensational event (real or imagined) of the fire, necessitating the rescue of the two babies and the momentary confusion over the identity of the babies being saved. Moreover, the opening sequence itself playfully borrows from the *film noir* style: signs of a murder, unknown gunman, unknown victim, old man planning the killing of 'Alfred'. Two temporal sequences are superimposed over each other, perhaps offering the audience some clue as to what has/is about to happen: the discovery of the murder when the enquiry is about to begin, juxtaposed with the earlier planning of the murder. American-inspired detective dramas litter the film, adding to the mystery and underpinning the influence and dominance of American film culture in Europe. Issues of identity raised by this relationship are intensified by Thomas' identifying with Toto, the character in the drama unfolding as the nusery burns. Moreover, Thomas' unfounded belief that he is the son of the wealthy business man and Alfred's father, Mr Kant, also underpins the allure of capitalism and material wealth.

The film continues to break linearity by cross-cutting from present to past and from present to future, interweaving in this way, one temporal sequence with another. Within both, past and future, there is further cross-cutting: for the past there are three different stages, very early childhood, Thomas prior to puberty, and finally Thomas when he is in his thirties. There also is a distinction between the 'objective' future – the crime to be committed – and imagined future of Thomas' overactive imagination.

The film operates on two levels. There is the film proper, Thomas' story as it unfolds. There is also the metafilm, the film of Toto the secret agent, as seen in the fragmented television episodes. The hero in the film, Thomas, copies the hero in the metafilm, Toto. But, in a spoof-like fashion, the film itself incorporates the *film noir* style of the metafilm. Its time frame moves from the 1950s (signalled through models of cars, clothes, and Charles Trenet's song *Boum sur Paris*, recorded in 1953), when post-war depression gave rise to *film noir* and Thomas was about ten years old, to the 1960s and, finally, the film ends beyond the present when Thomas is an old man and must, therefore, have reached the new millennium (2010 or even later). This projection into the future is signalled through a very basic futuristic setting.

The opening images lay the foundation for the ambiguity of the entire film. It exposes, on the one hand, Toto's belief that he has been taken by the wrong mother and, on the other, his ambition to become a private detective, 'Toto le héros'. Toto's life will unfold between these two poles; the belief that he is not 'Thomas' and the dream of becoming the private detective 'Toto'. Moreover, the three different stories surrounding the birth introduce the notion of fatality.

What identity can be constructed on such arbitrary occurrences? Thomas' two versions of his own birth, the birth in a maternity ward but taken by the wrong mother, and the particle picked up from the sea, reminiscent of Venus' birth, stress the non-biological birth, the 'not-belonging' to the parents. This not-belonging haunts Thomas throughout the film and his entire life. At the age of ten, following a dream of the fire in the nursery, Thomas confronts Alfred with the fact that his parents are not truly his parents. Alfred is outraged, hits Thomas and threatens to kill him if he dares to say this to anyone.

But soon the dream of heroism he secretly harbours also becomes linked to Alfred and his family. One night, Thomas is woken up by his father, a pilot, who comes to say good-bye to him before flying to England for some undefined mission, at the request of Mr Kant, Alfred's father. When his father fails to return from this mission, Thomas imagines that he is a prisoner of Mr Kant and that he, the private detective, Toto le héros, will rescue him. But some time later, Mr Kant announces the death of Thomas' father, which leaves the family impoverished. The 'killing' of his father at the hands of Mr Kant increases the discrepancy between the fate of the two children. The departure of Thomas' father is filmed with the attributes of *film noir* style: night, darkness, special atmosphere created by lighting and setting, rain, mystery, fear and disappearance of the hero.

The film plays further with Hollywood norms through its double plot line of a mission to be accomplished and a heterosexual romance. The mission is that of Toto, secret agent, and the heterosexual romance concerns Thomas' sister, Alice. Thomas is in love with his sister and even imagines that they might go to Egypt where brothers and sisters can marry each other. But he soon learns that Alice is in love with Alfred. Asking for proof of her love for him, Thomas dares her to set fire to the house of Alfred's parents. When, from his room he sees her cross the road with a can of petrol, he rushes outside just in time to see the explosion in which Alice disappears and dies.

Thomas will remain haunted by the image of his sister until one day, reminiscent of Alfred Hitchcock's *Vertigo* (1958), he meets her lookalike, the married Evelyne, with whom he falls in love. Evelyne, his new Alice, chooses to leave her husband and elope with Thomas.

They fix a date and place for the departure but things go wrong. Evelyne is delayed and, rather than wait for her, Thomas decides to go to her home. Coincidence has it that the husband she is leaving is Alfred. There is no escape from Alfred; every event that takes place in Thomas' life is inextricably connected to Alfred.

We might assume that Thomas is afflicted by the psychiatric disorder of a delusion of the double – a failure to distinguish between self and other – or that this is a case of pathological jealousy, since Thomas is envious of Alfred's rich parents and social success. Even when he finally ends up in an old people's home, Thomas remains haunted by his conviction that his life has been lived by someone else and that, therefore, nothing has happened in his life. The only way out then would seem to be to murder Alfred, forcefully taking back his life.

The film's central theme and basic story line, of a man haunted by the uncertainty of his own identity, may also be seen as a questioning of the struggle for identity of European/Belgian cinema. The re-occurring clips of detective American-like films remain a reminder of what extent the penetration of American cinema on European screens threaten the identity of the subject. Thomas' belief that he has been robbed of his identity may then be linked to the threat American film poses to European cinema as revealed already in the opening sequences of the film.

The problem of identity is intensified by Thomas' identification with Toto, the character in the American film. The intricately structured tale of someone haunted all his life by uncertainty about his own identity could then also be seen as a representation of the oppressive power of American cinema. Indeed, the film's playful integration of a *film noir* style corroborates this. But, while playing with the American paradigm, the film also emanates a more philosophical, specifically Belgian, trend whereby the influence of André Delvaux, Van Dormael's teacher, may be detected. As with Delvaux's work, a core question in Van Dormael's film concerns perceptual knowledge. How do we know that what we perceive is actually there? And how do we know that what we remember is real? And if we cannot be sure about the world we perceive, how can we then know ourselves? Delvaux's grappling with these questions through the medium of film has led to a highly original film language and style, in which images are often both literally and symbolically shrouded in mist. In several instances, a character is seen asleep or dozing off in a train and when he awakens reality seems illusory and neither character nor viewer is able to disentangle the fragile borderline between reality and dream, through the film's treatment of time and its conjuring with events and characters, amidst memory, dream, fantasy and reality.

There is more than an aesthetic value to this kind of cinematic magic realism, where images assume a dream-like quality. The viewers inevitably wonder about all the coincidences in *Toto le héros* that link Thomas and Alfred, about the many references to fire, to dreams and fantasies. In a more explicit way than in Delvaux's films, the question of identity comes to the fore. If in Delvaux's films the 'I' doubts the existence of the other and hence his own existence, in Van Dormael's film, this is pushed to the extreme of the subject thinking he is an other.

However, the film is clearly not trying to present a psychoanalytical case, it is presenting a quest for identity that mirrors that of European cinema. If, on the one hand, the film follows a specifically Belgian tradition, it also addresses the question of the 'invasion' of American cinema. The analogy that may be suggested here is the following: Alfred has robbed Thomas of his identity, Thomas plans to murder Alfred but this will not actually be a murder since Alfred's identity belongs to him. If we transpose this to the presence of American cinema in the opening of the film, this bizarre murder plot might suggest that Van Dormael denounces the imperialism of American cinema – Alfred and his father are wealthy capitalists and constitute an appropriate metaphor for American cinema.

The events that occur in the film seem a direct result of that power as represented by Mr Kant. The question of Thomas' belief that he has been robbed of his identity will be resolved when he, an old man in a nursing home, learns that there has been an assassination attempt on Alfred, linked to his firm's bankruptcy. He, 'Toto le héros', will finally be able to become the secret agent. However, on discovering that there is a new plan for the assassination of Alfred, he contrives an extremely complex murder story: rather than solve the murder, as Toto the detective would do, he stages a thriller-like story in which he will be the victim of the murder: only in this way can he really regain the life that belongs to him.

The theme of the 'double' that permeates the film will finally lead to oneness. Toto/Thomas and Alfred/Thomas will become one and, moreover, this Belgian/European film will close in an American *film noir* style. With this closure, Van Dormael interweaves the tradition of Belgian magic realism with a playful subversion of the basic codes of American *film noir*. In the complex plot Thomas has created, the film subverts the *film noir* code by an unusual permutation of roles between murderer and victim. While Thomas, the old man, planned the murder of Alfred in great detail, he abandons this plan and shifts to the role of victim: he will use Toto and the secret agent strategy for staging his own murder.

On the day of the planned assassination, Thomas/Toto goes to Alfred's house, asks for a cup of coffee and locks him in the kitchen. He then disguises himself as Alfred and, knowing the strategy devised by the would-be assassins, he takes the place of Alfred, as the victim of a murder. In this way, Thomas reasons, he will finally recover his identity at the moment of his death. The murderers shoot 'Alfred'. As he falls into a fountain his head becomes enveloped in a transparent net curtain, which he drags with him creating the effect of the covered heads in Magritte paintings. In being killed as Alfred, Thomas believes he has reclaimed his identity. However, the film closes with an ironic twist concerning identity: Alfred identifies the body as that of Thomas and the initial confusion is repeated: the ashes are labeled with Thomas' name. Thomas' desperate attempt to assign his own identity fails.

Toto le héros is about identity: that of Toto, of Belgium, of narrative and of cinema. The playful representation of mistaken identity has allowed Van Dormael to explore the constructing, deconstructing and reconstructing of the individual's existential doubt about the self. But in exploring this, he addresses the larger question of the identity of European cinema.

Lieve Spaas

DE NOORDERLINGEN THE NORTHERNERS

ALEX VAN WARMERDAM, THE NETHERLANDS, 1992

The black comedy *De Noorderlingen* (*The Northerners*, 1992) is the second feature film by director/screenwriter/actor Alex van Warmerdam, following the surprise success of his debut *Abel* (*Voyeur*, 1986). It is a beautifully crafted film that tells the strange story of a street in the middle of nowhere. The frustrated inhabitants can only express their sense of loss and longing for something more, in a nearby wood. This dark wood becomes a place of a manhunt, rape and murder. In *Abel*, Van Warmerdam's theatrical background resulted in the employment of artificiality and the film is absurdist in both subject matter and execution. Although the art direction of *The Northerners* presents an identifiable Holland circa 1960, Van Warmerdam once again creates a unique, personal vision of this world.

In the first scene, a family of the post-war 'Reconstruction Era' poses for a photographer. 'You have to look hopeful', says the photographer. 'Hopeful to what?' asks the father. 'To the future!' answers the photographer, annoyed. The photo with the hopefully smiling family reappears in the next scene, on a big building sign placed in the middle of a sand flat. On the billboard the Batavian Construction Company proudly announces the building of 2000 houses, to be ready in 1958. After this the number 1960 appears. This is both funny and disturbing, because the new housing development has been limited to only nine houses in the G. de Smetstraat. There is no pavement, just sand and a dark wood in the distance. In the meantime, a small tree has grown in a discarded concrete mixer; a symbol of the lack of hope for the future.

The period in which *The Northerners* takes place – the summer of 1960 – is the dividing line between the Reconstruction Era and the New Age. The building that took place during the Reconstruction Era is finished, but nothing has changed. The sexual revolution is gradually taking root in society, but everyone still goes to church. The world is neatly arranged. In addition to ordinary houses, the G. de Smetstraat features a school and a butcher's shop. The inhabitants struggle with the emptiness of the sand flat and with their repressed, lustful urges. The mysterious Fir wood offers shelter for those who look for seclusion, but in the end desire and lust will undermine and destroy the veneer of harmony that existed on the street.

In *The Northerners* Van Warmerdam created a very personal version of the Netherlands. He used archetypical Dutch iconography and traits, whilst avoiding clichés. The film represented the atmosphere of Holland in the early 1960s: houses with huge bay windows, the radios that are always playing, the street without cars, the first black-and-white television. There is little that is overly stylised. But behind the new facades lie hidden interiors of heavy oak tree furniture with Persian carpets, dimly lit by floor lamps. The crucifix overlooks the domestic peace. The meals are uninteresting. From behind the curtains, the inhabitants of the street leer at each other. There is no privacy. The story alternates between the street and the fir wood. The wood seems to be the edge of the world. Apart from the ringing of distant church bells and a regular bus service, there are hardly any signs of a world outside these two areas.

A pivotal character is 12-year-old Thomas, who is easily distracted by the events in the street. His father is the fat butcher, whose desires are rarely satiated. His wife cannot abide his wandering hands and prays to St Francis for both his and her redemption. On the other hand their neighbour, the hunter, has little time for sex, even though his wife desperately longs for a child. The hunter performs as a forester and, uninvited, oversees law and order in the wood. It is the projection of the desires of the people who live on the street and as a result is where the strangest of incients take place. Thomas, in particular, is sensitive to the strange events that take place in the wood. A mysterious girl in a white dress wanders through the wood and tempts him, while the bully, Fat Willy, terrorises him on his red motorbike.

The connecting link between these characters is Plagge, the postman (played by the director himself). In the wood he opens all the letters using the steam from a whistling kettle. The voyeuristic postman plays God, burning final notices and aware of everyone's private life. With only one look he prevents the butcher sleeping with his neighbour's wife. He acts as protector of the weak and avenger of the bullies' victims. He is in a permanent state of war with the hunter, who catches Plagge red-handed opening letters and reading a pornographic magazine. When Plagge runs from the police, the story takes a fatal turn. The sexually-frustrated butcher digs a big hole in which he traps a female cyclist. Thomas witnesses his father's crime. The short-sighted hunter accidentally shoots the mysterious girl and dumps her dead body in a pond in the wood. His wife leaves him and finally the hunter freezes to death, alone in the wood.

The outside world is represented by a continuous stream of reports on the war of independence in the Belgian Congo. The struggle between the two conquering leaders, Kasavubu and Lumumba, is sweeping the country. Sometimes, Thomas runs around in blackface, dressed up like Lumumba, with a hat in tiger print and black sunglasses. Then two missionaries visit the school in the street. They arrive to present an exhibition about Africa. A 'real Negro' forms the main attraction. The man sullenly sits in a cage only wearing a skirt of reeds. The teacher guides his pupils through the exhibition and tells his pupils that 'Negroes in general have a good sense of humour and are exceptionally loose-limbed.' As the class moves on, Thomas notices that 'the Negro' takes a cigarette from under his skirt and starts to smoke – much to the dismay of one of the missionaries. Thomas decides to set him free.

These characters are not just 'northerners' because their never-completed district is called the Northern Quarter. They are dour people. The atmosphere in the film is Calvinist – although the characters are Catholic. On the one hand Van Warmerdam ridicules religion within the home, whilst also showing the hold it can have over individuals, such as the butcher's wife, who experiences the full power of religious raptures. Ultimately, the characters are treated with dignity. The fat butcher in his shirt and pyjama trousers is at the same time hideous, laughable and deeply tragic. Thomas is an incomplete character, an unfinished personality who may never develop into a fully-rounded human being. Thomas becomes the key to the film; with his old-fashioned sweater and knee socks, he seems to represent the director when he was a boy.

In 1961 the Van Warmerdam family moved from the city of Haarlem, to a newly-built street on the border of Den Bosch, a city in the south of the Netherlands. There they were considered as 'northerners'. Behind their house was a sand flat with piles of bricks, where a new quarter would be built, two years later. The pavement still had to be constructed and on the way to Alex's school there was a mysterious wood. The Van Warmerdam brothers passed the wood daily, when they rode on their bicycles to the Catholic fraternity school. The three brothers Alex (b. 1952), Marc (b. 1954) and Vincent (b. 1956) formed a tightly-knit clan. Both Marc and Vincent would become important collaborators in the theatre productions and films of their eldest brother. On *The Northerners*, Marc was assistant director and Vincent composed the score.

The Van Warmerdam brothers grew up with theatre. Their father Peter worked as a stage-hand at the municipal theatre of Haarlem, and later became stage manager in theatres at Den Bosch and Ijmuiden. Peter was also active in amateur theatre, which inspired his sons. In the late 1960s they started out in theatre themselves. In 1969, after attending graphics school, Alex went to study at the Rietveld Academy in Amsterdam, which during the 1960s had become an open studio where students could freely develop their own style. The young Van Warmerdam showed a personal style and imagination. But his style became more and more mannerist and as a result of his dissatisfaction with his direction, Alex decided to return to the theatre, although he still paints theatre sets and posters (including the poster for *The Northerners*).

The theatrical background of Alex van Warmerdam was of crucial importance for the style of *The Northerners*. He did not pursue realism or nostalgia, instead magnifying various aspects of the post-war community to preposterous proportions. Images occasionally resemble a *tableau vivant*. The beehived, head-scarfed neighbours resemble an absurdist Greek choir; an example is their worshipping when the butcher's wife experiences a miracle. While Martha (Annet Malherbe) is praying for the statuette of Saint Francis of Assisi, a bird suddenly flies through the closed window. It is the bird that belongs on the shoulder of the saint. The statuette is soon to shake its head disapprovingly when the butcher offers his ill wife a sandwich with corned beef. This prompts Martha's hunger strike. Later, the statuette climbs down from its shelf for a chat with the fasting martyr. While Martha lies bedridden next to the front window, neighbours begin to pray for her on the pavement. Soon more and more pilgrims come to venerate her. Even the bishop visits the butcher's house to support Martha. Thomas and his father observe it with astonishment.

At the end of the 1960s, Alex and his brother Marc plunged into experimental theatre. They performed their street theatre shows at pop festivals and markets. In 1971 they met the band belonging to the brothers Dick and Rob Hauser. Alex, Marc and Jim van der Woude, a friend from Ijmuiden, were allowed to perform their acts in-between the group's performance. After two years of touring youth centres and schools, the theatre collective, known since 1972 as *Hauser Orkater*, began touring theatres. (Orkater means an amalgam of Orchestra and Theatre.) Over the next few years, *Hauser Orkater* took Dutch theatres by storm with their smart mix of theatre, music, mime and acrobatics. They created productions like *Op Avontuur* (*In search of Adventure*, 1974), *Famous Artists* (1976), and *Het Vermoeden* (*The Suspicion*, 1977). The 'comic couple' Jim van der Woude and Alex van Warmerdam established a grandiose, international reputation. *Hauser Orkater* disbanded in 1980, following performances of *Zie de Mannen Vallen* (*Watch the Men Fall*) in France where critics described their show as the finest foreign theatre production of the year.

Under the umbrella of the Orkater Foundation, the group divided into two troupes: *De Mexicaanse Hond* with the Van Warmerdam brothers and musician Thijs van der Poll, and *De Horde* with Jim van der Woude and the Hauser brothers. For *De Mexicaanse Hond*, Alex started to write scripts, direct, act and design sets and posters. This resulted in productions like *Broers* (*Brothers*, 1981), *Graniet* (*Granite*, 1982), *De Wet van Luisman* (*Luisman's Law*, 1984), *Onnozele Kinderen* (*Innocent Children*, 1986), *Kaatje is Verdronken* (*Cathy Has Drowned*, 1993), and *Adel Blank* (1999). Names and characters from these theatre productions would return in the films of Van Warmerdam. Fat Willy, for instance, is present in the theatre production *Leugenbroeders* (*The Brothers of the Lie*, 1987) and the name of the city quarter of *The Northerners*, *Het Noorderkwartier* (*The Northern Quarter*), was the title of a theatre production of 1989.

Alex van Warmerdam also acquired some film experience with *Hauser Orkater*. Frans Weisz, an experienced and well-known film director, turned two of their shows, *Entrée Brussels* (1978) and *Striptease* (1979) into films. In 1982 Alex and Frans Weisz also directed a television version of a production of *De Mexicaanse Hond*, *Granite*. Furthermore, Van Warmerdam, in cooperation with director Ottokar Votocek, made the short feature *De Stedeling* (*The Townsman*, 1984) for the VPRO television channel. Disappointed by the results of working with others, he decided to start directing himself. This led to *Abel*, which was only the second production of First Floor Features, a new and ambitious film production company of director Dick Maas and Laurens Geels, a former manager of *Hauser Orkater*. It is the tragicomic history of a family feud between a father, a mother and their grown-up son, who refuses to go outside. Van Warmerdam himself plays the title character. The film received positive reviews by the Dutch press and proved to be an impressive box-office success, attracting an audience of 400,000 in The Netherlands alone. At the Dutch Filmfestival in Utrecht, the film won two Golden Calves, the awards for the Best Film and Best Direction of the year. Four years later, the readers of the prominent newspaper *De Volkskrant* chose *Abel* as the best Dutch film of the 1980s.

As a result of this success, in 1992 expectations were high for Alex van Warmerdam's next film. *The Northerners* expanded its palette, but like *Abel*, remained interested in the war that raged behind the veneer of the happy family. *The Northerners* turned out to be formally more rigid, displaying more dry humour than its predecessor. The Netherlands in *The Northerners* is at the same time Catholic and Calvinist, stupid and small-minded but also highly imaginative and witty.

The simple style that Van Warmerdam used for *Abel* and which had been the result of his theatrical background was deliberately applied again for *The Northerners*. This is demonstrated, for example, in his preference for using establishing/long-shots. Van Warmerdam preferred to film a scene with only one camera set-up. *The Northerners* had an impressive budget – for a Dutch film – of 4.7 million Dutch guilders and was shot in the First Floor Film Factory, near the city of Almere. Although filmed in a studio, it posseses a realistic look. Nevertheless, there remained a degree of theatricality to the production. In such moments, Van Warmerdam chose to highlight the hyperreality of the film.

The inhabitants of the street are reduced to their most significant character traits, which are then magnified. Everyone is human and also an emblem. The 'Negro' is agile, the Butcher horny, the Boy innocent, and the Mother holy. Many characters bear a denominator instead of names. The group of actors, with whom Van Warmerdam often works, adapted perfectly to his directorial style. He does not work with an American-style constructed plot and is wary of psychologisation. He does not write forced confessions for his characters and loves situations in which he does not have to give explanations of how things started. With a humorous eye he observes the lethargic wanderings of the inhabitants of the G. de Smetstraat. At the end of the film he slowly moves the camera back into the wood and leaves his characters in their environment.

The emphasis in *The Northerners* is clearly on the visual. There are only 22 minutes of music in the film. Vincent van Warmerdam, the composer of the score, explained to the press that his brother preferred a minimum of music in his films. To Alex a film is a series of images in particular. In real life one does not hear music in dramatic situations either. From the start, Alex envisioned certain images. Some of them he adapted from his theatre productions, such as the one of a 'Negro' in a cage on a mission exhibition, an ice-cream man without customers and a postman who opens letters above a singing teakettle.

Together with director of photography Marc Felperlaan, Van Warmerdam invested nine months in developing a storyboard, in which every scene, every shot was laid out. He interpreted his reality like a mathematician: the dead straight street, the perpendicular fringe of the wood. The trunks seem to be planted in the wood mathematically. This game with horizontal and vertical lines is sometimes reminiscent of the work of painter Piet Mondriaan. With his straight lines and his plain *mise-en-scène*, Van Warmerdam has enlarged the artificial, stylised nature of the Dutch polder landscape as much as he did with the traits of his characters.

Some images stay on-screen for a very long time: the lonely street in the middle of the sand flat; the group of the inhabitants waiting silently on a small pavement for the bus. Van Warmerdam thus opens the eyes of the spectator to crazy and wonderful details. Particularly impressive is the dark, mysterious coniferous wood, recalling the legendary forest of Siegfried in *Die Nibelungen* (1924), the classic silent film of Fritz Lang. Like that magical forest, the wood of *The Northerners* contains only bare and artificially symmetrical trunks and no bushes, and the austere rows of fir trees seem to disappear in the dark. Van Warmerdam states in an interview that the wood in *The Northerners* was a dramaturgical theme for him: it is a fairytale wood, as unreal as the wood in the imagination of most people. When Thomas is waiting for the bus with the other inhabitants, he sees two tempting buttocks appear between the trees. The mysterious girl Agnes tries to lure him into the wood. In scenes like this, *The Northerners* resembles the surrealist beauty of a painting by René Magritte.

Both the design and the budget of *The Northerners* were ambitious. The set in the new First Floor Film Factory in Almere was one of the biggest film sets ever created in the Netherlands. But in spite of those efforts, the film got a mixed reception by the Dutch critics and attracted, in the Netherlands, only around 150,000 spectators. This result is not bad for a Dutch film, but the producers were probably disappointed, especially after the success of *Abel*. *The Northerners* won many awards though. At the Dutch Film Festival in Utrecht the film was awarded with two Golden Calves. Actor Rudolf Lucieer won a Golden Calf for his interpretation of the hunter and Van Warmerdam himself gained the award for Best Director. In Berlin the film was awarded with four Felix's, the European Film Awards. Rikke Jelier won for Best Art Direction and Vincent van Warmerdam was declared Film Composer of the Year ('Europäischer Filmkomponist des Jahres 1992'). Alex van Warmerdam himself gained a Felix as the director of the Best 'Young' Film (defined as a first or second direction of a feature film). This was a lucrative award, because it included 100,000 deutschmarks prize money. Furthermore, producer Laurens Geels was awarded an extra Felix. This was the first time in five years that the Netherlands was awarded a Felix. (Five years earlier, Johanna ter Steege gained the Felix for Best Actress in *The Vanishing*.) The four awards for *The Northerners* were milestones in the history of the Dutch cinema, and it helped the international distribution of the film. International reviews were mixed, although the majority were positive. In Paris *The Northerners* was shown for many weeks at the end of 1992 at the Studio Ursulines, filling this legendary art cinema to capacity many times. The film was also distributed in Italy, Great Britain, Sweden, Norway, Germany, Austria, Switzerland, Spain, the USA, Cuba and other countries.

One recurrent criticism was the ending of the film. Although Van Warmerdam probably meant it to be so, the ending of *The Northerners* is dissatisfying. There is no climax. Too many loose ends remain, like the growing group of pilgrims in the street or like the story of 'the Negro'. Furthermore, Van Warmerdam fails to tie the many storylines together well. Some characters suddenly drop out of the story, like the wife of the hunter or Fat Willy. In the end, *The Northerners* lacks not only a strong plot, but also a real central character. In fact, Thomas is not the main character, but rather Plagge, the all-knowing postman. In the beginning of the film he is the ideal guide to the audience, but in the middle he disappears out of the story and is not replaced sufficiently.

Some spectators had difficulties with the humour in *The Northerners*. In comparison with *Abel* the humour in *The Northerners* is much more vicious. Van Warmerdam really wanted the audience not to laugh too much. This shows a Calvinist streak, which is typical for many Dutch humourists. The action in *The Northerners* becomes increasingly painful, the humour blacker, until there is nothing left to laugh about. The characters are often sad figures, whose drippy lethargy seems to be typically Dutch. The humour is often created with visual means. Dialogues are used sparingly, but regularly, they are gems of absurdism. A sparkling example is the dialogue between the postman and the distrusting hunter about William the rabbit and his wife Carla who cannot have children. A slapstick scene follows, in which the two men fight for a letter in which it is written that the hunter is infertile. These scenes are labourious: much is told, but even more is left out.

Some critics have compared *The Northerners* to the films of Jacques Tati, auteur of brilliant comedies like *Jour de fête* (1949) and *Les vacances de monsieur Hulot* (*Monsieur Hulot's Holiday*, 1952). But the postman in *Jour de fête* was a birdbrain, who biked on cheerfully, while Plagge is a scoundrel, an anarchist in a uniform. Still, Van Warmerdam notes in interviews that he was inspired by the French actor/writer/director. Like Tati, Van Warmerdam avoids close-ups, because they are too pointed. When the main character in *Abel* pretends to be crazy, he is shown only in the background. The 'slapstick' scenes in *The Northerners* too are photographed in totals or medium-shots most of the time. Van Warmerdam invented many wonderful visual jokes in a Tati-like style, and edited the film – in cooperation with editor René Wiegmans – so cleverly that it really gets momentum, using the storytelling effect of the emphasis on strange noises. Particularly hilarious is the shrieking of a shammy that drives the butcher crazy when his shop girl is washing the windows and he is tempted by her busty appearance.

During the 1980s, many Dutch films had the same visual, black humour as *Hauser Orkater* once had in the theatre. Like *Abel* and *The Northerners*, these were films containing a lot of slapstick and a seemingly nostalgic art direction. By the end of the 1980s, so many absurdist comedies were produced in the Netherlands that one could speak of a Dutch School. Examples are *De Illusionist* (*The Illusionist*, 1983) and *De Wisselwachter* (*The Pointsman*, 1986) both directed by Jos Stelling, *Ei* (*Egg*, 1987) by Danniël Danniël, *De Orionnevel* (*The Nebula of Orion*, 1987) by Jurriën Rood, and *Han De Wit* (1990) by Joost Ranzijn. Some of these films starred former *Hauser Orkater* member Jim van der Woude. The films of Alex van Warmerdam are definitely among the highlights of this so-called Dutch School.

Today, Van Warmerdam keeps working both in theatre and cinema, and has also published the novel *De Hand van een Vreemde* (*The Hand of a Stranger*, 1987), which received positive reviews in the Dutch press. In 1995 his body of work was awarded with the prestigious Theatre Award of the Prince Bernhard Foundation. In his later films, *De Jurk* (*The Dress*, 1996) and *Kleine Teun* (*Little Tony*, 1998), based on the theatre piece of the same name of 1996, he continued to film in the style of *The Northerners*. The atmosphere became even more vicious: the fate of the characters can never be altered. For the general public these films were too morbid and they lacked the freshness of their predecessors. *The Northerners*, then, with its world of wonders and desire, rests unequalled.

Paul Van Yperen

C'EST ARRIVÉ PRÈS DE CHEZ VOUS MAN BITES DOG

RÉMY BELVAUX, ANDRÉ BONZEL & BENOÎT POELVOORDE, BELGIUM, 1992

The history of modern horror cinema has often been punctuated with low-budget productions that have managed to overcome their somewhat obscure origin through artistic recognition (*The Texas Chainsaw Massacre*, 1974), cult following (*Evil Dead*, 1982), or even wide popular success (*The Blair Witch Project*, 1999). *C'est arrivé près de chez vous* (*Man Bites Dog*, 1992), a horror comedy made in Belgium by three newcomers (Rémy Belvaux, André Bonzel and Benoît Poelvoorde) and released in its home country on 12 August 1992, is most certainly that kind of film. Its satirical and critical value acknowledged, it acquired a cult status through the personality of its main character, some striking sequences and clever dialogue, and – although strictly speaking not a popular phenomenon – it was a hit upon its release.

In 1989, three years before the release of *Man Bites Dog*, Belvaux, Bonzel and Poelvoorde worked together for the first time on *Pas de C4 pour Daniel-Daniel*, a short film that they produced themselves under the name Les Artistes Anonymes (Anonymous Artists). This schoolboy parody of spy films looked like a 13-minute-long trailer for a forthcoming film featuring a Belgian hero called Daniel-Daniel, and offered the opportunity for Benoît Poelvoorde to make what some might call his first one-man show. As with *Man Bites Dog*, central to the short was the mocking of cinematic/generic conventions. Although shot in 16mm, *Pas de C4 pour Daniel-Daniel* nevertheless had a CinemaScope aspect ratio which enhanced its around-the-world adventure-like feeling.

After this innocuous parody, the three friends decided to take the plunge and make their debut feature film in the same independent way. Mainly shot thanks to a profit-sharing system, *Man Bites Dog* had difficulty in getting financial aid, but received technical support (French director Patrick Grandperret kindly lent an editing table to the filmmakers) and found a distributor at the time of its Cannes screening. According to Claude Nouchy, who managed to distribute the film world-wide, it cost three millions Belgian francs. This time however, the subject matter found by Belvaux was not so overtly comical, as it addressed two topical issues: reality television and the serial killer phenomenon. The film offered a portrait of Ben, a young serial killer who is filmed and interviewed by a documentary film crew and makes a living by killing people of all ages and both sexes on an almost daily basis. In the course of the picture, the members of the technical team get to know Ben better, meeting his relatives and friends, and become increasingly mixed up in his criminal activities, so much that they commit murders and take part in a gang rape with him. Ben is eventually caught by the police and spends some time in jail, but manages to escape with the help of the crew. However, in the end they are all killed by an unseen sniper, finally leaving nothing but the sound of the camera.

In an attempt to understand this deceptively complex film, I will first analyse the basic aesthetic features of *Man Bites Dog* and tackle two major aspects of it, and then focus on the film's chief asset, its main character, briefly looking at the image and behaviour of the serial killer.

According to its three directors, the main aesthetic features of *Man Bites Dog* were first and foremost imposed by the shoestring budget that was at their disposal. Therefore, *Man Bites Dog* – whose original title, *C'est arrivé près de chez vous*, is the name of a column of the Belgian daily newspaper *Le Soir* – uses with great dexterity various techniques borrowed from what has been identified as the documentary genre, techniques that are not necessarily associated with high production values. By doing this, the film becomes part of the Belgian documentary tradition – albeit in a deliberately parodic and critical way. But it borrows not only from 'conventional' documentary, and more precisely from *cinéma direct* or *cinéma vérité*, but also from certain television shows. As Rémy Belvaux said in an interview in the French press book: 'We always referred to a Belgian programme called *Strip Tease*, which looks much more like a film than the reality shows do.'

The 16mm film stock used gave the film a grainy look, and a handheld camera was often used to film sequence shots that seem to capture a sense of the everyday. Moreover, shooting with a non-professional cast (mostly comprised of friends and family) on location in various Belgian cities (Brussels, Louvain and Namur) added a final touch of 'naturalistic' feeling to the film. The sound was recorded live and, although it was carefully written and planned, the film admittedly left some room for actors' improvisation, in addition to unplanned events that were included in the finished film. For instance, most dialogue spoken by the members of Ben's family were improvised from suggestions offered by the filmmakers and, at several points, profilmic events were clearly not planned: when two little boys playing with a plastic gun approach Ben, wearing the uniform of a dead postman, and again when Ben, fixing a drink for the crew, inadvertently trails the bottom of his jacket in a sink. Such details, that might at first seem only anecdotal, are nevertheless in total harmony with the film's aesthetic style and enhance the impression of reality over fiction.

The film was among the first in a tradition of films that were part of the sub-genre known as mock-documentary or mockumentary. In Jane Roscoe and Craig Hight's book on the subject, *Man Bites Dog* is a fictional text that 'appropriate[s] documentary codes and conventions and mimic[s] various documentary modes'. Like Rob Reiner's *This is Spinal Tap* (1984), for instance, *Man Bites Dog* can be read as a hoax because it employs various documentary traits in order to give its fictional world an enhanced sense of reality. However, the film is not only characterised by the imitation of documentary techniques, but also by a rather critical attitude towards documentary as a cinematic form and discourse, a stance that seems inherent to all mock-documentaries. As Roscoe and Hight argue: 'a defining characteristic of mock-documentary is an (often latent) reflexive stance toward documentary – a "mocking" of the genre's cultural status'. According to them, *Man Bites Dog* thus manages to render explicit the latent reflexivity of the form, becoming part of a 'Third Degree' of the genre. The films that belong to this category not only parody or criticise the discourse on factuality held by the documentary genre, but they strive to deconstruct it, to expose its internal assumptions and undermine them. Thus, *Man Bites Dog* examines the non-interventionist stance of the documentary genre. The genre conveys an impression of authenticity, since central to its concept is the assumption that the events we are witnessing are not staged (altered, faked, etc.) and would have been the same even if the film crew were not present. In this conception, the films are windows opened to the world, but we, documentarists and spectators, are supposed to stay safely in the house.

The plot presents a construction which is not based on events linked by a relation of cause and effect but on the growing involvement of the members of the documentary film crew in Ben's criminal activities. In the beginning, the crew watches Ben killing and getting rid of his victims' bodies from the safety of the off-screen position, which is quite naturally theirs. This invisible presence is made explicit by only two devices: the voice of an interviewer (Rémy, played by director Rémy Belvaux himself) is ocassionally heard on the soundtrack (particularly when the killer expresses his views), and the murderer looks off-screen towards his interlocutor. However, things soon cease to be so clear-cut, as the crew begin to appear on screen, and more importantly, participate in the murders themselves. Not only do members of the crew help to dispose of a body, but the filming apparatus (the zoom lens of the camera) becomes part of the killer's equipment. Moreover, it is the crew who challenge Ben to attack the occupants of a suburban home; an unusual target, which shares similar characteristics to a sequence in John McNaughton's *Henry: Portrait of a Serial Killer* (1986), and leads to Rémy aiding in the killing of a child. Lastly, when Ben sits in front of an editing table to watch what looks like one of the earlier sequences of the film, he can quite rightfully criticise the crew for not helping him to overpower a postman.

Through the mocking of the documentary's non-interventionist stance, the desire of the spectator is virulently criticised throughout the film. At one point, Ben and the crew drunkenly break into an apartment, interrupting a couple as they are making love, and rape the woman in front of her husband beffore killing them both. The next morning, the camera pans across the room, showing the horribly mutilated corpses as well as the sleeping murderers, lying peacefully on the floor. For the very first time, the camera is not held by a diegetic character. As this formal break suggests, this much talked about gang-rape sequence is anything but unmotivated. Something new happened here, but what exactly? Until this point, the position of the spectator was divided between witnessing the atrocities that they could simultaneously condemn and desire/enjoy. However, after this event, to avoid being complicit, the audience are compelled to distance themselves from the action and think about what came before. *Man Bites Dog* is interesting because it shows that we, like the documentary film crew, have crossed the line; we have lost our foundation stone and are no longer at a remove from the events.

Like other examples of mock-documentaries, the film aims to blur the boundaries between fact and fiction, and, as far as the representation of violence is concerned, this blurring is somewhat problematic. Any discussion of *Man Bites Dog* has to engage at one point or another with the complex reception of a film which convincingly manages to combine a horrific subject matter and its documentary style. Interestingly, André Bonzel, the film's director of photography, claimed that it was made in black-and-white, not for economic reasons (the developing was in fact much more expensive than for colour film stock), but because it produced a further distanciating effect, while simultaneously being reminiscent of the photographs from newspapers. However, perhaps *Man Bites Dog* can be better understood as a film that activates a complex range of interpretations for the audience.

At first sight, the various atrocities committed in the film appear to be understood by the viewers mostly as events which bear no relation at all to reality itself. However, the horrific nature of these events combined with the film's aesthetic choices tends at the same time to transform *Man Bites Dog* into a film which is extremely close to the definition of so-called 'snuff movies': films showing real murders for the gratification of those viewing them. Although the film employs various editing approaches, such as jump cuts during the interviews and montage sequences that feature a succession of murders, the main killings are always shown in sequence shots that seem to leave no place for fakery. According to the *cinéma vérité* movement, the documentary form is able to capture the unfolding of reality, and recording a real murder in continuity (that is, without ever stopping the camera), for the purpose of entertainment, is nothing less than making a snuff movie.

A brief analysis of the first sequence of *Man Bites Dog* provides a case in point. The opening scene is composed of a single shot showing Ben aboard a train rushing at a woman, dragging her in a nearby compartment and strangling her. The texture of the black-and-white image (traditionally codified as more 'real' than colour) and of live sound, the restrained acting of the actress, the absence of music, and the quickness of the event itself, tend to make us think that nothing had been staged, that the cameraman just filmed what happened, in front of him. Because of the initial position of this sequence, that is to say the lack of context, it can therefore be quite legitimately assumed by the audience (or, at least, by part of it) that they are not only seeing a murder but, more precisely, witnessing one.

In addition to this the profile of Ben, the main character, is a curious one. Much like John Doe in David Fincher's *Se7en* (1995), he lacks any significant profile. Doe is conscious of his difference and thus provides the police with a substitute, Victor, a hypothetical murderer who fulfills their expectations of a killer. As Richard Dyer has pointed out: 'Allen/Victor had a strict Christian fundamentalist upbringing (evoking the widespread psychoanalytic model of the repression in childhood of natural instincts that later come out in destructive forms); he has a history of mental illness and petty crime; he is sexually perverted.'

How does Ben fit into this pervasive conventional model? He has no identifiable religious background, he is clearly disturbed but not mad, and his sex life is not directly addressed in the film. Nevertheless, this character partly fits the usual profile of serial murderers: he is a middle-aged white man, with no distinguishing features, and he seems to live a perfectly normal life, as all the sequences presenting his familial environment and his social life tend to demonstrate. Moreover, the success and cult status of the film is attributable – at least to a certain extent – to the extroversion of its serial killer; Ben behaves like a genuine showman when confronted with the diegetic camera. In fact, Ben can be successively boastful and communicative, make vulgar or racist remarks, say things in a pedantic tone and, having sudden fits of enthusiasm, even recite poetry at the most inappropriate moment (such as when tracking down a rival in a disused factory). Ben's heightened egocentricity and the media's manipulation are brought to the fore by what seems to be at first only a joke: at one point, Ben learns that the crew does not have enough money to finish the film, and he declares straight away that he will give them all they need (or even work overtime) and that they might very well turn it into a 'saga'.

One important point to stress is that, according to the usual theoretical distinction made by the FBI between disorganised and organised killers, Ben appears to be a mixture of both categories. For instance, Ben does not know his victims and conceals their bodies like organised serial offenders might, and he also depersonalises them and displays sudden bursts of violence. As such, *Man Bites Dog* could be said to rid itself of this referentiality to actual murderers in favour of an economical/ideological representation of the phenomenon. Most contemporary serial killer narratives tend to present a character who kills in order to satisfy his impulses and/or surmount a trauma rooted in their past, overcome an inferiority complex, or else become famous: such is the case of, respectively, *Henry: Portrait of a Serial Killer*, Dominic Sena's *Kalifornia* (1993) and Oliver Stone's *Natural Born Killers* (1994). Against all expectations, there is seemingly nothing of the kind in *Man Bites Dog*. Ben's serial killing appears to be a way of earning a living, so much so that most of the time it seems to be his only purpose. After the protracted killing of the family in their home, it appears that no money can be found in the house (the assailants only get their hands on a few credit cards, which Ben considers too dangerous to use). Moreover, killing a child is anything but a profitable business because, as Ben cynically puts it while he is suffocating one with Remy's invaluable help:

Ben:	I don't like infanticide.
Rémy:	Why not?
Ben:	Kids aren't good business, Rémy. In theory, they're not bankable, understand?

The rationalisation of the serial killer's acts is interesting, but has been mostly overlooked by critics. In the first minutes of *Man Bites Dog*, a rather cheerful interview with Ben, sitting in a bar, is jarringly interrupted by the first montage sequence of the film. This sequence, which enables us to see various killings in a short space of time, looked at carefully, brings to the fore an element which is central to the film: serial killing is shown to be at least partly functioning in the same way as capitalism. Ben appears to act at random. However, he works hard to choose the method that is the most appropriate and economical to achieve his goal. Hence, causing a heart attack in order to kill an old woman permits him to go unnoticed but also, as Ben remarks with a demonstrative pride, to save bullets. He often changes his modus operandi (he shoots his victims, strangles them, frightens them to death) without showing evidence of any 'artistic' inventiveness: being the skilled capitalist he is, Ben only sees to it that the productivity of his murders is as high as possible. His criminal activity then makes explicit some of the fundamental implications of the capitalist economy: a person gets rich at the expense of others, depriving them of the fruit of their work, and hence of themselves. The victims' bodies, wrapped in impersonal white sheets, are interchangeable. Once Ben has obtained the money, bodies do not have to be touched or transformed (i.e. maimed, arranged according to some pattern), only thrown away.

All of this makes *Man Bites Dog* a very peculiar film, one that stands out in every way (within the Belgian documentary tradition, and the horror and serial-killer genres). That it remained a one-off is equally strange. After this sometimes controversial but often well-perceived feat, Belvaux, Bonzel and Poelvoorde never worked together again. Poelvoorde became a comic actor, whilst Bonzel went on to be director of photography on another feature film, *L'Amour, l'argent, l'amour* (*Love, Money, Love*, Richard Gröning, 2000), albeit eight years later. And Belvaux simply disappeared from the film world. However, *Man Bites Dog* has unquestionably become something of a classic; in terms of success, cult status and critical value, it still stands alone in the landscape of Belgian horror cinema.

Frank Lafond

KARAKTER CHARACTER

MIKE VAN DIEM, THE NETHERLANDS, 1997

Karakter (*Character*, 1997) was the very successful feature debut of young Dutch director Mike van Diem. Based on a novel and a short story of the Dutch 'modernist' writer, Ferdinand Bordewijk (1884–1965), the film is distinctively different in narrative strategy and technique, although both film and novel have a similar multi-layered structure. A young man is dominated by the struggle to free himself from the separate influence of his father and mother, both impressing and forceful figures in their own way. As well as a coming-of-age story with several subplots, such as a sad love story of suppressed emotions, a period piece of port town Rotterdam in the 1930s and a story of class struggle between the proletarian workers in the slums and the upper class, *Character* is a symbolic story of the struggle between a son and his overbearing parents.

Set in Rotterdam during the 1920s, the film tells the tale of an ambitious young lawyer, Katadreuffe (Fedja Van Huêt), who is arrested after the city's most feared bailiff, Dreverhaven (Jan Decleir) is found dead. The young man was the last to see the bailiff alive, and the police suspect him of murder, against his claims of innocence. Through a series of flashbacks during a police interrogation, Katadreuffe tells the story of his life. His mother, Joba (Betty Schuurman), had been raped by her employer Dreverhaven, and as a result gave birth to a son. A proud and stubborn woman, she refused to marry Dreverhaven and chose to raise her son with a firm hand, in dignified poverty. To make ends meet, she takes a lodger, Jan Maan (Hans Kesting). As a young adult, Katadreuffe wants to prove to his stern and silent mother that he can take care of himself. His first effort in business, a tobacco store, proved to be a disaster, after he was cheated and left bankrupt. He had a large debt with a bank that was owned by his father. Eager to climb the social ladder, Katadreuffe sensed the power possessed by his lawyer; a discovery that prompts his decision to enter the legal practice. All the time, his father attempted to hinder his ascent, but against all odds, he becomes a lawyer. Katadreuffe had reason to hate Dreverhaven, but was it enough to murder him? This question remains open for the spectator to decide. The police find out that Dreverhaven has killed himself and so release Katadreuffe. However, the news confirms his suspicions that he may also possess the desire for self-destruction.

Character's appearance is of an accessible mainstream feature. The edgy opening sequence is designed to build up a slight suspense about what happened exactly after the fade-out. The story is then developed in a sweeping and straightforward manner through a clearly recognisable flashback structure. There is little need for explanation. Still, a further exploration is interesting, because *Character* is, in a Dutch perspective, a very uncommon film. Furthermore, it is possible to compare the feature with the novel and short story by Bordewijk. The same story is presented in different forms and choices which were made to differ from each other in a significant way. And, there is the unusual subtle love story, with the melancholic undertone of suppressed feelings, set in the arena of the harsh business world of the lawyers' office.

Producer and co-scriptwriter Laurens Geels initiated the adaptation of the novel *Karakter*, a classic of Dutch literature. The film soon transformed into an ambitious project, co-produced with the Belgian company Kladaradatsch! and with an unusually high budget of 7 million Dutch guilders. The shooting period was lengthy for a typical Dutch production (lasting 71 days over the summer and autumn of 1996) and took place across a number of locations: Hamburg, Wroclaw, Antwerp, Ghent and places in the Netherlands.

It is very remarkable that such a prestigious project was left in the hands of a crew who, like director Mike van Diem and cinematographer Rogier Stoffers, were making their debut. Van Diem (b. 1959) originally studied Dutch language and literature at the University of Utrecht, but soon discovered that his main passion was cinema, so he transferred to the Dutch Film School in Amsterdam. He completed his successful student film *Alaska* in 1989, with Stoffers, whom he knew from his college years in Utrecht. After his graduation he decided to make his feature debut with a mainstream movie, as opposed to opting for the usual route of a low-budget, independent production. His determination and talent earned him a position at the production company First Floor Features, famous for the several box-office hits directed by Dick Maas (*Flodder*, 1986; *Amsterdamned*, 1987) and also for rare art features, such as *De Noorderlingen* (*The Northerners*, 1992). He developed several scripts for First Floor Features, the most promising of which was the Hollywood project, *Across the Street*, although it was eventually abandoned. In between, he worked as assistant director with Ronald Beer on the set of *My Blue Heaven* (1990) and directed eight episodes of the Dutch television series *Pleidooi* (*Plea*). A drama that took place in a lawyers' office, it re-united Van Diem with Stoffers who, after *Character*, has successfully worked with international directors like Philip Kaufman (*Quills*, 2000) and Michael Apted (*Enough*, 2002).

The cast of *Character* also featured a number of new actors, including the lead, Fedja van Huêt. At 14, he had had small roles in *Terug naar Oegstgeest* (*Return to Oegstgeest*, Theo van Gogh, 1987) and *Advocaat van de Hanen* (*Punk Lawyer*, Gerrit van Elst, 1996), but his part in *Character* marked his real debut. He had the difficult task of playing a young man whose emotions remain mostly hidden, but whose personality changes dramatically. His character was where the story's main theme, of overcoming one's own demons, was played out. The changes were reflected in the attitudes of those around him, most notably his mother and scornful and bitter father. There was also his love interest, Miss Lorna te George, played by Tamar van den Dop. She represented the tragic side to Katadreuffe, whose desire for social acceptability closed him off to any hope of happiness with another person.

Jan Decleir has been seen as the Flemish Gerard Depardieu. Both actors are frequently cast as the rambunctious character, with a passion for life. In the 1970s, Decleir won fame in the Netherlands for his part in the television drama *Sil de Strandjutter* (1976). But theatre audiences already knew him from his work with the company *Internationale Nieuwe Scène*, which filtered political action theatre through the techniques of the Comedia dell'Arte. His first success in cinema came early, as the male lead in *Mira* (1971). *Character* was conceived as the Dutch response to the Flemish box-office hit and Oscar-nominee *Daens* (Stijn Coninx, 1992), a period piece in which Decleir played the lead part. In *Character* he explored a much darker character. Betty Schuurman was also better known as a theatre actress. Before her appearance in *Character*, she had only played a part in *De Schaduwlopers* (*The Shadow Walkers*, Peter Dop, 1995). Tamar van den Dop graduated from the Drama School of Maastricht in 1993. She achieved national fame with her lead role in the television drama series *Zwarte Sneeuw* (*Black Snow*, Maarten Treurniet, 1996). Recently she directed the short feature *Lot* (2002), a visual poem about four generations of women.

The author of *Karakter* the novel, Bordewijk, knew the workings of a lawyers' office intimately. For six years he was a junior partner for a firm in Rotterdam, then becoming an independent lawyer in the nearby city of Schiedam. He used this experience to capture the setting and atmosphere of his novel. In 1928, he published the short story *Dreverhaven en Katadreuffe*, as a serial in the liberal weekly *De Vrijheid*. Another variation on the theme of father and son relations was used in the story *De man in de hoek* (*The Man in the Corner*), in which a wealthy businessman suddenly encounters his illegitimate son during a ride in a streetcar.

Bordewijk is regarded as one of the very few Dutch modernist writers and a representative of the Nieuwe Zakelijkheid (New Realism). His style is dominated by short sentences, a language without emotion, written in a sober, realistic way. He is best known for the short novels *Blokken* (1931) and *Bint* (1934). The latter, an unsentimental portrait of a cruel teacher, was regarded as a classic amongst literature classes in Dutch high schools. The label of the modernist writer does, however, give an incomplete picture of a more versatile and complex creative mind. Bordewijk was, for example, one of the few Dutch writers who wrote fantasy stories. *Karakter* was written in the summer of 1937, during a family holiday. The novel was first published as a serial in the spring of 1938 in the prestigious literary weekly *De Gids*. Its publication as a book followed in September 1938. The novel sold reasonably well – within two years there was need for a sixth print. Following his death in 1965, the English publisher Peer Owen published an English translation as part of a cultural project of the Council of Europe.

Karakter tells its story in chronological order, from the birth of Jacob Katadreuffe (1903) until his graduation as a lawyer (1931). His self-taught schooling took place in three stages: his matriculation, his bachelorship in law and his master's degree. The story in the novel is told through an omniscient narrator, and allows for numerous temporal elipses. Bordewijk composed a subtle time structure, moving both forward and backwards in time. The language used was short and at times forceful, with almost cinematic descriptions of the settings and detailed information about the lighting. The omniscient narrator moralises and comments both on the action and the characters. Dutch literature has a tradition of naturalistic fiction, such as *Van de Koele Meren des Doods* (*Hedwig; the Quiet Lakes*, written by Frederik van Eeden (filmed by Nouchka van Brakel in 1982), or *Eline Vere* by Louis Couperus (filmed by Harry Kümel in 1991)). The action and characters of these novels are imprinted with an irreversible sense of fate. By curious coincidence, these novels are all psychologically detailed portraits of female characters. By contrast, *Karakter* is about a man and features a more contemporary language. Nevertheless, Bordewijk remains part of this naturalistic tradition.

In an interview for *De Filmkrant*, Mike van Diem stated: 'What struck me in the novel is the way in which the protagonists communicate with each other, or rather not communicate, how they ruin themselves with their incapability to show emotions. It is a story of someone who wants to escape from his origins, who tries to tear away from his parents. In my view, it is a struggle that we all fight.' *Character* is by no means a faithful adaptation of the novel. To begin with, the narrative features a frame-story. The ending was also changed. The first sequence is told from the point of view of the son, Jakob Katadreuffe. The shots before the credits feature a restless moving camera, which reflects the agitated mood of the young man. For the last time, he climbs to the office of his father, the bailiff Dreverhaven, to confront him once and for all.

The sequence ends with the son diving over the father's desk, as he attacks him. The image is frozen in time, before the screen fades to black. The spectator is left with the question: what happened next?

We move forward in time. Katadreuffe is in prison and the police suspect him of murdering Dreverhaven. Through the interrogation, the film tells the story of his life. The story is told from Katadreuffe's point of view. In reality, the images are presented by an effective narrator and not an emotionally distraught man. Though the voice may be Katadreuffe's, the confidence with which the story is told is most certainly that of the novel's authorial presence. This is most evident near the end of the film, when the story is almost over. The first scene is repeated, and we see the confrontation again, but this time from the point of view of Dreverhaven. Suddenly we see an old man, a human being instead of a threatening figure. In the novel, this last confrontation is left to the last chapter, as the climax of the story. The film presents a much bleaker ending. Only in the last shots does it become clear what happened to Dreverhaven: he has killed himself by jumping from his office. In both the novel and film, Dreverhaven is seen to personify evil. He is possessed by the urge of possessing as much material wealth as possible and combines this vice with the abuse of power. The debts of Katadreuffe and the threat of his bankruptcy are a striking metaphor of the struggle to break free of any inherited greed. Katadreuffe attacks his father, they fight fiercely, and both are left bleeding from their injuries. They have become unable to express their love or affection.

The moment of revelation, or turning point, in both the film and novel, is the scene in which Katadreuffe sees five shining brass nameplates next to the door of the lawyers' office. His ambition to be the sixth 'shining sun' fills him with 'life'. However, before this scene, there is a lengthy account of his early life (30 minutes) and the events around his first bankruptcy (leading up to the end of the first hour). By comparison, Bordewijk narrates Katadreuffe's early years briefly: his youth is covered in just three chapters and his first bankruptcy in four. His first year at the lawyers' office is described in more detail in five chapters, after which the stage is set for the struggle between the father and son, which dominates the remaining sixteen chapters.

In an interview for the *Vprogids*, Van Diem explained that 'there are many genres mixed in the film. The courthouse scenes look somewhat as a parody of *Plea*. I filmed these scenes in a television fashion, with lots of different shots. But there are also elements of a thriller and even a western. For example, when Dreverhaven is standing on the steps of his home, with a big crowd around him, that is like John Wayne as a sheriff who addresses his town-folk.' Indeed, there are many reverberations of other films in *Character*. The figure of Dreverhaven can be associated with a western character, with his silence, long cape and black hat. The confrontation between him and a desperate tenant during a brutal eviction, against the background of a riot has the feeling of a classic shoot-out. Dreverhaven's gloomy office also harks back to the expressionistic set-designs of 1920s German cinema. Likewise, the Dutch police behave more like fascists in a war movie. This can be seen in the black suits they wear, although this could also be a nod to the bureaucratic hell of a Kafka story. The scenes in the slums are reminiscent of other Dutch films set amongst the working classes during the interbellum, like *Rooie Sien* (*Red Sien*, Frans Weisz, 1975) or *Ciske de Rat* (*Ciske the Rat*, Guido Pieters, 1984) or a film like *Katy Tippel* (Paul Verhoeven, 1975), set at the end of the nineteenth century.

The lawyers' office is also the location of the sad love story of suppressed emotions. The relationship between Katadreuffe and Miss Te George begins with their first encounter on the staircase outside the lawyers' office. There is no romantic music or intimation of any blooming romance, but the intimation of a possible relationship is present. Some time later Miss Te George walks Katadreuffe to his room in the attic. She opens a roof-door which had never been opened before and at that moment her physical act signifies the more metaphorical act of making emotional contact with Katadreuffe. This idyllic image returns later in the film, then as a melancholic memory. Katadreuffe is obsessed with his urge to succeed in life. He has no time for the love which is granted to him. In the novel his fear of sexual intimacy is explicitly mentioned, in the film this remains implicit (just as there is no hint of eroticism whatsoever, which is exceptional in a Dutch film). And yet, Katadreuffe silently suffers the pain of jealousy, when he encounters Miss Te George on the beach with another man. She is dressed in a dazzling white dress and is pleased to see him, but he does not know how to deal with his feelings. His desire to succeed dominates his life and everything is subservient or irrelevant in relation to it. As Van Diem stated in an interview: 'At the first viewing the most touching scene for me was Katadreuffe's speech about the importance of getting a position in the world, ignoring the love of Miss Te George completely.' This is demonstrated by the camera which literally passes from him, talking, to her. An ultimate moment of not-saying, where one can tell from the face of Tamar van den Dop that she is breaking apart inside, while she keeps on smiling. At screen-tests this was the big issue: 'actresses with high reputations could not play the part, Tamar was the only one.' After this, a melancholy overcomes Katadreuffe . There is a short farewell between the two in the corridor of the office, following the graduation party that Miss Te George organised and in which she realised that her love would never be requited. Katadreuffe only realises his mistake too late, and only when his mother points it out to him, as they are out walking in a park. They encounter Miss Te George, who is pushing a pram. Katadreuffe's mother remarks that he was as stupid as an owl to let her go.

There is also the relationship between Katadreuffe and his mentor, De Gankelaar. All too aware of his pupil's ambition and its destructiveness, he remarks with insulted, angry insight that Katadreuffe is too narrow-minded to accept even the smallest gifts. In the film their (somewhat more than professional) relationship ends in the hall of the courtyard. De Gankelaar yells the harsh truth at the top of his lungs: 'From whom did you inherit this? This useless self-torment? Who taught you this? People who cannot accept gifts are people who don't have anything to give! Nothing!' Surprisingly, it was not his father, but his mother who imbued in him this misguided lesson, highlighting that his life has not only been damaged by the estranged patriarch.

Released in April 1997, *Character* was critically acclaimed by most Dutch reviewers. The influential film critic Hans Beerekamp (*NRC/Handelsblad*) was the notable exception. His main objection was that *Character* aimed too low, resulting in a visually impressive, but simplistic film. Along with the soccer comedy, *All Stars* (Jean van de Velde, 1997), it was one of the year's biggest commercial successes. It was also successful on the festival circuit and was screened at the Cannes Film Festival. In the United States the film premiered March 1998 on six prints, with a return of $37,268. The international trade press reacted with positive reviews. *Screen International* stated that '*Character* is a Dutch film like Hollywood doesn't make anymore', whilst *Variety* called it 'a lushly mounted historical drama [which] boasts a rich evocation of 1920s Holland, solid thesping and assured, dynamic handling by debuting helmer Mike van Diem'. It went on to win the Golden Calf for Best Film at the Nederlands Filmfestival and the following year it was awarded the Academy Award for Best Foreign Film, cementing van Diem's position as an exciting new Dutch filmmaker.

Peter Bosma

TWEE KOFFERS VOL LEFT LUGGAGE

JEROEN KRABBÉ, THE NETHERLANDS/BELGIUM, 1998

Upon its release in 1998 *Twee Koffers Vol* (*Left Luggage*) was almost unanimously derided by the popular press. Film critics attacked the film for its clichéd storyline, overwrought performances and reliance on heavy-handed sentimentality in the place of any genuine emotional weight. All of which is arguably true. However, such a negative reaction should not obstruct the exploration of some intriguing themes the film raises. Though its approach may be less than subtle, the film is surprisingly complex in what it has to say about contemporary European Jewish identity. And despite negative press in the United States, the film was nominated for the Golden Bear and won three other awards (including a special award for Isabella Rossellini) at the 1998 Berlin Film Festival, won both the Grolsch Film Award at the Nederlands Filmfestival and the Emden Film Award at the Emden International Film Festival, and was nominated for the British Independent Film Awards in the 'Best Foreign Independent Film – English Language' category.

Left Luggage, a Dutch/Belgian/British co-production, was the directorial debut of Jeroen Krabbé, the Dutch actor who had made a name for himself, firstly with Paul Verhoeven in *Soldaat van oranje* (*Soldier of Orange*, 1977), *Spetters* (1980) and *De Vierde man* (*The Fourth Man*, 1983), and then in Hollywood in *The Living Daylights* (John Glen, 1987), *Kafka* (Steven Soderbergh, 1991), *The Prince of Tides* (Barbra Streisand, 1991) and *The Fugitive* (Andrew Davis, 1993). Based on the novel *The Shovel and the Loom* by Dutch author Carl Friedman, the film tells the story of Chaja (Laura Fraser), a 20-year-old Jewish girl in Antwerp in the early 1970s. Her parents, both survivors of Auschwitz, have chosen to deal with their past differently. Her mother (Marianne Sägebrecht) wants nothing more than to put any memories behind her, immersing herself in her hobby of weaving rugs and baking cakes, while her father (Maximilian Schell) is obsessed with finding the two suitcases of family mementos he buried, shortly before he was taken by the Nazis. Chaja was raised with virtually no Jewish identity, and is further alienated from her culture by the embarrassment she experiences from her two neurotic parents and their Jewish neighbours. 'I'm fed up with this whole *Jewish* thing', she confides to her friend, the Orthodox Jew, Mr Apfelschnitt (Chaim Topol).

However, it is through Mr Apfelschnitt that Chaja is offered the job of nanny in the Kalman household, a Hassidic family. At first, Mrs Kalman (Isabella Rossellini) is dubious about Chaja's appropriateness, as she refuses to conform to the strict and traditional world of the Hassidim. Mr Kalman (Jeroen Krabbé) is even more suspect of this *gomer* (Yiddish for 'whore'). Of the Kalmans' five children, Chaja soon bonds with Simcha (Adam Monty), the family's red-headed four-year-old, who has never spoken a word. Taking the boy and the Kalmans' infant twins to the park everyday, Chaja and Simcha soon find a bond growing between them and she is the first person he feels he can talk to.

Chaja also comes into conflict with the anti-Semitic concierge (David Bradley) of the Kalmans' apartment building. When he tries to frighten Simcha by locking him in the lift, Chaja comes to the young boy's rescue, but in the melée with the concierge tears his uniform. Demanding compensation for the ruined garment, Chaja is asked by the Kalmans not to visit them until the concierge has calmed down. Simcha, missing his nanny and confidant, takes solace in visiting the park, but one day plays too close to the duck pond and drowns. The film ends with Simcha's funeral. While the rest of the Hassidic community blames Chaja for Simcha's death, the Kalmans recognise the happiness she gave Simcha in the weeks up to his death.

Chaja is a free spirit; a rebellious independent young woman. She is presented as 'a modern girl', very much a product of the student radicalism that spread across Europe in the late 1960s and early 1970s. Her gentile boyfriend is a Marxist radical who views being able to pay the rent and even washing his socks as bourgeois. In stark contrast are her parents, whose conservatism is highlighted when we first see her return to their apartment, at the beginning of the film. On seeing her attire and in particular, her tight jeans, Chaja's mother comments that wearing them would likely 'cause cancer'.

Chaja is visibly embarrassed by her parents: her mother criticises her long flowing hair as being unkempt and points to her own, seemingly immovable, coiffured hairstyle as exemplary for a nice young Jewish girl. To Chaja, her mother no longer lives in a real world; it is a self-contained little ghetto where you can hear the neighbours arguing through the walls. There is a strong sense of the environment in which Chaja grew up. She was permanently surrounded by the same people; an extended community of largely secular Jews, many of whom, like her parents, were probably survivors of the Holocaust. Despite their wartime experiences, no one ever talks about what it was like in the concentration camps. The only exception is Chaja's father, with whom she has an ambivalent relationship. After an initial prologue, showing, in stark monochrome, Chaja's father burying the suitcases, the film cuts to seven-year-old Chaja

(Lana Broekaert), sitting on her father's lap, being told the tale of the suitcases. The story, so central to her father's way of dealing with the past, has become the stuff of family folklore. Yet despite her love for her father, Chaja is obviously embarrassed by his obsession with the past.

Chaja's parents represent the dichotomy of contemporary European Jewish response to the Holocaust: an obsession with the past, and the wholesale denial of the events that shaped their lives resulting in an attempt to put the past behind them. This dichotomy is exemplified when Chaja's family are sat around the dinner table. Chaja's parents are at either end, while she sits between them. Opposite Chaja is an old photograph of a woman, next to which is a memorial candle (*Yertzheit*). The dinner is the commemoration of Chaja's aunt, Selma, who committed suicide after surviving Auschwitz. Chaja's mother believes the act is sick and accuses her husband of obsessively dwelling on the past, while she is accused of wanting to forget what happened to them. Chaja is trapped between these positions, just as she is caught between her parents.

In a larger sense, Chaja's position (literally and figuratively) can also be seen as representing contemporary Jewish identity within Europe. European Jews (if not all Europeans to some extent) can be seen to grapple with an obsession with Europe's Nazi past (coming from and living within cultures where their very existence was and continues to be in jeopardy, among those who wanted – or at least did little to prevent – their extinction), with a desire to move forward, creating a new Europe out of the ashes. The specific Jewish cultural presence in Amsterdam and Antwerp, as cornerstones of the diamond industry, but also within a larger social context, caught between tradition and innovation, is a significant factor in the visibility and status of this conflict. Chaja's ambivalence, if not her outright hostility, toward Jews at the beginning of the film, echoes this.

Chaja, as the embodiment of contemporary Jewish Europe, also finds herself in conflict with tradition, as embodied in the Hassidic family who employ her. The Kalmans' life is alien to her, as she was raised (as many secular Jews have been, in Europe and North America) to view Hasidim with embarrassment and contempt. To an outsider, even a Jewish outsider, Hasidic Jews, with their strange clothes and insular communitiesm, seem at odds with modernity's breaking down of the *shtetl*/peasant mentality. And for more modern Jews, the insularity of Hasidic communities is viewed as, not only an embarrassment, but maintaining the kind of cultural prejudices which fuels anti-Semitism in the first place.

There is an old joke which summarises the feeling of many modern Jews towards the Hasidim: A modern Jew is on a crowded train. The only seat available is opposite a Hasidic

Jew, which he reluctantly takes. The modern Jew keeps glaring at the Hasidic Jew. After a few minutes, the Hasidic Jew asks if there is a problem. The modern Jew says: 'It is you people who make me ashamed of being Jewish. You hold onto the worst stereotypes of our people. You refuse to assimilate or enter the modern world. You still believe its 1804, rather that 2004.' The Hasidic Jew thinks for a minute and then says: 'I'm sorry, but I think you are mistaken. I'm not a Jew, I'm Amish.' The modern Jew says: 'Oh, I'm so sorry! I think it's wonderful how you people keep your traditions alive!' The paradox here is obvious: modern Jews, who view Hasidic Jews with contempt and embarrasment, tend to celebrate other cultures than those groups who try to keep their traditons alive. Such is also Chaja's position at the beginning of the film.

As a literary/filmic creation, Chaja-as-protagonist is opposed by a variety of antagonists, each of whose position is symbolic of a particular aspect in Chaja's coming of age. Already noted is the opposition between Chaja and her mother (thin vs. fat, flowing hair vs. fixed hair) and with her father (obsession with the past vs. awareness only of the present); similar troubled relationships exist with the Kalmans themselves (modern inclusion vs. Hasidic polarity). Mrs Kalman acts as an antagonist to Chaja insofar as she refuses to wear trousers ('it is forbidden to dress like a man'), to fight back against the concierge's anti-Semitism (active vs. passive), and to uphold Orthodox Jewish traditions. Mr Kalman is more overtly dismissive of Chaja. Even as the film nears its close, he refuses to even look directly at her. These roles structurally replace one another in the film: firstly, Chaja is opposed to her mother in defining who she is as a *woman*, then by her father in who she is as a member of *that family*. Chaja finds herself in opposition with Mrs Kalman in defining who she is as a *Jewish woman*, and then by Mr Kalman as a member of *that Jewish family*. Each of these relationships acts, structurally, as building blocks for the emergence of Chaja as an adult, at the end of the film.

In between these protagonist/antagonist relationships are mentor/guide characters that assist Chaja in negotiating her troubled relationships. Both Apfelschnitt and Simcha help her develop, whilst being seen to develop themselves, through her. But what is significant about both these roles, beyond what they symbolise for Chaja is how, once again, they replace one another. Apfelschnitt is Chaja's mentor in negotiating her relationship with her parents (particularly her father), whilst Simcha helps her deal with Mr and Mrs Kalman.

Chaja is caught at the centre of a cultural identity matrix: between the past and the future, and modernity and tradition. If we can see Chaja as symbolic of the position of contemporary Jews in Europe, they too could be seen to find themselves at the heart of this labyrinthine position: to hold onto aspects of tradition or embrace modernity's breakdown of those pre-existing cultural categories; to obsess over the past (particularly the Holocaust) or to put the past behind oneself, and build a new life for the future. These are polarised positions, and the film does not advocate choosing any of them. However, rather than essentialist categories of cultural identity, they are presented as positions on a spectrum. In this respect, Chaja is able to explore the extremes available to her, before finding herself a more central and moderate position. The character of Mr Apfelschnitt is very much her guide in the first stage of this process. He is an Orthodox Jew (we never see him without a *yarmulke* and, in one sequence, we see him put on *tefillin*), yet lives among more modern Jews like Chaja's family. It is Apfelschnitt who gets Chaja her job as a nanny with the Kalmans, and so he must have some connection with the Hasidic world too. While Apfelschnitt may be on the more traditional side of the centre, he enables Chaja to position herself on the more modern side, whilst ensuring free movement between the extremes.

The key to Apfelschnitt's position, and what motivates Chaja to discover her own Jewish identity, is the idea of understanding: of her parents' particular obsessions, of Jewish traditions (within the context of the Hasidic household), and ultimately of understanding herself as a Jew. There is a significant sequence towards the end of the film. Not understanding why Mr Kalman is so critical of Simcha for an error made in his asking of the Passover 'Four Questions' (the *Manishtinah*), she rows with the patriarch, following him into his study, a place forbidden for anyone to enter, other than himself. There she sees an old photograph on the wall, which Mr Kalman explains was taken of him, his father, and his younger brother, who Simcha bears a remarkable resemblance to. Kalman further explains that both his father and brother were hung by the Nazis for refusing to spit on the Torah. It is because he sees his brother when he looks at Simcha that he has difficulty relating to his young son. Though Kalman is not exonerated from the way he treats Simcha by his disclosure, Chaja at least understands the man a little more. Chaja's experiences with the Kalmans also aids her understanding of her parents, and as a result, herself. When Chaja follows the Simcha's funeral procession to the cemetery, maintaining a discreet distance from the family, she catches Mr Kalman's eye and for a brief moment, the two exchange a meaningful glance. He finally understands the joy she brought to his family.

This bittersweet aspect of *Left Luggage* was the primary focus for critics' attacks on the film. Many accused the film of being overly sentimental and emotionally manipulative. However, this could be seen as an essential aspect of its emergent *Jewishness*. The Yiddish term, *shund*, effectively meaning 'trash', came to be used in referring to a kind of vernacular genre of Yiddish-language drama and film in the early parts of the twentieth century. In film particularly, *shund* dramas were exceptionally popular throughout Yiddish-speaking communities in Europe and amongst North American Jewish immigrants. These *shund* dramas were overwrought melodramas, often focusing on the silent and steadfast suffering of a matriarch, in the face of family tragedies. In the Polish film *A brievele der mamen* (*A Letter to Mother*, 1938, Joseph Green), for example, the matriarch suffers silently as her husband abandons her, along with his youngest son, for America; her daughter runs off with her dance instructor spurning her engagement to the son of their neighbour; her eldest son (who can never decide on a career) dies in World War One, and her home is destroyed by enemy planes. Eventually she emigrates to America and attempts to find her youngest son in New York, who has now become a famous singer. She goes to see him perform, but before she can reveal her identity to him, she is hit by a car. On her deathbed, her son comes to see her and, taking his hand, she passes away. Such overwrought drama, watched by an unaccustomed audience, would be an easy target for derision.

While *Left Luggage* is not strictly a *shund* drama, in those moments of its most melodramatic excesses, it possesses elements of Yiddish drama. Rather than criticising the film for its overwrought emotions, it could be argued that an audience needs to embrace those moments as a kind of 'paracinematic excess'. In the same way that horror fans wait for moments of excess gore, fans of Yiddish drama wait for scenes of emotional pathos. Again, the scene at Simcha's gravesite is exemplary. Mr Kalman, who for most of the film shows no emotion other than disappointment, is allowed by Krabbé to weep silently. It is the one time he looks at Chaja without judgment and in their exchange of looks, his acceptance of what she has given his family is finally recognised.

The character of Simcha also exemplifies Jewish ideas, or at least is symbolic of them. A *simcha* in Jewish tradition is a 'blessed event' – a wedding, or the birth of a child – and something to be celebrated. But Simcha also functions as *simcha* for the Kalman family and for Chaja. He is the agency through which Chaja learns – and more importantly learns to accept – her own Jewish identity. His resemblance to his dead uncle also allows Kalman to accept the past. And he finally teaches both his own family and Chaja to be less suspicious of people who are different.

So why does Simcha die? There is a traditional Hasidic belief that one dies when one's role on Earth has been completed, when one has achieved one's goal in life. There is a paradox here: how can a four-year-old child have completed what he was preordained to accomplish? To answer this, one must shift paradigmatically away from an egocentric internal sense of accomplishment, to a more social and socially-responsive paradigm. Within this belief tradition, it is not what one does with one's life, but the effect one has on others, which is most significant. Simcha allowed Chaja to become more self-aware of her own Jewish identity, and Kalman to become more responsive as a father, as a result making both Chaja and Kalman more of a *mentsch* – in Yiddish, a good person. Simcha, then, parallels Apfelschnitt's role as Chaja's guide in allowing these alienated adults to feel more connected to their own humanity. And when Simcha dies, Apfelschnitt returns to the narrative to act as Chaja's guide in the mourning process.

The film itself fulfils a role similar to Simcha's, for the audience. In criticising the film for its melodramatic excesses, certain reviewers overlooked a central tenet: to see *Left Luggage* as a self-contained *objet d'art* is to miss seeing the film for its affectation. It may be *shmaltzy*, but one is nevertheless moved by it. We may rage at being so emotionally manipulated, but we *have* felt the emotion. These emotional affectations may be presented crudely and appear overly 'simple'. But that is *shund*.

The film's lack of subtlety can be considered its greatest strength. Everything in the movie is hyperbolic. Chaja is just too lively, her mother is too bizarre, her father too obsessed with the past, Simcha is too cute and Mr Kalman too distant. Even the anti-Semitic concierge is portrayed too broadly. These caricatures are not meant to be 'real people', but are embodiments of culturally specific ideas. In this case, of Jewish ideas.

Criticising *Left Luggage* for being clichéd is perhaps unfair. Certainly, it is a contrived story, but that reveals the film's literary source material. In addition, it would be a mistake to see the film as undermining verisimilitude, for at no time does it imply that it should be read in such a way. All these criticisms would be better directed at Friedman's novel, than the film. For what the film does is to bring to life the discourses implicit in Friedman's prose, not as any kind of definitive overview, but as an interpretation. *Left Luggage* is a film of Jewish ideas and culture, a Western European Jewish culture, related to that of the Low Countries, which has attempted to rebuild itself out of the ashes of the Holocaust and in doing so, like Chaja herself, attempts to understand what it means to be a Jew.

Mikel J. Koven

ROSETTA

LUC & JEAN-PIERRE DARDENNE, BELGIUM, 1999

Rosetta (Dardenne Brothers, 1999) was the fourth feature film directed by the talented brothers Luc (born 1954, a university-trained philosopher) and Jean-Pierre Dardenne (born 1951, a trained actor), who were presented with the Palme D'Or at the Cannes Film Festival in 1999. Such prestige has elevated the Dardennes into the gallery of acclaimed independent filmmakers and, of course, placed them in the smaller grouping of sibling filmmakers that include the Taviani and Coen Brothers, both of whom were also awarded Cannes' most coveted prize (for *Padre Padrone* (1977) and *Barton Fink* (1991), respectively).

Rosetta is the name of the central character. An 18-year-old girl living in a decrepit caravan with her alcoholic mother, the film follows her struggle for work and a place in society. Her life is tough, an unending series of mishaps and tragedies, from which she attempts to struggle out of, impulsively and more often than not agressively, finding any way she can to escape her miserable family life and be accepted within a seemingly antisocial society. The result makes for striking and involving cinema.

Rosetta does not stand alone in the Dardenne oeuvre. It is, more or less, the logical successor of previous efforts. In considering a number of the other films made by the Dardennes, it becomes clearer how *Rosetta* completes their oeuvre. After a period of directing insightful socio-political documentaries between 1975 and 1985 (*Lorsque le bateau de léon M. Descendit la Meuse pour la première fois/While the boat of Leon M. descends the river Meuse for the first time*; *Pour que la guerre s'achève*; *Les murs devaient s'écrouler/Walls will come tumbling down*; *R... ne répond plus/R... doesn't respond anymore*; *Leçons d'une université volante/Lessons from a University*, and others) the brothers made their fiction debut with *Falsch* (*False*, 1986). Since they set up their production company, Collectif Dérives, in 1975, they have produced sixty documentaries, most of them dealing with the working-class movement and, with the inclusion of their most recent film, *Le Fils* (*The Son*, 2002), they have produced and directed five feature films.

Looking at how *False* was adapted from the play by the Belgian dramatist René Kalisky, one gets the impression that the directors wanted to mark some distance from their earlier documentary work. As a result, *False* is a high-quality picture with specific avant-garde and experimental overtones. As a result, it was seen as too mannered and lacking personal social engagement, elements which were so demonstratively present in all their earlier documentaries. The story of the Jewish doctor Joseph Falsch (meaning 'false' in German) and his family, as they struggle with the ghosts from their past, the film is set in a deserted airport that serves as a stylised *huis clos*. Following this, the Dardennes made *Il court… il court le monde* (*He Runs… He Runs the World*, 1987), a ten-minute short that deals with the issues of speed, images, movement and cinema.

This artistic intermezzo was followed by *Je pense à vous* (*I Think of You*, 1992), which looked at what happened to life in the Dardennes' home region of Seraing during the 1980s, reflecting the general collapse of the steel industry in French-speaking Belgium. Inspired by Belgium's documentary pioneer Henri Storck and with the help of screenwriter Jean Gruault (former screenwriter of François Truffaut and Alain Resnais), the Dardenne brothers intended to clarify in this film the tragic consequences of the industrial crisis for one family, and one person in particular. As such, *I Think of You* is a forerunner of the deeply personal trajectories of their later films. As they always concentrated their documentaries on the workplace, where people come together, each wanting to belong to that common place of recognition, the Dardenne brothers gradually moved to focusing on one individual within those groups. *I Think of You* tells the story of steelworker Fabrice whose happiness, with his family, his job and his friends, is ruptured because the factory where he works is being closed down. As with *Rosetta*, the story begins with trouble at work. Fabrice becomes jealous and aggressive, seeking comfort in alcohol and soon finds himself in a downward spiral.

The personal story of Fabrice acts as a metaphor for the collective economic disaster that struck the whole Belgian region of Liège and Seraing during and after the 1970s. On an even larger scale, the Dardennes represented the huge impact of the neo-liberal, global free market and its terrible consequences (decline of heavy industry and permanent unemployment) on individuals. *I Think of You* is a strong and visually beautiful call for respect and hope. It is the first film in which the Dardennes demonstrate their qualities as makers of realist fictions. However, the documentary content is more powerful than the supplied fictional elements which sometimes appear too anecdotal. Whereas *False* was criticised as too intellectual, *I Think of You* was found to be too sentimental and even too romantic. Both *False* and *I Think of You* were commercial failures, but *I Think of You* was also a disappointment for the directors themselves. According to their own standards they had made too many 'Belgian compromises'.

Both financial disasters resulted in a few years of silent reflection. In 1996, Luc and Jean-Pierre Dardenne surprised friend and foe with *La Promesse* (*The Promise*), a film that is neither mannered nor sentimental, but touching in its plainness, directness and humanity. The story of the fifteen-year-old Igor whose initiatiation into the world of moral consciousness recalls auteur cinema or what François Truffaut defined as cinema in the first person singular. Set in their home region of Seraing, along the river Meuse, *The Promise* builds on, albeit more appealingly, what was already apparent in a few Dardenne documentaries and in *I Think of You*. Igor, played by a non-professional actor (Jérémie Renier), is the son of Roger (Olivier Gourmet) who is an insensitive employer on a dilapidated building site exploiting illegal immigrants. The carefree teenage son participates in the slave-trading business of his father until an accident causes the death of Hamidou (Rasmane Ouédraogo), an African worker from Burkina Faso. The father wants to hide the truth, but the son's conscience is disturbed and he is forced to betray his father. He keeps the promise he made to the dying Hamidou: to guarantee the well-being of his wife and child. In order to respect the dead man's last will and following his growing moral consciousness, Igor turns against the paternal authority, showing honest human dignity and responsibility.

With *The Promise* the Dardennes achieved a style in which their themes were presented clearly and with conviction. Like *Rosetta* after it, *The Promise* is a documentary-style report of the everyday struggle of a 'socially excluded' individual, confronted with the moral question of necessary betrayal. The actors' performances, which are restrained, perfectly serve the very intense story. Characters are always in motion and the restless camera, aimed at, and sometimes taking the place of a character, follows every move in order to make the physical bearings more pronounced.

The Promise is a parable of human dignity, one that can be compared with the *Dekalog* stories of Krzysztof Kieslowski (1988) or Roberto Rossellini's *Germania anno zero* (1947). In an interview with *Sight and Sound* Jean-Pierre Dardenne explained why they were admirers of Kieslowski's work and vision: 'we've never seen [Kieslowski's] documentaries, but what's fascinating in his films, especially in the *Dekalog*, is that there's always real doubt at the centre. It's there in the way he tells a story, the way a character enters the frame. You never know whom to trust and the characters don't seem to trust themselves.' *The Promise* was both a popular and a critical success. The many prizes won by the Dardenne Brothers (in Cannes, Namur, Geneva, Potsdam, Frankfurt, Valladolid, Tehran) compensated for the earlier disappointments. They had found their personal formula and with that they finally found their public and critical support. With *The Promise*, the Dardenne Brothers also launched their very specific way of casting, rehearsing and shooting their stories. Instead of working with casting directors, they expressed an interest in working with unknown faces, bodies and voices. This places more emphasis on pre-production. For example, the original complicity between father and son in *The Promise* needed to be a real complicity, lived rather than acted by the interpreting actors (this very specific and problematic father-son relationship is comparable to the father-son relation in Vittorio de Sica's *The Bicycle Thieves* (*Ladri di Biciclette*, 1948)). Because the Dardennes like to tell their stories through the character's motions and emotions, they insist on rehearsing a great deal and on filming a large number of takes in order to find the footage with the rhythm they are looking for. Events occuring on the set can intrude into what the directing team has already in mind, which can be challenging work for all concerned, both in front of and behind the camera.

The successor of *The Promise*, *Rosetta*, demonstrates the brothers' search for concise direction and a cinema as *coup de poing*. *Rosetta is* the image, and the image is her action. The story of Rosetta, a young woman on the wild and raw run in life and society, is a personal homage to the pure, authentic cinema of Roberto Rossellini and also very reminiscent of the ascetic masterpiece of Robert Bresson, *Mouchette* (1967). Unlike *Mouchette*, *Rosetta* does not end in a fatality. Rosetta is not a girl anymore, but she is not yet a woman. As observed by Lieve Spaas and much like Igor in *The Promise*, *Rosetta* is always in motion. From the very first sighting of her, the audience witness a character in constant motion. Rosetta runs violently through the corridors of the factory where she has worked and now is fired without explanation. She is furious and the restless, handheld camera follows her fury. The camera is like the brutal world all around her; a heavy, troubled weight on her shoulders. She finds her alcoholic mother in the old caravan where they both live. The world has reversed and the daughter finds herself taking care of a mother (Anne Yernaux) who prostitutes herself in exchange for beer. Rosetta refuses any generosity or compassion. She does not want to beg. She wants to work honestly for her living and is determined to find a new job to survive. A normal life is what she desires the most. Rosetta meets Riquet (Fabrizio Rongione), a young man who sells waffles. On his recommendation Rosetta is offered a job in the little waffle factory. The scene in which Rosetta and Riquet are together, eating French toasts, is the only moment in the whole film where music is heard and some affection in a tentative friendship becomes possible. Such formal austerity, refusing to compromise, to 'soften the blow' of the situation, stands in stark comparison with the works of Mike Leigh (*Secrets and Lies*, 1996; *Career Girls*, 1997), Ken Loach (*Raining Stones*, 1993) or

Mark Herman (*Brassed Off*, 1996). They all deal with similar themes, but tell them in very different ways.

The radical style used by the Dardennes features a shortage of moderating humour. But their consistent radicalism in form, produces a more powerful emotional effect on audiences. When Riquet comes closer, his musical attempts offer an opportunity for the two to dance. However, it is Rosetta who chooses to distance herself from him and finds herself back in her isolated situation. In the next scene she lies motionless in bed, holding an astonishing conversation with herself: 'Your name is Rosetta. My name is Rosetta. You have found a job. I have found a job. You have found a friend. I have found a friend. You have a normal life. I have a normal life. You won't fall into the rut. I won't fall into the rut. Good night. Good night.' In this extraordinary scene, Rosetta, remarkably portrayed by Emilie Dequenne, looks desperate and rough but at the same time attests to an inner strength and a determination to continue her battle for normalcy and some semblance of human dignity. Later on, she loses her job after having discovered that Riquet is cheating his boss (Olivier Gourmet). And again she finds herself without work. As she will do anything to have proper work and contact with society, she betrays her potential friend Riquet. Like in *The Promise*, betrayal functions, at least to Rosetta, as a moral dilemma on the way of making her living as a human being and not as an animal. She gets Riquet's job and sells waffles, and for a while she seems happy to feel the dignity of having work. While she's working, the always-moving camera stops to look at her, a young woman who now belongs to society. But Riquet returns to seek revenge on Rosetta (or Rosetta's conscience). Rosetta returns home to find her mother passed out. She gives up her work, and tries to gas herself. But the gas runs out and she is forced to go out and buy another gas canister. When she drags the canistar to the caravan, she breaks down and for the first time in the film, she bursts into tears. At that very moment, the emotional apotheosis of the motion picture, Riquet appears. Unknowingly he interrupts her suicide attempt and offers her help. It is only in that final scene that Rosetta is willing to need and feel somebody. It took her an entire film to become a true human being.

The Promise, Rosetta and *The Son* are trajectory films, in which a main character has to travel a very hard journey from surviving to some kind of normal life. Each of those films offers that pure, very difficult journey, the development of a person to change life in living. In an interview with *Sight and Sound* Luc Dardenne described *Rosetta* as a war film and Rosetta herself as a warrior: 'in writing the screenplay we decided Rosetta would live in a space divided into three. First you have the war zone: the world in which she's fighting to find a job and a place. Then there's the camp: the caravan site where she lives and has her little rituals – setting her fish-hooks and so forth – and her mother, because she's an alcoholic, is like a wounded soldier, a casualty, confined to camp. Then between those two spaces is the frontier: the motorway she crosses continually to get from the camp to the workplace. Once we'd established this in the writing we had to decide on our shooting style. And we decided to follow Rosetta as you would follow a soldier in a war, which means the camera never knows which way she's going to turn. Of course the action is still directed, but the camera never prefigures what Rosetta is doing – it can't look before she looks, and so on. In essence, though, this idea of war comes from our sense that having a job today is a war – you have to fight to get one and usually getting one means taking away someone else's.'

More than a war film, *Rosetta* is a synthesis of the documentary history particular to Belgian filmmaking and the beginnings of the Dardenne filmmaking, combined with stories told in the post-World War Two tradition of European *cinéma d'auteur*. This synthesis proved to be the key to its worldwide success. In addition to the Palme d'Or, the film also garnered the prize for Best Actress at Cannes (debutante Emilie Dequenne shared the prize with the equally non-professional Séverine Caneele, who starred in Bruno Dumont's sober *L'Humanité*). The jury at Cannes, chaired by Canadian director David Cronenberg, applauded *Rosetta* because the film presented a current fringe which, in the jury's opinion would be the next centre of film making; a film that offers hope for the future of cinema. The film showed that cinema can change the world and has still the desire to do so. As Truffaut's *Les Quatre Cent Coups* (*The 400 Blows*, 1959) initiated the social debate on how to treat 'difficult children' in a more human way in France, so *Rosetta* prompted in Belgium a debate on employment problems and opportunities for young people. Belgium's then minister of labour, Laurette Onkelinx, conceived the 'Rosetta Plan', a currently on-going project to stimulate young, unskilled people on the labour market.

Rosetta has paved the way for a new, larger audience for the Dardennes' cinema, with their follow-up film building on earlier triumphs. At Cannes 2002, Olivier Gourmet, the longtime Dardenne collaborator, whose conviction emphasised the emotional honesty of his roles as the heartless father in *The Promise* and the understanding waffle-baker boss in *Rosetta*, received the prize for Best Actor in *The Son*. In contrast to his earlier roles, he plays a lonely, uncommunicative carpentry instructor in a rehabilitation centre for young delinquents. He refuses a new teen as his apprentice but begins to pursue the young man who, as it turns out, killed his son five years before. Once again, the camera follows the silent, mysterious main character, Olivier. And although Olivier's face remains expressionless, and his playing style neutral, by the end of the film, the camera's probing reveals the inner cracks; the emotional core of a mourning man.

The Promise, Rosetta and *The Son* also established the Dardenne Brothers as authentic *auteurs*, a notion which Annette Insdorf describes as essential in developing a personal vision of the world, which progresses from film to film. With these three films, Jean-Pierre & Luc Dardenne are probably the most celebrated living Belgian directors. Moreover, they can be seen as continuing the trend of recent international successes of Belgian (Flemish as well as French-speaking) features and, even more important, *cinéma d'auteur* of Belgian feature cinema during the last decade. This trend was introduced in the early and mid-1980s by Jaco Van Dormael's *Toto le héros* (*Toto the hero*) and *Le huitième jour* (*The Eighth Day*, 1996). During that period, films like *Daens* (Stijn Coninx, 1992) and *Farinelli, il castrato* (Gérard Corbiau, 1994) were nominated for Academy Awards and won prizes at international festivals, and the low-budget *C'est arrivé près de chez vous* (*Man Bites Dog*) was the controversial revelation at Cannes in 1992.

However, although Van Dormael turned the eyes of Francophone cinephiles towards new French-speaking Belgian cinema, there is a significant difference between the films of Van Dormael and the Dardennes. Van Dormael is an artist proceeding from a typical Belgian cinema tradition, known as magic realism. This was adapted from literature and the works of authors such as Johan Daisne, Hubert Lampo and Jean Ray. Their works were adapted by two Belgian filmmakers, Harry Kümel (with *Malpertuis*, 1974) and André Delvaux, most notably in *De man die zijn haar kort liet knippen* (*The Man Who Had His Hair Cut Short*, 1965) and *Un soir, un train* (*One Night … a Train*, 1968). They can be considered the masters of a cinema in which pure fantasy, poetic mystery and a completely imagined world arises out of a very recognisable and tangible reality. Just like Alain Berliner and his recent films *Ma vie en rose* (*My Life in Pink*, 1997) and *Le mur* (*The Wall*, 1998), Van Dormael is a disciple of magic realism in cinema that even goes back to Charles Dekeukeleire's surrealistic classic *Het kwade oog* (*The Evil Eye*, 1937). A constant in this kind of cinema is the representation of problematic cultural (Belgium – Wallonia – Flanders) and personal identities. In each of these films, the audience is faced with outcast characters or disturbed personalities. It seems as if the imagination presents itself as a rich escape route and a refuge for a complex personal and collective reality, representing Belgium as place similar to a labyrinth, where human beings do not always know where they are and to which community they belong. And even when the generation of Van Dormael and Berliner have abandoned the strong literary origins of Delvaux's films, their pictures are undoubtedly a tribute to the magic realism in Belgian literature, the realistic surrealism in plastic arts and animated film (René Magritte, Paul Delvaux, Raoul Servais, etc.) and the absurdities of real Belgian life.

It is more fitting to place the Dardennes in another tradition of Belgian feature cinema: that of the documentary. It was documentary pioneer Robert J. Flaherty who declared that the Belgian documentaries of Henri Storck, Charles Dekeukeleire and others were the most interesting in the world. Storck is undoubtedly the defining figure here. Like Dekeukeleire, he made various forms of documentaries representing a rich and varied image of Belgian identity, creating sensation with his social protest and commitment. *Misère au Borinage* (co-directed with Joris Ivens, 1934) and the notable *Les Maisons de la misère* (*Houses of Misery*, 1937) can be considered the model revolutionary documentary films. It is a kind of revolutionary humanism – a term originally used by film critic André Bazin to portray Italian neorealism – that characterised the social protest films of Henri Storck. These ethics, where the documentary maker takes side with the most vulnerable but resistant human beings – so peculiar to the work and vision of the neorealist Roberto Rossellini – is unquestionably present in the outstanding documentary work of many Belgian filmmakers. Paul Meyer's *Déjà s'envole la fleur maigre* (*The Lank Flower Has Already Flown*, aka *Children of the Borinage*, 1960), Patric Jean's *Les Enfants du Borinage – Lettre à Henri Storck* (*Kids from the Coal Land – A Letter to Henri Storck*, 1998) and even the Dardennes' own *While the boat of Leon M. descends the river Meuse for the first time* deal with the same social problems and show similar human beings fighting for a dignified living. It is easy to see how Storck influenced the Dardenne Brothers. But in their cinematic reflection on both individual's and the working class' struggle for valuable life, the Dardenne Brothers are not only inspired by the Storck model. They also collaborated with the filmmaker and veteran of the resistance movement in Belgium, Frans Buyens, who produced social documentaries about the subject of concentration camps and the awareness of the horrors perpetrated by the Nazis (for example, *Open Dialoog/Open dialogue*, 1971).

In a biofilmography dedicated to Luc and Jean-Pierre Dardenne by Louis Héliot, they officially deny reincarnating the Belgian documentary tradition. They want to be passionate and free filmmakers before being representatives of any Belgian cinema tradition. And even though they were born and continue to live and work in Wallonia, they claim their film fatherland is situated elsewhere, in the territories of Roberto Rossellini, Kenji Mizoguchi, John Cassavetes, Maurice Pialat and Krzysztof Kieslowski. They want to make films like they feel it, without asking whether they belong to this or that film movement or film school. Nevertheless,

The Promise, *Rosetta* and *The Son* demonstrate the actuality and history of Belgian documentary tradition, and of course the personal documentary history of the Dardenne Brothers themselves. The way they make films, their personal style, their manner to tell the stories of Igor, Rosetta or Olivier may owe more to the *cinéma d'auteur* of Kieslowski, Rossellini and others than to Storck's or Buyens' documentary forms. But the Dardenne's idea of the world – their ethical concerns – is the reality of Belgium, Wallonia and more specifically problematic (young) life in Seraing close by the river La Meuse. At the same time their idea of cinema – their aesthetic potential – is developed through the greatest *cinéma d'auteur* in the world.

Wouter Hessels

FILMOGRAPHY

MAUDITE SOIT LA GUERRE WAR IS HELL **1914**
Director: Alfred Machin
Producer: Belge Cinéma Film
Screenplay: Alfred Machin
Camera: Jacques Bizeuil, Paul Flon
Cast: Suzanne Berni (Lidia Modzel), Baert (Adolphe Hardeff), Albert Henderickx (Sigismond Modzel), Nadia D'Angely (Mother Modzel), Fernand Crommelynck (Father Modzel), Henri Goidsen (Lt Maxim)

ZUIDERZEE 1930–33
Director: Joris Ivens
Screenplay: Joris Ivens
Camera: Joris Ivens
Editor: Joris Ivens, Helen Van Dongen

NIEUWE GRONDEN NEW EARTH **1933**
Director: Joris Ivens
Screenplay: Joris Ivens
Camera: Joris Ivens, Helen Van Dongen, John Fernhout, Piet Huisken, Eli Lotar
Editors: Joris Ivens, Helen Van Dongen
Music: Hanns Eisler

MISÈRE AU BORINAGE BORINAGE **1934**
Directors: Joris Ivens, Henri Storck
Producer: Education par L'image (Jean Fonteyne)
Screenplay: Joris Ivens and Henri Storck
Camera: François Rents
Editor: Helen Van Dongen

DE WITTE WHITEY **1934**
Director: Jan Vanderheyden
Producer: Jan Vanderheyden (Jan Vanderheyden-Film p.v.b.a.)
Screenplay: Edith Kiel (book: Ernest Claes)
Camera: Ewald Daub
Editor: Walter Van Bonhorst
Music: Renaat Veremans
Cast: Jef Bruyninckx (De Witte), Magda Janssens (Mother), Jef Van Leemput (Father), Gaston Smet (Niske), Nora Oosterwijk (Treske)

KOMEDIE OM GELD THE TROUBLE WITH MONEY **1936**
Director: Max Ophüls
Producer: Will Tuschinski
Screenplay: Christine Van Meeteren, Max Ophüls, Walter Schlee

Camera: Eugen Schüfftan
Editors: Gerald Bensdorg, Nol Van Es
Music: Heinz Lachmann, Max Tak
Cast: Herman Bouber (Brand), Matthieu Van Eysden (Ferdinand), Rini Otte (Willy), Cor Ruys (Moorman), Edwin Gubbins Doorenbos (Speaker)

GLAS GLASS **1958**
Director: Bert Haanstra
Producers: Bert Haanstra, George K. Arthur
Screenplay: Bert Haanstra
Camera: Edouard Van Der Enden
Editors: Bert Haanstra, Ralph Sendon
Music: Pim Jacobs

DE MAN DIE ZIJN HAAR KORT LIET KNIPPEN THE MAN WHO HAD HIS HAIR CUT SHORT **1965**
Director: André Delvaux
Producers: Paul Louyet, Jos Op De Beeck
Screenplay: André Delvaux, Anna De Pagter (book: Johan Daisne)
Camera: Ghislain Cloquet
Editor: Suzanne Baron
Music: Frédéric Devreese
Cast: Senne Rouffaer (Govert), Beata Tyszkiewicz (Fran), Hector Camerlynck (Prof. Mato), Hilde Uytterlinden (Beps), Annemarie Van Dijk (Corra)

MIRA OF DE TELEURGANG VAN DE WATERHOEK MIRA **1971**
Director: Fons Rademakers
Producer: Jan Van Raemdonck
Screenplay: Hugo Claus (book: Stijn Streuvels)
Camera: Edouard Van der Enden
Editors: Jan Dop, Kees Linthorst, Hetty Konink
Music: Georges Delerue
Cast: Willeke Van Ammelrooy (Mira), Carlos Van Lanckere (Broeke), Jan Decleir (Sander), Luc Ponette (Maurice), Roger Bolders (Sieper), Freek De Jonge (Treute)

LES LÈVRES ROUGES DAUGHTERS OF DARKNESS **1971**
Director: Harry Kümel
Producers: Paul Collet, Henry Lange (Showking Films, Maya Films)
Screenplay: Pierre Drouot, Jean Ferry, Harry Kümel
Camera: Edouard Van der Enden
Editors: Gust Verschueren, Denis Bonan, Daniel De Valck, Edith Schumann
Music: François De Roubaix
Cast: Delphine Seyrig (Comtesse Bathory), Andrea Rau (Ilona), Danièle Ouimet (Valerie), John Karlen (Stefan), Fons Rademakers ('Mother')

TURKS FRUIT TURKISH DELIGHT **1973**
Director: Paul Verhoeven
Producer: Rob Houwer
Screenplay: Gerard Soeteman (book: Jan Wolkers)
Camera: Jan De Bont

Editor: Jan Bosdriesz
Music: Rogier Van Otterloo
Cast: Monique Van De Ven (Olga Stapels), Rutger Hauer (Erik Vonk), Tonny Huurdeman (Mother), Wim van den Brink (Father), Hans Boskamp (store manager), Dolf De Vries (Paul) Manfred De Graaf (Henny)

MARIKEN VAN NIEUMEGHEN MARIKEN 1974
Director: Jos Stelling
Producers: Rob Du Mee, Jos Stelling
Screenplay: Jos Stelling (Dialogues: Mies Bouwhuis)
Camera: Ernest Bresser
Editor: Jan Bosdriesz
Music: Ruud Bos
Cast: Ronnie Montaigne (Mariken), Sander Bais (Moenen), Diet van Hulst (Berthe), Jan Harms, Wil Hildebrand, Menno Jetten, Leo Koenen (Four Men)

JEANNE DIELMAN 23 QUAI DU COMMERCE 1080 BRUXELLES JEANNE DIELMAN 1975
Director: Chantal Akerman
Producers: Corinne Jénart, Evelyne Paul
Screenplay: Chantal Akerman
Camera: Babette Mangolte
Editor: Patricia Canino
Cast: Delphine Seyrig (Jeanne), Jan Decorte (Sylvain), Henri Storck (first client), Jacques Doniol-Valcroze (second client), Yves Bical (third client)

SOLDAAT VAN ORANJE SOLDIER OF ORANGE 1975
Director: Paul Verhoeven
Producer: Rob Houwer
Screenplay: Erik Hazelhoff Roelfzema, Kees Holierhoek, Gerard Soeteman, Paul Verhoeven (book: Erik Hazelhoff Roelfzema)
Camera: Jost Vacano
Editor: Jane Sperr
Music: Rogier Van Otterloo
Cast: Rutger Hauer (Erik Lanshof), Jeroen Krabbé (Guus Lejeune), Derek De Lint (Alex), Peter Faber (Will), Edward Fox (Colonel Rafelli), Susan Penhaligon (Susan), Lex Van Delden (Nico), Huib Rooymans (Jan), Dolf De Vries (Jacques), Edy Habbema (Robby), Belinda Meuldijk (Esther)

TWEE VROUWEN TWICE A WOMAN 1979
Director: George Sluizer
Producers: Anne Lordon, George Sluizer
Screenplay: Jurriën Rood, George Sluizer (book: Harry Mulisch)
Camera: Mat van Hensbergen
Editor: Leo De Boer
Music: Willem Breuker
Cast: Bibi Andersson (Laura), Sandra Dumas (Sylvia), Anthony Perkins (Alfred), Charles Gormley (Eric), Gregor Frenkel Frank (Roeblyov)

DE STILTE ROND CHRISTINE M A QUESTION OF SILENCE 1982
Director: Marleen Gorris
Producer: Matthijs Van Heijningen

Screenplay: Marleen Gorris
Camera: Frans Bromet
Editor: Hans Van Dongen
Music: Lodewijk de Boer, Martijn Hasebos
Cast: Edda Barends (Christine M.), Nelly Frijda (An), Henriette Tol (Andrea), Cox Habbema (Janine), Eddie Brugman (Ruud Van Den Bos)

CRAZY LOVE 1987
Director: Dominique Deruddere
Producer: Erwin Provoost
Screenplay: Dominique Deruddere, Marc Didden (books: Charles Bukowski)
Camera: Willy Stassen
Editor: Ludo Troch
Music: Raymond Van Het Groenewoud
Cast: Josse De Pauw (Harry Voss), Geert Hunaerts (Young Harry), Michael Pas (Stan), Gene Bervoets (Jeff), Amid Chakir (Bill), Florence Beliard (Princess)

SPOORLOOS THE VANISHING 1987
Director: George Sluizer
Producers: Anne Lordon, George Sluizer
Screenplay: George Sluizer, Tim Krabbé (book: Tim Krabbé)
Camera: Toni Kuhn
Editor: Lin Friedman, George Sluizer
Music: Henny Vrienten
Cast: Gene Bervoets (Rex Hofman), Johanna ter Steege (Saskia Wagter), Raymond Lemorne (Bernard-Pierre Donnadieu), Gwen Eckhaus (Lieneke), Benadette Le Saché (Simone Lemorne)

A WOPBOBALOOBOP A LOPBAMBOOM 1989
Director: Andy Bausch
Producers: Andy Bausch, Jürgen Tröster
Screenplay: Andy Bausch, Armand Strainchamps, Michel Treinen
Camera: Klaus-Peter Weber
Music: Maggie Parke, Gast Waltzing
Cast: Birol Uenel (Rocco), Thierry Van Werveke (Petz), Desirée Nosbusch (Vero), Sabine Berg (Anke), Jochen Senf (Bruno), Serge Wolf (Daniel)

TOTO LE HÉROS TOTO THE HERO 1991
Director: Jaco Van Dormael
Producers: Pierre Drouot, Philippe Dussart, Dany Gays, Luciano Gloor
Screenplay: Jaco Van Dormael
Camera: Walther Van Den Ende
Editor: Susanna Rossberg
Music: Pierre Van Dormael, Charles Trenet
Cast: Michel Bouquet (Thomas as an old man), Jo De Backer (Thomas as an adult), Thomas Godet (Thomas as a young boy), Gisela Uhlen (Evelyne as an old woman), Mireille Perrier (Evelyne as a young woman), Pascal Duquenne (Célestin), Sandrine Blancke (Alice), Peter Böhlke (Alfred as an old man), Didier De Neck (Mr Kant).

DE NOORDERLINGEN THE NORTHERNERS 1992
Director: Alex van Warmerdam

Producers: Laurens Geels, Dick Maas
Screenplay: Laurens Geels, Dick Maas
Camera: Marc Felperlaan
Editor: René Wiegmans
Music: Vincent van Warmerdam
Cast: Leonard Lucieer (Thomas), Jack·Wouterse (Jacob, the Butcher), Annet Malherbe (Martha, his wife), Rudolf Lucieer (Anton, the Hunter), Loes Wouterson (Elisabeth, his wife), Alex van Warmerdam (Plagge, the Postman), Dary Somé (the Black Man), Veerle Dobbelaere (Agnes, the Girl), Theo van Gogh (Fat Willy)

C'EST ARRIVÉ PRÈS DE CHEZ VOUS MAN BITES DOG 1992
Directors: Rémy Belvaux, André Bonzel, and Benoît Poelvoorde
Producers: Rémy Belvaux, André Bonzel, and Benoît Poelvoorde
Screenplay: Rémy Belvaux, André Bonzel, and Benoît Poelvoorde, Vincent Tavier
Camera: André Bonzel
Editors: Rémy Belvaux, Eric Dardill
Music: Jean-Marc Chenut, Laurence Dufrene
Cast: Benoît Poelvoorde, (Ben), André Bonzel (André, cameraman), Rémy Belvaux (Rémy, interviewer), Jacqueline Poelvoorde-Pappaert (Ben's mother), Nelly Pappaert, (Ben's grandmother), Hector Pappaert (Ben's grandfather)

KARAKTER CHARACTER 1997
Director: Mike Van Diem
Producers: Laurens Geels, Sam Cerulus, Noël Swinnen
Screenplay: Mike van Diem, Laurens Geels, Ruud van Megen (book: Ferdinand Bordewijk)
Camera: Rogier Stoffers
Editor: Jessica De Koning
Music: Het Paleis van Boem
Cast: Jan Decleir (Dreverhaven), Fedja van Huêt (Katadreuffe), Betty Schuurman (Joba), Tamar van den Dop (Lorna te George), Hans Kesting (Jan Maan), Victor Löw (De Gankelaar)

TWEE KOFFERS VOL LEFT LUGGAGE 1998
Director: Jeroen Krabbé
Producers: Ate De Jong, Hans Post, Dave Schram, Rudy Verzyck, Dirk Impens, Jeroen Krabbé, Maria Peters
Screenplay: Edwin De Vries (book: Carl Friedman)
Camera: Walther Van Den Ende
Editor: Edgar Burcksen
Music: Henny Vrienten, Keith Allison, Erik Satie
Cast: Laura Fraser (Chaya), Adam Monty (Simcha), Jeroen Krabbé (Mr Kalman), Isabella Rossellini (Mrs Kalman), Chaim Topol (Mr. Apfelschnitt), Marianne Sägebrecht (Chaya's mother), Maximilian Schell (Chaya's father)

ROSETTA 1999
Directors: Luc & Jean-Pierre Dardenne
Producers: Luc & Jean-Pierre Dardenne, Michèle & Laurent Pétin, Arlette Zylberberg
Screenplay: Luc & Jean-Pierre Dardenne
Camera: Benoît Dervaux
Editor: Marie-Hélène Dozo
Cast: Emilie Dequenne (Rosetta), Fabrizio Rongione (Riquet), Anne Yernaux (The mother), Olivier Gourmet (The employer), Frédéric Bodson (The factory boss)

BIBLIOGRAPHY compiled by Ernest Mathijs

The following bibliography serves two functions. First, it lists every work cited in the text (as far as the source is known). Second, it attempts to guide the reader to the most essential reading materials available on Low Countries cinema. Although I have tried to include as many materials as possible, I did have to apply some limitations. Books, articles and clippings dealing with specific films or filmmakers, other than the ones discussed in the book, have been left out. Reviews of particular films have only been included if they were quoted or referred to in the book.

I would also like to point the reader to three reputed institutions that collect most writings on cinema of the Low Countries: the Royal Film Archive of Belgium, The Dutch Filmmuseum and the Luxembourgian CNA (Centre National de l'Audiovisuelle) They harbour well-equipped libraries of international repute. Their collections include not only books and journals but also, importantly, reviews (covering most of the national magazine and newspaper press) press kits, brochures, production documents, government studies, filmographies, catalogues, festival publications and photographs. They also actively support research and regularly publish professional guides and collections on national cinema. Information on these institutions can be accessed online through:

Royal Film Archive of Belgium: http://www.ledoux.be
Dutch Filmmuseum: http://www.filmmuseum.nl (also see http://www.nfdb.nl)
CNA Luxembourg: http://www.cna.public.lu/index.html

Aitkin, I. (1996) 'Cultural Problems in the Study of European Cinema and the Role of Questions on Cultural Indentity', in W. Everett (ed.) *European Identity in Cinema*. Exeter: Intellect, 75–82.

Anon. (1989–1997) *Jaarboek Mediageschiedenis*, continued as *Tijdschrift voor Mediageschiedenis*. All articles with summaries in English.

____ (1988) 'The Vanishing', *Dutch Film 1987–88*, The Hague: Government Publishing Office, 170.

____ (1995) *Les premiers temps du cinema en Belgique* (special issue of *Revue Belge du cinema*), 38–9.

____ (1996) 'Luc et Jean-Pierre Dardenne, vingt ans de travail en cinéma et vidéo', *Revue Belge du cinema*, 41.

____ (1996) 'Interview met Mike Van Diem', *de Filmkrant*, 169, 10.

____ (1997) 'Interview met Mike van Diem', *de Vprogids* (5 April).

____ (1997) 'Character', *Variety*, 367, 4, 68.

____ (1997) 'Interview met Mike Van Diem', *Vrij Nederland* (12 April).

____ (1998) 'Character', *Screen International*, 1148, 27.

Ansen, D. (1979) 'Last tango in the lowlands', *Newsweek* (9 August).

Asper, H. G. (1998) *Max Ophüls. Eine Biographie*. Berlin: Dieter Bertz Verlag.

Aumont, J. (1990) 'L'Homme au crâne rasé', in G. Jungblut, P. Leboutte, D. Païni (eds) *Une Encyclopédie des cinémas de Belgique*. Paris/Crisnée: Musée d'Art Moderne de la Ville de Paris/Editions Yellow Now, 127–9.

Bakker, K. (ed.) (1999) *Joris Ivens and the Documentary Context*. Amsterdam: Amsterdam University Press.

Bauman, Z. (1998) 'Identity – Then, Now, what For?', *Polish Sociological Review*, 123.

____ (1999) *Culture as Praxis*. London: Sage.

____ (2001) 'Identity in the Globalising World', *Social Anthropology*, 9, 2, 121–9.

Bergstrom, J. (1977) 'Jeanne Dielman 23 Quai du Commerce, 1080 Bruxelles by Chantal Akerman', *Camera Obscura*, 2, 114–21.

Bertina, B. J. (1987) 'de picturale fantasieën van een gedreven cameraregisseur', *Jaarboek film 1987*, Houten: Unieboek.

Bishoff, R. (1988) *Hollywood in Holland: de geschiedenis van de filmfabriek Hollandia 1912-1923*. Amsterdam: Thoth.

Blom, I. (1995) 'L'Artère nord-sud. Jean Desmet, distributeur hollando-belge, et la Belgique', *Revue belge du cinéma*, 38/39, 25-8.

_____ (2003) *Jean Desmet and the Early Dutch Film Trade*. Amsterdam: Amsterdam University Press.

Blom, J. C. H. and E. Lamberts (eds) (1999) *History of the Low Countries*. London: Berghahn Books.

Bolen, F. (1971) *D'un certain cinéma belge*. Brussels: Ministery of Culture.

_____ (1978) *Histoire authentique, anecdotique, floklorique et critique du cinema Belge depuis ses plus lointaines origines*. Brussels: Memo & Codec.

Bono, F. (1992) 'De Hollandse school door Italiaanse ogen', *Skrien*, 186, 54-7.

Borgomano, L. and A. Nysenholc (1988) *André Delvaux. Une Oeuvre. Un Film. L'Oeuvre au noir*. Brussels: Labor.

Bouineau, J-M. (2001) *Paul Verhoeven: Beyond Flesh and Blood*. Paris: Le Cinephage.

Bredschneyder, F. (1964) 'Bert Haanstra en de 'candid camera', Alleman', *Film & Televisie* (May–June), 38-9.

Brismée, J. (1995) *Cinema: One Hundred Years' Movies in Belgium*. Liège: Mardaga.

Burgelman, J-C. (1987) 'Impact of Politics on the Structure and Development of Belgian Broadcasting', *Historical Journal of Film, Radio and Television*, 7, 1, 35-46.

Burgelman, J-C. and C. Pauwels (1992) 'Audiovisual Policy and Cultural Identity in Small European States: The Challenge of a Unified Market', *Media, Culture and Society*, 14, 2, 169-83.

Bush, W. S. (1914)'War is Hell', *Moving Picture World* (9 May), 800-3.

Ciment, M. (1966) 'Le Silence du monde: l'homme au crâne rasé', *Positif*, 58, 53-6.

Coleman, J. (1979) 'Review of *Jeanne Dielman 23 Quai du Commerce 1080 Bruxelles*', *New Statesman* (1 June).

Convents, G. (1988) 'Documentaries and Propaganda before 1914: A View on Early Cinema and Colonial History', *Framework*, 35, 104-13.

_____ (2000) *Van kinetoscoop tot café ciné. De eerste jaren van de film in België*. Leuven: Universitaire Pers.

_____ (1995) 'Le cinéma et la premiere guerre mondiale en Belgique. Quelques aspects inconnus', *Revue belge du cinéma*, 38/39, 29-36.

Cook, R. and B. Mortan (2002) *The Penguin Guide to Jazz on CD*. London: Penguin Books.

Courtmans, G. (1973) 'Le cinema cochon', *Special* (29 August 1973), 39.

Cowie, P. (1979) *Dutch Cinema*. London: Tantivy Press

Daems, J. (1996) *Teder testament: de films van Bert Haanstra*. Leuven: Acco.

Davay, P. (1973) *Cinéma de Belgique*. Gembloux: Duculot.

De Kuyper, E. (ed.) (1995) *Alfred Machin: Cinéaste/Filmmaker*. Brussels: Belgian Royal Film Archive.

De Laet, D. (1995) *Fantasy and Science Fiction in Belgian Films*. Brussels: Peymey Diffusion.

De Laet, D. and Y. Varende (1980) *Beyond the Seventh Art: History of the Belgian Strip Cartoon*. Brussels: Ministry of Foreign Affairs.

De Lauretis, T. (1984) *Alice Doesn't: Feminism, Semiotics, Cinema*. London: Macmillan Press.

Delcorde, J. (1959) *Le film belge a l'étranger*. Brussels: Ministry of Education.

Delvaux, A. (1991) 'Vlaamse Film: Identiteitscrisis?', special issue, *Academia Analecta*, 51, 1.

De Rover, F. (1976) 'Twee vrouwen over tijd', *De Gids*, 139, 352-65.

Dibbets, K. and F. van der Maden (eds) (1986) *Geschiedenis van de Nederlandse film en bioscoop tot 1940*. Weesp: Wereldvenster.

Dibbets, K. (1993) *Sprekende films: de komst van de geluidsfilm in Nederland, 1928-1933*. Amsterdam: Cramwinckel.

_____ (1993) 'De ontdekking van de Nederlandse film', *Argus*, 2, 49-60.

_____ (1995) 'Filmgeschiedschrijving in Nederland', in J. C. H. Blom and H. Wijfjes (eds) *Mediageschiedenis: kansen en perspectieven*. Amsterdam: KNAW, 103-14.

_____ (2003) *Netherlands Cinema History*. http://www.xs4all.nl/kd/ (Accessed 18 June 2003).

Dittrich, K. (1987) *Achter het doek. Duitse emigranten in de Nederlandse speelfilm in de jaren dertig*. Houten: Het Wereldvenster. (In German: *Der niederländische Spielfilm der dreissiger Jahre und die deutsche Filmemigration*. Amsterdam: Rodopi).

Donaldson, G. (1997) *Of Joy and Sorrow: A Filmography of Dutch Silent Fiction*. Trowbridge: Flicks Books.

Doniger, W. (2002) 'Lacan's Ghost', *London Review of Books*, 24, 1, 7-8.

Donner, J. H. (1979) 'Film', *NRC Handelsblad* (11 June).

Dubois, P. and E. Arnoldy (eds.) (1995) *Ça tourne depuis cent ans; une histoire du cinéma francophone de Belgique.* Brussels: Communauté française de Belgique/Wallonie.

Dubroux, D., Th. Giraud and L. Skorecki (1977) 'Entretien avec Chantal Akerman', *Cahiers du Cinema*, 278, 34–42.

Dyer, R. and G. Vincendeau (eds.) (1992) *Popular European Cinema.* New York: Routledge.

Dyer, R. (1999) *Seven.* London: British Film Institute.

Ebert, R. (1991) 'The Vanishing', *Chicago Sun Times* (25 January).

Eisler, H. (1947) *Composing for the Films.* New York: Oxford.

Eksteins, M. (1995) 'The Cultural Impact of the Great War', in K. Dibbets and B. Hogenkamp (eds) *Film and the First World War.* Amsterdam: Amsterdam University Press.

Elhem, Ph. and M. Vanhellemont (eds) (1989) *Le cinéma belge francophone des années 80.* Brussels: Cinegie-Europe.

Engelen, L. (2002) 'Anticipatie of representatie? De representatie van de oorlog in Alfred Machin's Maudite soit la guerre', *Tijdschrift voor Media Geschiedenis*, 5, 1, 4–27.

Erens, P. (1990) (ed.) *Issues in Feminist Film Criticism.* Indiana: Indiana University Press.

Everaerts, J. P. (2000) *Film in Belgie. Een permanente revolte.* Brussels: Mediadoc.

Fens, K. (1975) 'Twee vrouwen', *de Volkskrant*, (8 November).

Ferguson, O. (1971 [1936]) 'Guest Artist', in R. Wilson (ed.) *The Film Criticism of Otis Ferguson.* Philadelphia: Temple University Press, 125–6.

Foster, G. A. (ed.) (2003) *Identity and Memory: The Films of Chantal Akerman* (2nd edn.) Carbondale, IL: Southern Illinois University Press.

Fowler, C. (2001) 'Sites of Contestation: the Place of Alfred Machin in Early Belgian Cinema', *Historical Journal of Film, Radio and Television*, 21, 4, 347–59.

____ (2002) 'Doing Time: Chantal Akerman's Woman Sitting Down After Killing', *Vertigo*, 2, 2, 48.

____ (2003) 'All Night Long; the Ambivalent Text of "Belgianicity"', in G. A. Foster (ed.) *Identity and Memory: The Films of Chantal Akerman* (2nd edn.) Carbondale, IL: Southern Illinois University Press, 77–93.

François C. (1993) 'Von Petticoat, Punk und Pappnasen', in *Zelluloid Cowboy.* Luxembourg: Editions Phi, 59.

Frodon, J-M. (1998) *La projection nationale, cinéma et nation.* Paris: Odile Jacob.

Gab (1934) 'De Witte wordt verfilmd', *Wereldrevue* (05 April 1934).

Gallagher, T. (2003) 'Max Ophuls: A New Art But Who Notices?', *Film International*, http://www.filmint.nu/eng.html.

Gans, C. (1992) 'Interview des Artistes Anonymes', Original French press book, n.p.

Geens, P. (1986) *Naslagwerk over de Vlaamse film.* Brussels: CIAM.

Geeraerts, D. and M. Van Hoogenbemt (eds.) (1982) *Krisis in de Belgische film/La Crise dans le film belge.* Mechelen: Donut Productions.

Goedegebuure, J. (1976) 'Liefdesromans als leesvoer', *Tirade*, 20, 215/216, 288–302.

Haakman, A. (1975a) 'Interview with Jos Stelling and Ernest Bresser', *Skoop*, 10, 9, 3–7.

____ (1975b) 'Jan Bosdriesz over de afwerking van Mariken van Nieumeghen', *Skoop*, 10, 9, 12.

____ (1975c) 'Wat Paul Verhoeven wil: Interview', *Skoop*, 9, 2, 3–11.

Hall, S. (1996) 'Who Needs Identity?', in S. Hall and P. Du Gay (eds) *Questions of Cultural Identity.* London: Sage.

Hartl, J. (1975) 'Yes but what is the film about?', *Seattle Washington Times* (27 October).

Héliot, L. (1999) *Bio-Filmo Luc & Jean-Pierre Dardenne.* Brussels: Scope Editions.

Hermes, J. (2002) 'Family matters: Recent Dutch television crime drama', Unpublished essay.

Hinson, H. (1991) 'The Vanishing', *Washington Post* (8 March).

Hofstede, B. (2000) *Dutch Film Abroad: The International Position of Dutch Film.* Amsterdam: Boekmanstichting.

Hogenkamp, B. (1988) *De Nederlandse documentaire film 1920–1940.* Van Gennep: Amsterdam.

____ (1997) 'Herinneringen aan Bert Haanstra (1916–1997)', *DIFA-Nieuwsbrief*, 25, 2.

Hogenkamp, B. and H. Storck (1983) *De Borinage: De mijnwerkersstaking van 1932 en de film van Joris Ivens en Henri Storck.* Amsterdam/Leuven: Van Gennep/Kritak. (Republished and translated as: Hogenkamp, B. and H. Storck (1984) *Le Borinage: La grève des mineurs de 1932 et le film de Joris Ivens et Henri Storck.* Brussels: Revue Belge du Cinéma).

Howe, D. (1991) 'The Vanishing', *Washington Post* (8 March).

Hulsker, J. (1933) 'Joris Ivens', *Cinema Quarterly*, 1, 148–51.

Indiana, G. (1983) 'Getting Ready for the Golden Eighties: A Conversation with Chantal Akerman', *ArtForum* (Summer), 55–61.

Insdorf, A. (1996) *François Truffaut*. London: Cambridge University Press.

Ivens, J. (1969 [1944]) *The Camera and I*. New York: International Publishers.

Ivens, J. and R. Destanque (1982) *Joris Ivens ou la mémoire d'un regard*. Paris: Éditions BFB.

Jungblut, G, P. Leboutte and D. Païni, (eds) *Une Encyclopédie des cinémas de Belgique*. Paris/Crisnée: Musée d'Art Moderne de la Ville de Paris/Editions Yellow Now.

Kelly, R. (2000) 'Wage Warrior', *Sight and Sound*, 10, 2, 22–4.

Kinder, M. (1979) 'Reflections on 'Jeanne Dielman' in P. Erens (ed.) *Sexual Stratagems: The World of Women in Film*. New York: Horizon Press, 248–57.

Kossman, E. H. (1978) *The Low Countries, 1780–1940*. Oxford: Oxford University Press.

Kristeva, J. (1982) *Powers of Horror: An Essay in Abjection*. New York: Columbia University Press.

Lacassin, F. (2001) *Alfred Machin de la jungle à l'écran*. Paris: Dreamland éditeur.

Labio, C. (ed.) (2003) *Belgian Memories: Yale French Studies, 102*. New Have: Yale University Press.

Lafond, F. (2002a) 'Faking it? or the Spectator's Response to *Man Bites Dog*', Unpublished manuscript.

_____ (2002b) 'Aux frontières du réel: Les limites/excès de la représentation réaliste du meurtre dans le film d'horreur', *Simulacres*, 7, 82–7.

_____ (2003) 'The Life and Crimes of Ben; or When a Serial Killer Meets a Film Crew in *Man Bites Dog*', *Post Script: Essays in Film and the Humanities*, 22, 2, 92–102.

Lakeland, M. J. (1977) 'The Color of Jeanne Dielman', *Camera Obscura*, 3–4, 216–18.

Lesch, P. (1995) *Germaine Damar; Ein Luxemburger Star im deutschen Film der 50er Jahre*. Dudelange: Ministery of Cultural Affairs.

_____ (2002) *Heim ins UFA-Reich? NS-Filmpolitik und die Rezeption deutscher Filme in Luemburg 1933–1944*. Trier: Wissenschaftlicher Verlag Trier.

Linssen, C. (1999) *Het gaat om de film! Een nieuwe geschiedenis van de Nederlandsche Filmliga, 1927–1933*. Amsterdam: Filmmuseum.

Linthorst, G. (1993) 'Bert Haanstra, de milde blik van een observator', *Ons Erfdeel*, 1, 91–8.

Loader, J. (1977) 'Jeanne Dielman: Death in Installments', *Jump Cut*, 16, 10–12.

Longfellow, B. (1989) 'Love Letters to the Mother: The Work of Chantal Akerman', *Canadian Journal of Political and Social Theory*, 13, 1–2, 73–90.

Mairesse, E. (1977) 'A propos des films de Chantal Akerman: un temps-atmosphère', *Cahiers du Cinéma*, 281, 60–1.

Margulies, I. (1996) *Nothing Happens: Chantal Akerman's Hyperrealist Everyday*. Durham, NC: Duke University Press.

Maslin, J. (1991) 'Review/Film; How Evil Can One Person Be?', *New York Times* (25 January).

Mathijs, E. (2004a) 'Alternative Belgian Cinema and Cultural Identity: S. and the Affaire Dutroux', in E. Mathijs & X. Mendik (eds) *Alternative Europe: Eurotrash and Exploitation Cinema Since 1945*. London: Wallflower Press, 64–75.

_____ (2004b) '"Nobody is Innocent": Cinema and Sexuality in Contemporary Belgian Culture', *Social Semiotics*, 14, 1, 85–101.

_____ (2004c) '*Man Bites Dog* and the Critical Reception of Belgian Horror (in) Cinema', in S. J. Schneider & T. Williams (eds) *Horror International*. Detroit: Wayne State University Press, forthcoming.

McNeil, S. (1993) '"We'll Never Get Enough": *Man Bites Dog*, Documentary Theory and Other Andalusian Ethics', *Cinema Papers*, 95, 28–31.

Melchior-Bonnet, S. (2001) *The Mirror: A History*. London: Routledge.

Milne, T. (1972) 'Countries of the Mind', *Sight and Sound*, 41, 2, 74–7.

Monaco, J. (ed.) (1991) *Encyclopedia of Film*. London: Perigree Books, 4–5.

Morlion, F. (1932) *Filmleiding*. Leuven: Davidsfonds.

_____ (1934a) 'De Witte' *De Standaard* (8 June 1934).

_____ (1934b) 'De Witte', *Liga* (August).

Mosley, P. (1992) 'Literature, Film, Music: Julien Gracq's Le Roi Cophetua and André Delvaux's Rendezvous à Bray',

Literature/Film Quarterly, 20, 2, 138–45.

_____ (1994) 'From Book to Film: André Delvaux's Alchemy of the Image', in _The French Review_, 67, 5, 813–23.

_____ (2001) _Split Screen: Belgian Cinema and Cultural Identity_. New York: SUNY Press.

_____ (2003) Anxiety, Memory, Place in Belgian Cinema', in C. Labio (ed.) _Belgian Memories: Yale French Studies_, 102, New Have: Yale University Press, 160–75.

Murphy, J. (1986) 'A Question of Silence', in C. Brunsdon (ed.) _Films for Women_. London: British Film Institute, 99–108.

Murray, S. (1991) 'Vanishing act makes Lambs look tame', _Atlanta Journal and Constitution_ (27 December).

Nichols, B. (1981) _Ideology and the Image: Social Representation in the Cinema and Other Media_. Bloomington: Indiana University Press.

Nysenholc, A. (ed.) (1985) _André Delvaux ou les visages de l'imaginaire_. Brussels: Editions de l'Université libre de Bruxelles.

Ophüls, M. (1936) 'Der Kampf', in _New Theatre and Film_, 3, 10, 16; reprinted in Kline, H. (1984) _New Theatre and Film 1934 to 1937: An Anthology_. HBJ Publishers: London.

_____ (1959) _Spiel im Dasein. Ein Rückblende_. Stuttgart: Henry Goverts Verlag.

Patterson, P. and M. Farber. (1979) 'Beyond the New Wave: I. Kitchen Without Kitsch', _Film Comment_, 13, 6, 47–50.

Peeters, Ch., T. Thijssens and H. Webers (2000) _De economische impact van de film in Vlaanderen_, Dordrecht: Kluwer.

Pilowsky, M. (2000) '_Spoorloos (The Vanishing)_', in S. Pendergast and T. Pendergast (eds) _The International Directory of Films and Filmmakers, 4th Edition_. Farmington Hills, MI: St. James Press, 1136.

Perlmutter, R. (1979) 'Feminine Absence: A Political Aesthetic in Chantal Akerman's _Jeanne Dielman 23 Quai du Commerce 1080 Bruxelles_', _Quarterly Review of Film Studies_, 4, 2, 125–33.

Pleij, H. (1975) 'Wat Zien ik in de middeleeuwen', _De Gids_, 138, 1/2, 131.

Quart, B. (1984) 'A Question of Silence', _Cineaste_, 13, 3, 45–7.

Queval, J. (1976) _Henri Storck ou la traversée du cinéma_. Brussels: Festival National du Film Belge.

Ramanathan, G. (1992) 'Murder as Speech: Narrative Subjectivity in Marleen Gorris's _Question of Silence_', in _Genders_, 15, 58–71.

Reijnhoudt, B. (1994) _The Difficult Road to the Restauration of the Films of Joris Ivens_. Amsterdam: Nederlands Filmmuseum.

Rich, B. R. (1983) 'Up Against the Kitchen Wall: Chantal Akerman's Meta-Cinema', _The Village Voice_ (29 March), 1, 51.

_____ (1984) 'In the name of Feminist Film Criticism', in P. Steven (ed.) _Jump Cut: Hollywood, Politics and Counter-Cinema_. Toronto: Between the Lines.

Root, J. (1985) 'Distributing _A Question of Silence_: A Cautionary Tale', _Screen_, 26, 1, 58–64.

Roscoe, J. and Hight, C. (2001) _Faking it: Mock-documentary and the Subversion of Factuality_. Manchester: Manchester University Press.

Rosenberg, J. (1983) _Women's Reflections: The Feminist Film Movement_. Michigan: UMI Research Press.

Ross, M. (2002) '_Turkish Delight_ and Representation of Cultural Identity in Holland and the Benelux', Unpublished Essay, University of Wales, Aberystwyth.

Rotha, P. (1952) _Documentary Film_. London: Faber & Faber.

Roud, R. (1967) 'The Man Who Had His Hair Cut Short', _Sight and Sound_, 36, 2, 93–4.

Schiweck, I. (2002) _Weil wir lieber im Kino sitzen als in Sack und Asche: der deutsche Spielfilm in den besetzten Niederlanden, 1940-1945_. Münster-New York: Waxmann.

Schneider, S. J. (2002) 'Repackaging Rage: _The Vanishing_ and _Nightwatch_', _Kinema: A Journal for Film and Audiovisual Media_, 17, 47–66.

_____ (2004) 'When the vow breaks: Marriage, masculinity and repression in Dutch thriller cinema', in L. Badley, R. Barton Palmer and S. J. Schneider (eds) _Traditions in World Cinema_. Edinburgh: Edinburgh University Press: forthcoming.

Schneider, S. J. and K. Sweeney (2004) 'Genre Bending and Gender Bonding in Dutch Horror Cinema: Masculinity and Repression in Dutch "Thriller" Cinema', in S. J. Schneider and T. Williams (eds) Horror International. Detroit: Wayne State University Press, forthcoming.

Schoots, H. (2000) [1995] *Living Dangerously: A Biography of Joris Ivens*. Amsterdam: Amsterdam University Press.

Schuhmacher, W. J. (1977) 'Is *Soldaat van Oranje* de beste Nederlandse film aller tijden?', *Knack* (26 October).

Sedgwick, E. K. (1985) *Between Men: English Literature and Male Homosocial Desire*. New York: Columbia University Press.

Simons, J. and P. Delpeut (1985) 'Ik probeer het te zien, niet te bedenken: een interview met Paul Verhoeven', *Skrien*, 143, 10–16.

Singer, B. (1989-90) 'Jeanne Dielman: Cinematic Interrogation and Amplification', *Millenium Film Journal*, 22, 56–75.

Smelik, A. (1998) *And the Mirror Cracked: Feminist Cinema and Film Theory*. London: Macmillan.

Sojcher, F. (1999) *La kermesse héroique du cinema belge (Three volumes)*. Paris: L'Harmattan.

Soren, D. (1979) *Unreal Reality: The Cinema of Harry Kümel*. Columbia, MI: Lucas Brothers.

Spaas, L. (2000) *The Francophone Film: A Struggle for Identity*. Manchester/New York: Manchester University Press.

Stallaert, R. (1989) *Rode Glamour*. Ghent: Ludion.

Stelling, J. (1975) 'Ik film omdat het moet: Interview met Jos Stelling', *Elsevier*, (11 January), 56.

Stufkens, A. (ed.) (2002) *Cinema Without Borders: The Films of Joris Ivens*. Nijmegen: European Foundation Joris Ivens.

Sweeney, K. (2002) 'The Horrific in Sluizer's *The Vanishing*', *Post Script: Essays in Film and the Humanities*, 21, 3, 90–110.

Tanghe, G. (1965) 'Alleman, een juweel van montage!', *Film & Televisie* (October), 8–11.

Ten Bert, H. (1987) *Bert Haanstra*. CK Videos: Amsterdam.

Thomas, P. (1995) *Un siècle de cinema Belge*. Ottignies: Quorum.

Thompson, D. (2002) 'Auteur of Darkness', *Sight and Sound*, 12, 8, 16–18.

Thomson, H. (1971) 'Film: Artistic Vampires', *New York Times* (29 May 1971).

Thys, M. (ed.) (1999) *Belgian Cinema – Le cinéma belge – De Belgische film*. Ghent: Ludion.

Treilhou, M. C. (1976) 'Chantal Akerman: 'La vie, il faut la mettre en scène…', *Cinéma*, 76, 206, 89–93.

Urbano, C. (1995) 'A Question of Narrative', *CineAction*, 37.

Valenti, T. F. (2001) *Paul Verhoeven: carne y sangre*. Barcelona: Glénat.

Van Beusekom, A. (2001) *Kunst en amusement: reacties op de film als een nieuw medium in Nederland, 1895–1940*. Haarlem: Arcadia.

Van Bueren, P. (1979) '*Twee vrouwen*', *de Volkskrant* (23 May).

Van Bueren, P. and R.A.F. Proper (1979) 'Harry Mulisch over *Twee vrouwen*', *Skoop*, 15, 4, 12–14.

Van Den Heuvel, Ch. (1982) 'Itinéraires du cinéma de Belgique des origins à nos jours', *Revue Belge du cinema*, 2 (Winter).

Van Der Paardt, R. (1989) '*Twee vrouwen* en de Orpheustraditie', *Literatuur*, 1, 10-16.

Van der Poel, D. C. (1936) 'Een Komedie om geld', *De Groene Amsterdammer* (31 October), Folder Nederlands Filmmuseum.

Van De Westelaken, G. (1975) 'Interview met Harry Kümel', *Skoop*, 11, 4, 29–41.

Van Driel, H. (2003) 'Dutch Literature and Film', http://let.uvt.nl/cgi-bin/filmlit/filmlit (Accessed 4 June 2003).

Van Gelder, H. (1996) *Abraham Tuschinski*. Amsterdam: Nijgh en Van Ditmar.

Van Ieperen, A. (1978) '*Twee vrouwen* verfilmd voor wereldmarkt', *NRC Handelsblad* (25 July).

_____ (1999) 'No Trains No Planes', *Vrij Nederland* (3 April), 71.

Van Scheers, R. (1996) *Paul Verhoeven: The Authorized Biography*. London: Faber and Faber.

Verdaasdonk, D. (1990) *Beroep filmregisseur: het verkrijgen van continuïteit in een artistiek beroep*. Zeist: Kerckebosch.

Verschooten, G. (1985) *Harry Kümel*. Brussels: Fantasy Films.

Vincendeau, G. (ed.) (1995) *Encyclopedia of European Cinema*. London: Cassell/British Film Institute.

Vincendeau, G. (1998) 'Issues in European Cinema', in J. Hill and P. Church Gibson (eds) *The Oxford Guide to Film Studies*. Oxford: Oxford University Press, 440–8.

Vrielynck, R. (1980) *Beyond the Seventh Art: Animated Cartoons in Belgium*. Brussels: Ministery of Foreign Affairs.

Wakeman, J. (ed.) (1988) *World Film Directors*, volume 2. New York: H. W. Wilson, 250–5.

Walker, J. (ed.) (1995) *Halliwell's Filmgoer's Companion*. London: HarperCollins.

Waugh, Th. (1981) 'Joris Ivens and the Evolution of the Radical Documentary', unpublished Ph.D. thesis, Columbia

University.

_____ (1999) 'Joris Ivens and the Legacy of Committed Documentary', in K. Bakker (ed.) *Joris Ivens and the Documentary Context*. Amsterdam: Amsterdam University Press, 171–82.

White, S. (1995) *The Cinema of Max Ophuls: Magisterial Vision and the Figure of Woman*. New York: Columbia University Press.

Wolff, J. Ph. (1998) *Production is key in the film industry: evaluatie van het speelfilmbeleid in het kader van het mediabeleid van de Europese Unie*. Lelystad: Stichting IVIO.

Yakir, D. (1977) 'Interview with André Delvaux', *Sight and Sound*, 46, 2, 90–3.

Zaagsma, F. (1979) 'Twee 'keukenmeiden'-vrouwen', *Het Parool* (23 May).

Zimmerman, B. (1981) 'Lesbian Vampires: *Daughters of Darkness*', *Jump Cut*, 24/25, 23–4.

INDEX